Censorship, Translation and English Language F

Approaches to Translation Studies

Founded by

James S. Holmes

Edited by

Henri Bloemen
Cees Koster
Ton Naaijkens

VOLUME 41

The titles published in this series are listed at *brill.com/atts*

Censorship, Translation and English Language Fiction in People's Poland

By

Robert Looby

BRILL

RODOPI

LEIDEN | BOSTON

Cover illustration: Artistic vision of communist censorship, analog picture taken in 1982 in Poland. Artist: Jacek Halicki.

Library of Congress Control Number: 2015934113

ISSN 0169-0523
ISBN 978-90-04-29305-2 (paperback)
ISBN 978-90-04-29306-9 (e-book)

This book is printed on acid-free paper.

Printed by Printforce, the Netherlands

Contents

Chapter 1
Censors

No censor ever changed a text as much as its translator. The censor may decide to replace every instance of "East Germany" with "The German Democratic Republic" and be content to leave it at that. The translator must make thousands of such decisions. As the conviction grew that translation, like censoring, is re-writing, it was inevitable that translators eventually attracted the label of "tacit censors" (Gibbels 2009) or "censorial agents" (Sherry 2013). Translators are not alone: editors, publishers and authors themselves can be added to the list of suspected censors. The publisher wants marketable books, the editor wants a tidy prose style, and the author...? The author wanted to write something more personal, more lyrical, but that was drummed out of him at school, at work, by the passing years of failure, on the creative writing course. But all of these people and processes are also productive. Without that profit-driven publisher, the pedantic, blue-pencilling editor, and the self-disciplined author with his humdrum education, his life-experience, his MA in creative writing and his constant redrafting, there would be no book for any censor to censor, translator to translate or critic to criticise.[1] George Orwell recognised that censorship should not be understood narrowly as a state institution, writing in "The Prevention of Literature": "Any writer or journalist who wants to retain his integrity finds himself thwarted by the general drift of society rather than by active persecution" (Orwell 1998, vol. 17: 371).

In People's Poland[2] the censor was only one part of an entire system of state control, encompassing selection, translation, editing, distribution, censorship and reception, and running from the Party's Central Committee right down to primary schools bringing up children to be good socialist citizens, some of whom would become authors, critics, translators and censors. Francis Couvares declines to give a consistent definition of censorship because it can be understood so broadly – from official, "prior restraint" to the "conscious and unconscious editorial evasions and silences practised by writers, [film] directors, and other personnel involved in the production of cultural commodities". Drawing on Jansen, Couvares writes "censorship has come to be reconceived not as one or more discrete acts of repressive control over free expression, but as a 'normal' and 'constitutive' part, indeed, a very condition, of free expression" (Couvares 2006: 10). There is little doubt that censorship is "constitutive". It is hard to argue that there can be complete freedom of expression or of action. From the first time an adult tells a child "Don't..." the die is cast. Socialisation begins, our behaviour is constrained and though we rebel, our rebellion is determined by the status quo. Or consider the journalist's weapon: the unkind review. In the wrong hands it can kill a play on opening night, silence an erring translator, or elevate a mediocrity. In the right hands it can do all of the above. If a bad review is a form of censorship, then it follows that to minimize censorship all reviews should be favourable. But that, of course, would be censorship. The answer to the question of "what is censorship?" is, David Tribe observed, "almost anything" (Tribe 1973: 17).

Helen Freshwater expresses some scepticism about the use of a "Foucauldian definition of censorship as a productive force. [...] If censorship is constitutive, operating at the most basic level of discourse and comprehension, how are we to assess it?" (Freshwater 2004: 230). She advocates acknowledging the different forms censorship can take, from unkind reviews to worse, and analysing "censorious events" "with critical emphasis upon their socio-historical specificity" (Freshwater 2004: 242). Beate Müller also warns against an extremely broad definition of censorship, fearing that, as Manfred Pfister said in the context of intertextuality, it will be of "little heuristic potential" (Müller 2004: 10). Müller suggests using a "family resemblance" model of censorship, recognising that some practices are more central to censorship while others are more peripheral, perhaps specific to certain times and places (Müller 2004: 15).

What we are accustomed to calling censorship (leaving aside banning) often takes the form of a superficial cutting and tweaking, sometimes of individual words. It is a "blunt instrument" (Rockett 2004: 17). If the censor is good enough to record that he or she changed "Gypsy" to "vagabond" or "god" to "God" the researcher's job is easy enough: simply combing through the archives will answer most of our questions. Roald Dahl changed the colour of the Oompa-Loompas in *Charlie and the Chocolate Factory* from black to orange when he re-issued the book and a simple comparison of earlier and later editions will confirm this – though it will not tell us why he made the change or at whose instigation. But when it is the translator who makes the changes things are more complicated. In such cases, Piotr Kuhiwczak claims, "the act of censorship remains largely invisible". He admits that a comparison with the source text can be made but "even an expert would find it difficult to determine whether the translation deviates from the original because of linguistic and cultural difference or because of some other, more sinister considerations" (Kuhiwczak 2011: 363). The use of a particular word (or idiom, mood, tense, voice, part of speech, grammatical construction – not to mention a translation strategy such as domestication) means an alternative is rejected and this may strike some as censorship. Guy Phelps, on the subject of hidden censorship in the cinema, writes, "The whole complex structure of the film industry ensures that there are numerous points in the process whereby films are made and presented to the public when it is hard to distinguish decision-making from censorship" (Phelps 1975: 251). He has in mind various commercial and moral pressures on filmmakers but translation is surely one such point of decision-making in the book world.

In *Censorship in Soviet Literature* Herman Ermolaev unproblematically counts off changes, e.g.: "...18 political and 108 puritanical revisions [...] nearly all of them deletions" (Ermolaev 1997: 102). Ermolaev was generally comparing successive editions of books; it is more difficult when the comparison is between a book and its translation. As Freshwater points out, much depends on the socio-historic context. For example, one could argue that the consistent translation of regionalisms or other indicators of non-standard English into standard literary Polish is nothing more than conforming to norms of "good" Polish. It is praiseworthy or blameworthy, according to one's own opinion, but it is hardly censorship. However, if this translation strategy is to be found in a book translated at the height of Stalinism in Poland things take on a new complexion. In 1950, Stalin overturned Nikolai Marr's thesis that since language is part of the "superstructure" it must change when the socio-economic base changes. Stalin now claimed that social and economic changes did *not* change languages. Furthermore, dialects could not be regarded as languages and were "unfit as means of communication for the whole of society" (Ermolaev 1997: 100). Stalin may have had in mind the multilingual USSR but when the Great Linguist spoke Poles had to listen. Stalin had his thoughts published in *Marxism and Questions of Linguistics* in August 1950 (Ermolaev 1997: 101). The Polish translation appeared before the year was out. The Soviet censors, Ermolaev writes, went on an "all-out purge of jargon, dialecticisms, vulgarisms, curses, obscenities, coarse words and neologisms. All these elements were believed to diminish the effectiveness of literary works in communicating political and ideological messages to the broad masses" (Ermolaev 1997: 100-101). Polish translations of the post-war period are also usually poorer in swear words, obscenities, vulgarisms and dialecticisms than their English language originals. Perhaps, then, the substitution of clearly marked regional and social speech markers in an English source text (ST) with a variety of Polish read (if not actually spoken) and understood by all Poles in the target text (TT) is not such an innocent choice after all. The government censor need not have changed the translator's text; it would have been enough for the translator to come across *Marxism and Questions of*

Linguistics and draw her own conclusions about what would be a wise way to continue in the translation business.

Another difficulty in deciding whether a given change on the journey from one language to another is translational or censorious is the fact that the translator and the critic may simply have understood the texts, languages and cultures differently. For example: what is the "standard English" referred to above? On the answer to that question depends one's judgment of whether the Polish translation deviates from it. One's own ideology, of which one is not always aware, comes into play too. If the working class English of the original is translated into non-standard Polish some might see this as patronising the working class ("don't they talk funny"); others might see it as preserving their separate identity. The problem is well described in the editors' introduction of *Translation Right or Wrong*:

> Every agent in the process of making, judging or studying translations needs to be evaluated; none of us is neutral, standing outside the process. As bias, ideology and position cannot be eliminated, they must be acknowledged and factored into the discussion (Bayó Belenguer et al 2013: 14).

The text must be interpreted to be translated. The critic has no right – even with the benefit of hindsight – to set, *ex cathedra*, his interpretation above that of the translator. The second last story in Sherwood Anderson's *Winesburg, Ohio* is called "Sophistication". The Polish translator chose to call it "Smutek przemijania" ("The Sadness of Passing"). I would argue that "Sophistication" ("wytworność", or "wyrafinowanie") is a far more appropriate title since the story contains the line "'There is no one here fit to associate with a girl of Helen's breeding,' she [Helen's mother] said" (Anderson 1946: 177).[3] To my mind this is crucial to the story, whose title is therefore – in this reading – ironic (Winesburg is, at least on the surface, small-town, unsophisticated America, and Helen and her daughter are big fish in a very small pool). This gives me no right to accuse the translator of suppressing or censoring a given reading (the one I happen to prefer) of the story. As Bayó Belenguer et al say, I do not stand "outside the process".

Some of these problems can be illustrated by the translation into English of the opening lines from a post-war short story by Polish writer Sławomir Mrożek called "W podróży" ("On a Journey"). The historical context and one's own interpretation of the story's meaning combine to make any assessment of the extent of censorship in the translation difficult – and this is a translation published *west* of the Iron Curtain. "On a Journey" is an absurd story in which the narrator is driven in a horse-drawn coach to a part of the country where human beings are used to transmit messages by shouting to each other in relay instead of using telegraph wires.

Zaraz za N. wjechaliśmy między płaskie, podmokłe łąki, wśród których nieliczne rżyska świeciły jak głowy rekrutów. Kolaska pędziła raźno mimo wybojów i błota. Daleko, na wysokości uszu końskich, ciągnęło się pasmo boru. Dokoła było pusto, jak zwykle o tej porze roku. Dopiero gdyśmy jechali czas jakiś, zobaczyłem przed nami sylwetkę człowieka, którą coraz lepiej mogłem rozpoznać – w miarę jakeśmy się do niego zbliżali. Był to mężczyzna o pospolitej twarzy, w mundurze funkcjonariusza poczt. Stał nieruchomo przy drodze, a kiedyśmy go mijali, obrzucił nas obojętnym spojrzeniem. Ledwo straciłem go z oczu, gdy przed nami ukazał się następny, w podobnym uniformie, również stojący bez poruszenia (Mrożek 2000: 138).

This short extract (a discussion and translation to follow) presents the translator with a multitude of decisions, any one of which could be attacked on the grounds of being "censorship". It begins with "Just after N—". This has the unmistakeable feel of nineteenth century Russian literature. Gogol's *Dead Souls*, for example, begins in the "provincial town of NN—". However, "N—" may just mean "Unknown" (Russian: *Neizvestnyi*; Polish: "nieznany") and so straight away the translator faces a dilemma: keep the intertextual reference (translate it as "N", as is done in translations of Gogol) or assume that the resemblance is coincidental, that "N" simply means "unknown", and translate it as, say, "X". In the context of twentieth century Polish-Russian relations, changing just this one letter might be seen as censorship: an attempt to suppress a reading of the story that understands provincial socialist Poland as being like provincial Tsarist Russia. The passage also compares the fields of stubble to the heads of recruits. Should the translator, as translators often do, "explicitate" this by writing "army recruits"? Is it possible that Mrożek (or his readers) had in mind recruits to the party? By translating the word as "army recruits" this avenue of interpretation is – if not closed off – narrowed somewhat. Polish readers of the times, used to censorship, had a tendency to seek out allusions even where none had been intended. For example, although the only details suggesting the period are the horse-drawn carriage and the mention of telegraphs, and although no country is mentioned, it almost certainly would be read as a comment on contemporary Poland. The "recruits" example and some of the following may seem far-fetched, but translators must at least consider such options, even if only to immediately reject most of them.

The narrator's language is a little literary and old-fashioned. For "fast" he has "raźno" instead of the more usual "szybko"; much use is made of mobile verb endings ("jakeśmy, gdyśmy"); the syntax of "dopiero gdyśmy jechali czas jakiś" ("only when we had been travelling for some time") is markedly more literary than the alternative "dopiero po jakimś czasie". A decision to make the narrator more direct and colloquial in translation has a knock-on effect that could be labelled censorship. There is a contrast between the narrator's careful speech and that of his coach driver, who speaks in clipped sentences, e.g. "Na służbie" ([They are] "on duty") (Mrożek 2000:

139), and colloquially, e.g. "Najgorzej, jak sobie który podpije" ("The worst is when one of them gets drunk") (Mrożek 2000: 140). The driver's speech is also interspersed with word like "wio" and "hetta" (Mrożek 2000: 140), addressed to the horses. Weakening this contrast by making the narrator more colloquial or by correcting or standardising the driver's speech alters the story's emphasis. In the original, the narrator comes across as a member of the intelligentsia visiting the provinces, a place where wire for telegraphs is stolen, wood for the poles is missing, and an absurdly labour-intensive and corruption-prone alternative to telegraphs is used instead. By having outsider and local speak the same language the contrast between the normality of the outside world and the absurdity of this province, for which we are inclined to read modern, socialist Poland, is weakened. Although very slight, the effect is there: the political import is watered down and the hapless translator may be branded a censor for what are or might appear to be purely linguistic decisions. While few might be willing to hand out (and fewer to receive) such criticism the picture might change if it were the case that official or semi-official policy (in Poland) was to standardise language. The perils of reading too closely are revealed when we turn to Konrad Syrop's translation of the story. Here is the excerpt:

> Just after B— the road took us among damp, flat meadows. Only here and there the expanse of green was broken by a stubble field. In spite of mud and potholes the chaise was moving at a brisk pace. Far ahead, level with the ears of the horses, a blue band of the forest was stretching across the horizon. As one would expect at that time of the year, there was not a soul in sight.
>   Only after we had travelled for a while did I see the first human being. As we approached his features became clear; he was a man with an ordinary face and he wore a Post Office uniform. He was standing still at the side of the road, and as we passed he threw us an indifferent glance. No sooner had we left him behind than I noticed another one, in a similar uniform, also standing motionless on the verge (Mrożek 2010: 131).

The narrator's language is a little less literary in translation. Barring specific vocabulary items ("chaise" for "kolaska"), it is also less old fashioned. For example, the word "bór" in the original, which is uncommon today, is translated simply as "forest". Additionally, the coachman's speech, later in the story, is somewhat standardised and instead of reproducing his words to the horses the translator writes, "and he urged the horses on" (Mrożek 2010: 132) or omits the word. Where in the original the coachman says the wireless telegraphs are "postępowsze" (Mrożek 2000: 141), in translation they are "more modern" (Mrożek 2010: 135). However, "postępowsze" is less correct than "bardziej postępowe" and it could (not should!) be translated as "progressiver" or perhaps "more progressive-like". Mrożek has mangled a favourite word of People's Poland propaganda, "postępowy", in the coachman's mouth: so much for progress; so much for modernising the countryside; so much for improving education. This might be seen as nitpicking, and no doubt some will disagree with my entire assessment of the story and the role of language in it, but it illustrates the hazards of reading too much into decisions made by the translator and crying "censor" at the ones you don't like.

Syrop's translation was first published in a collection called *The Elephant* in London in 1962 but paradoxically he may have been less free of institutional Polish censorship than Mrożek, whose ties with Poland had not yet been broken. If Syrop had clarified any of the Aesopian language in the stories Mrożek might have suffered repercussions. Smuggling criticism of People's Poland past the censor was risky enough: the last thing Mrożek needed was some westerner to give the game away by pointing out allusions the censor had missed. So perhaps this is why the English version of the story takes place "Just after B—" not N— and makes no mention of recruits' heads. This example illustrates an inevitable limitation of this book. There is no handy rule to tell us what is "innocent" translation and what is censorship. Take, for example, the decision to translate and publish in Britain this story by this writer and not, say *Numer 16 produkuje* ("Number 16 is Producing") by Jan Wilczek. Mrożek is by common consent a better writer but it is surely no coincidence that he satirises People's Poland while Wilczek glorifies it. No decisions are innocent but which are guiltier is in the eye of the beholder. A judgment must be made, influenced by all kinds of non-literary considerations and tainted by one's own opinion on the meaning of the text.

In Kevin Rockett's discussion of the Irish Film Censor's decision to cut part of the 1946 film *Gilda* he writes:

> The superficial reading of the scene by the censors failed to appreciate the subversive nature of the song ['Put the Blame on Mame' performed by Rita Hayworth] and its performance in which the visual and the aural textures undercut its voyeurism. Such a literal reading of the 'performance' also fails to take into account the destabilizing of the narrative through (dance) movement (Rockett 2004: 128).

Two comments might be made here. Firstly, Rockett may be wrong and the textures do not undercut the voyeurism. Secondly, it is possible the censor did appreciate the subtleties of the scene but banned it anyway, fearing or assuming its audience would not.

In her assessment of four German translations of Wollstonecraft's *Vindication of the Rights of Women* Elisabeth Gibbels notes that the translator's replacement of the first person plural pronoun with "the male-connotating impersonal 'man' further makes the text male-addressing" (Gibbels 2009: 66). Is this censorship? It might be if one associates the impersonal pronoun (*man*, in German) with the male of the species (*Mann* in German) but not everyone must. Katarzyna Jakubiak, in her discussion of

Polish performances of *A Raisin in the Sun,* claims it is a misreading of the play to interpret the skin-colour of the African American Younger family as merely incidental and to assume the play is about middle-class aspirations. This is what many early critics did (Jakubiak 2011: 559). If the play is understood "incorrectly" then staging it with an all white cast might be understood as censorship, since one would be writing African Americans out of the picture. But what if the early critics were right? Would an all white cast then cease to be censorship? Or perhaps it was never censorship in the first place?

The point is not that Rockett, Gibbels and Jakubiak are wrong but that the subjective element cannot be taken out of a discussion of censorship and translation. There are not many scholars who would insist that there is always one and only one correct way to translate anything. Even with archival evidence, it is difficult to disentangle ordinary translation decisions from decisions imposed by the censor, by self-censorship, by "the system", or by Orwell's "general drift of society". And yet some attempt must be made if a book on censorship and translation is to be written at all. If censorship is defined as broadly as translation it ceases to have any useful meaning. "All translation is censorship" does not tell us anything about the differences between translating in the USSR and in the USA. If we know the rules the translators and censors operated under we should be able to deduce which changes were politically motivated (censorship understood narrowly) and which were not. However, the rules actually used by censors often have to be deduced from the products of that same censorship. The approach of this book, therefore, is to compare target texts to their source texts and to present and analyse the differences between them, taking into account any archival evidence and the wider social and historical context. Reference is made to other means of control such as limited print runs, bans and critical reception but the emphasis will be on how censorship affected what was actually translated and published.

In practice, many of the changes detailed in the rest of this book can be located quite uncontroversially on any spectrum ranging from conventionally understood translation to censorship, as when the word "ass" (Stalin's ass, to be precise) is not translated. In any case, the reader will have the opportunity to make his or her mind up – always aware that the data, including all back translations, has been selected and presented by me. A wide range of primary texts has been chosen for study: it includes classics, genre fiction, children's books and literary fiction. The sample is wide enough to avoid the risk of reading too much into the idiosyncrasies of a small number of translators.

Annette Kuhn rejects what she calls the "prohibition/institutions" model of censorship research. Such research is doable but the "focus on concrete institutions – even when these are not confined to censorship bodies – *isolates* censorship practices from their broader social and historical conditions of existence and effectivity" (Kuhn 1988: 4). However, in the case of Poland, the censorship office is an elephant in the room that really cannot be ignored and it is that elephant to which we now turn.

In Poland, in September 1944, the newly created Department – later Ministry – for Information and Propaganda was given responsibility for, among other things, radio, cinema, propaganda, the press and publishing (Nałęcz 1994: 11-12). Newspapers were already being censored in 1944: permission was given to publish on condition there was no criticism of the Soviet Union or of Polish Communist leader Bolesław Bierut (Nałęcz 1994: 12). The country had not yet been fully liberated from the Germans when the USSR sent two specialists from their own censorship body, *Glavlit*, to advise on the establishment of a censorship regime. They were unhappy with what they found, reporting in December 1944 that the "Censorship Decree", formulated three months earlier in Poland, was anti-Soviet and left out radio, maps, museums, public lectures, films, exhibitions and foreign literature (Różdżyński 1994: 8). Although there is evidence that advisers exaggerated their success and importance in their reports (Rzendowski 1994), the oversights they mention were corrected and an order from the Minister for Public Security institutionalised press censorship in Poland on January 19th 1945 (Nałęcz 1994: 27). Although this order refers to the "Central Office of Press Control" the Russian advisers referred to it in a report home as the "Central Office of Press, Cinema, Radio etc. Control" (Różdżyński 1994: 8). In July 1946, this was to become the *Główny Urząd Kontroli Prasy, Publikacji i Widowisk* (GUKPPiW), the Main Office for Control of the Press, Publications and Public Performances, which censored virtually everything intended for publication in Poland until 1989. The Censorship Office steadily increased its powers as the state moved to nationalise publishing and take control of paper allocation, theatre repertoires and personnel in the years after the war. In discriminating against private publishers (by reducing print-runs, refusing permission to publish and recommending that no paper be allocated – even to books that were not "censorable" just "bad") the Censorship Office played a part in the nationalisation of publishing (Nowak 2012: 149).

As well as criticism of the Soviet Union, the censors targeted falsehoods, military and state secrets concerning industrial and military capabilities, newspaper articles attacking government policy or the policy of its allies, and incitement to racial hatred (Ciećwierz 1989: 106-107). At a meeting of censors in June 1949, a Warsaw censor condemned "Catholicism, bourgeois liberalism, formalism in art and literature and all influence of western thought – including the sciences". There were calls for "worthless" books "distracting [attention] from contemporary problems" like *Anne of*

Green Gables not to be re-issued (Nałęcz 1994: 24). Censorship should be attuned to the likely readers of a given publication – intelligentsia or working class – and books should be prefaced in such a way as to "make them ours" (Nałęcz 1994: 25), according to one speaker.

Mazurkiewicz dates the advent of socialist realism in Poland to 1947, if not earlier (Mazurkiewicz 2009: 110-111), but 1949 marked the official turn in Polish culture towards this doctrine in the arts with the Fourth General Meeting of Poland's Writers' Union in January in the town of Szczecin. Literature was, among other things, to accommodate Marxist theories of society and be engaged in socialist construction (Fik 1989: 113). In April, at the plenum of the Central Committee of the Polish United Workers' Party devoted to culture, there was talk of an "ideological offensive" and criticism of formalism in art, cosmopolitanism and fascination with the West (Fik 1989: 117). Throughout the year, in various forums, there were more condemnations of formalism and abstractionism in art for their decadence as well as encouragement of artistically weak but socially engaged plays (Fik 1989: 117-119). Before the nationalisation of book publishing (almost complete by 1950) the censor played a part in enforcing socialist realism but from then on it was mainly the publishers who took over the task (Nowak 2012: 131).

The effects of the Stalinisation of culture on translated literature in Poland are described by Bates (2011). In general, however, the choice of books for translation was affected more than the way they were translated. This was censorship by selection rather than by the scissors and it remained important throughout the existence of People's Poland. From 1949, state publishers could not make their own, independent choices of books: plans had to be submitted to the authorities for approval (Kondek 1999: 27). English and American literature was passed over in favour of Soviet books, with the result that the thaw in 1956 brought a flood of the western translations Polish readers had been deprived of.

Despite the regimentation, the censorship, and the enforcement of socialist realism Stalinism did benefit literature in some ways. Among the first concerns of the new authorities in post-war Poland was primary schooling. Efforts were also made to educate adults and to stamp out illiteracy. In 1946 89.1% of children aged 7 to 13 were in primary school; in 1957/8 the figure was 98.4%. By 1960, illiteracy had been reduced from around 15% in 1939 to 2.7%, though it should be noted that inter-war Poland had made great strides in this area too (Czarnik 1993: 29; see also Werblan 2009: 87). These successes meant that many people were exposed to literature for the first time and the official books periodical *Nowe Książki* ("New Books") rated the books it reviewed according to their difficulty. Grade I° meant a book was suitable for beginning readers, grade I books were suitable for readers who had been to primary school, grade II meant some "intellectual preparation" was needed, and grade III was for books for advanced readers and academics ('Adnotacje' 1952: 198). It was thought that "new readers" would need guidance and there is much evidence of paternalism – not to say condescension – in the censorship archives, as when one censor generously writes of a 1950 edition of a Turgenev short story collection that "the stories, despite their naturalism, are of educational value" (G-148, 31/68: 319).[4] Concern that readers – new or otherwise – might not understand novels "correctly" is reflected, too, in prefaces and other critical apparatus often added to books for the readers' instruction. As John Bates puts it:

> In the longer term, the education system, supplied with ideologically correct interpretations of past and contemporary works of Polish literature by trusted Party literary critics and scholars, was to regulate the literary tastes and understanding of the new state's citizens. In this way, via a complex of factors both material and socio-psychological, the Party developed a system of control designed to condition the literary work from its initial conception in the author's mind until its final consumption by the reader (Bates 2004a: 13).

For example, one of the censors who reviewed German writer Anna Seghers's *Die Gefährten* in 1950 expressed the fear that readers might gain the impression that the Polish-Soviet war (1919-1920) was an act of Russian aggression and not a "just war of liberation". He/she adds, "The translator's infrequent comments are insufficient and often outdated and naïve [...].These comments should be supplemented and the opportunity to provide the appropriate political interpretation should be taken" (G-145, 31/26: 374). Nevil Shute's *On the Beach* was only permitted, in 1968, when the publishers expanded the afterword by the addition of comments on the absurdity of the book's idea that China might go to war against the USSR over uninhabited parts of eastern Siberia. This decision was consulted with the Party's Central Committee (K-lvi859).

To begin with, in the 1940s, books, especially fiction, enjoyed relative freedom as the authorities concentrated on the press (Bates 2011: 61). This was followed, as we have seen, by a clampdown, which eased with 1956's promises of democratisation: there were instances of the censors themselves protesting against censorship and in favour of democratisation (Skórzyński 1991: 104-105) and for some months there was virtually no censorship, with even calls for the dissolution of the Party going uncensored (Adamowski and Kozieł 1999: 62). However, when First Secretary Gomułka was replaced in 1970 by Edward Gierek it was again possible for the new leader to offer relaxation of censorship as a carrot to intellectuals. Still later, during the so-called "carnival" period of Solidarity (from mid-1980 to late 1981) there was a sharp reduction in the activity of the censorship office (Wojsław 2013: 204), with *Tygodnik Solidarności* (*Solidarity Weekly*) newspaper even publishing an interview with a former censor. In July 1981, a change in the law allowed publishers the right to appeal decisions and to indicate parts of their texts that had been cut. It also meant that the Censorship Office (now without the word "press" in its name) could not blacklist authors (K-lvi864). Furthermore, all works published before 1918, as well as re-issues of books that had been published in People's Poland, were released from censorship. The introduction of martial law in December that year led to further restrictions (the 1981 law was suspended and *Tygodnik Solidarności* ceased publishing). The Cultural Division of the Central Committee concluded in 1984 that there should be a big increase in translations of contemporary literature from socialist countries and that western books for translation should meet higher artistic and ideological standards than hitherto. Also – though this would concern Polish books rather than translations – all publishers' plans for 1984 and 1985 should be evaluated with an aim to eliminating opposition writers and fast-tracking loyal writers (K-lvi669).

However, in 1986-1987 censorship again eased in Poland (Remmer 1989: 423). Evidence of this more liberal attitude in the late 1980s can be seen, for example, in the publication in issue 1 of *Literatura na Świecie* ("World Literature") in 1986 of several extracts of George Orwell's prose (though not *1984* or *Animal Farm*) along with a piece by Anthony Burgess called "1985" and an article by Wacław Sadkowski entitled "After 1984". According to Jacek Bocheński, the Censorship Office functioned merely as a confiscator of books in the final years of People's Poland, as state power was breaking down (Bocheński 1995: 62). Bocheński is backed up by Piotr Siemion, the translator of Thomas Pynchon's *The Crying of Lot 49* (which passed the censors with no problems and appeared in 1990). Siemion claims that by then "nobody had any illusions" about the course of events ('The Obsolescence of Vice' 2010: n. pag.). In November 1988, it was suggested in a Party document that the authorities were not so weak that they could not withstand some "dissenting" ("nieprawomyślne") books. Since the authorities were being criticised "in life" ("w życiu") (presumably in newspapers and at rallies and so on) they could also be criticised in literature. Criticism of Marxism should be allowed, the document continued, because forbidden fruit tastes sweetest (K-lvi356).

What remained constant throughout the years was the wide latitude of interpretation of the law on what constituted censorable material. Stefan Kisielewski stresses the vagueness ("ogólnikowość") of the 1946 law establishing the GUKPPiW as well as the subsequent amendments, up until the early 1980s (Kisielewski 1983: 83; Ciećwierz 1989: 107). This was also a feature of British censorship of "offences of opinion" (O'Higgins 1972: 17).

It allowed censors to adjust their tactics to the prevailing politics. Paradoxically, this vagueness was sometimes accompanied by extraordinary detail, as can be seen in the surviving daily instructions to censors, especially in the 1970s. In 1972, among many, many other things, censors were instructed not to pass any information – usually "until further notice" – on the Fiat 126 car made under licence in Poland, the new postal rates, or the film *Diabeł* ("Devil") directed by Andrzej Żuławski, which "for the Polish viewer and reader *does not exist*" (G-1130, 176/35: 52; emphasis in original). When instructions this detailed and specific can be issued and obeyed, the precise wording of the censorship law of 1946, with its talk of protecting the Polish political system, not revealing state secrets, preventing the dissemination of falsehoods and protecting morals (Dziennik Ustaw 1946, nr. 34, poz. 210: Dekret o utworzeniu GUKPPiW) seems less important than the law's actual results in the form of published texts. Indications given in the early days about the course to be taken do remain relevant throughout the following years but it is clear that anything the authorities did not like could be censored and it is more profitable to study the actual results of censorship than the stated rules of the game.

Kondek refers to the difficulties planners faced due to the changing party line during the early 1950s (Kondek 1999: 46). Foreign writers and their translators were not unaffected by day to day changes of tack. A planned new edition of Steinbeck's *Grapes of Wrath* in 1967 was stopped because of Steinbeck's position on the Vietnam War, as was *Travels With Charley*, which was not published in a Polish translation until 1991 (K-lvi857; K-lvi859). Ursula Le Guin's *Wizard of Earthsea* was translated by Stanisław Barańczak but a note from 1980 in the archives of the Party's Central Committee suggests that crediting *Anna* Barańczak was considered: Stanisław was blacklisted for his opposition to the regime (K-lvi863). The translation appeared with Stanisław's name in 1983 but the foreword, by Stanisław Lem, is dated 1976, which may indicate that publication was held up for many years. Books were often banned because of the author's politics rather than their contents. Also, writing *about* blacklisted authors was generally forbidden, though the censors seem to have been less rigorous in applying this to translated fiction, where one will find mention of novels that were banned in Poland. A censor's review of Carl Zuckmayer's autobiographical *Als wär's ein Stück von mir* demands the cutting of a reference to George Orwell (G-863, 101/3: 188) but, for example, the 1978 translation of John Updike's *Museums and Women* mentions Henry Miller's *Tropic of Cancer*, which had been banned in Poland only the year before. In 1986 *Literatura na świecie* published a transcript of a public meeting with Kurt Vonnegut and William Styron which includes (i.e. was permitted by the censor to include) a question about Vonnegut's *Mother Night*, which was then only available in "second circulation", or *samizdat* ('Styron i Vonnegut' 1986: 301). Blacklisting was commoner in the late 1970s (Bocheński 1995: 63), when, for example, Barańczak's translation of e.e. cummings's poems was delayed (according to *Zapis* magazine ('Kronika' 1977: 211) by the publisher rather than the censor, though if Barańczak was blacklisted it seems academic whether the publisher stopped the book or the censor). A volume of Barańczak's translations appeared in 1983.

For the first ten years of its existence, there was no mention in the press of the Censorship Office with the first hints appearing in late 1955 and taking the form of references to publishing delays. Such articles themselves were censored (Woźniak-Łabieniec 2013: 89-91), though a 1956 article by Andrzej Braun did mention the Censorship Office by name (Woźniak-Łabieniec 2013: 93). The authorities were sensitive to all accusations of censorship, not just mentions of the Censorship Office. On the pages of *Film* magazine, one writer tried to claim that until recently the Ministry for Culture and Art had only approved of realistic art, while formalist tendencies were condemned. This was cut by the censor in 1957 (G-508, 39/21) even though it was patently obvious that such had been the case: there had been numerous proud public pronouncements to the effect. It should come as no surprise that long passages concerning work in the Kraków censorship office were cut from an article intended for journalism students (and with a print run of just 380) in 1973 (G-1124, 176/29: 90). In 1978, *Polityka* magazine published a report on the Polish Writers' Union convention from which the censor removed the information that delegates criticised the work of the Censorship Office (G-1342, 229/21: 122). Even in 1987, by which time publishers were permitted to mark the intervention of censors in parentheses in the text, the censor was still sensitive to the issue, cutting from an article the following: "They [a newspaper] wanted to print it but the censors, of course, pulled it, and there was not even a trace of it since back then [i.e. before 1981] you could not mark the place in brackets..." (K-lvi871).

The GUKPPiW collection in the National Archive is large (163 running metres) but patchy.[5] For example, reviews are grouped in files by year and publisher but many are missing. Or one finds the 1971 file for a given publisher, which contains a request for permission to publish a given book's jacket and flyleaf (they were also subject to censorship), but there is no trace of the review of the book itself, even though it is the correct file since reviews of other books put out in 1971 by the same publisher are present. In addition, a lot of GUKPPiW reports (from the 1980s) are to be found not in the censors' files but in those of the Party's Central Committee. Thus, it would not do to say "there is no record of writer/book X in the archives".[6]

Whether because of cooling ardour, poor record keeping, deliberate destruction or a combination of all three, the reviews of foreign books in later years are fewer and more perfunctory. From 1949 there are at least four reviews each of Albert Maltz's *The Underground Stream (Te trzy dni*, in its Polish version) and Howard Fast's *Conceived in Liberty (Bitwa pod Valley Forge)* (G-145, 31/23). Less dedication is visible in the 1960s and 1970s, with the reviews of many foreign books impossible to find. If a book *is* on file there is often only one, very short review. Earlier reviews often have a fairly detailed summary, some character description, perhaps some general reservations, and mention of the book's ideological value (or lack of), while after the 1950s one often finds the briefest of reviews and a laconic "no censorial reservations". The occasional flash of communist zeal is still to be seen, as in the review of *The Great Gatsby*, in which the censor approves of the afterword, which states that American bourgeois society is as closed to Gatsby as Polish bourgeois society is to Wokulski in Prus's nineteenth century novel *The Doll (Lalka)*. The censor adds: "The author does not discuss other social problems" (G-736, 68/126: 296). More typical, though, is the case of Elisabeth Gaskell's *Cranford*, which earns a six-line review in 1970 (G-861, 101/1: 71), while the review from 1971 of a Frank O'Connor short story collection can be quoted in full:

> The petit-bourgeois world is the theme of the stories by the Irish writer contained in the publication reviewed here. They are reminiscences from the childhood years of the writer and stories about people gathered in a small Irish town. The book is a contribution to the development of Ireland's own national culture. I have no reservations connected with censorship issues (G-918, 121/8: 146).

Occasionally one finds an initial review by a branch office of GUKPPiW but by 1950 (Bates 2011: 62-63) the publishing industry had been highly centralised in Warsaw. For every non-periodical publication two separate reviews were written, sometimes more in controversial cases. There was also a follow-up (*wtórna*) review, after publication, to decide if and how the book should be re-issued (Budrowska 2009: 24). Some books had from 10 to 20 reviews but foreign writers in general exercised the censors much less than Polish writers, whose books, as might be expected, struck closer to home.

The archives contain few manuscripts of novels, though shorter works and sometimes plays can be found (Budrowska 2013: 41, 93).[7] If the censor wanted a change made she marked it in her copy of the book and on the review form she noted the page number and a very brief description (sometimes no description) of the change. The censor had two copies of the book but both were destroyed after publication, leaving only the altered book in circulation (Drewnowski 1998: 20). On the review form, which was not always used, was a section for the censor's superior to enter her final decision. Occasionally this contains a note to the effect that after an informal word with the publisher some problem or other was solved, a hint of the amount of state control that escaped written records. According to Stanisław Siekierski censorship decisions were usually transmitted verbally, either over the phone or in person (Siekierski 1998: 35).[8] A former employee claimed the Censorship Office was less bureaucratic in the 1960s than the 1970s and instructions were often telephoned (Łopieńska 1981: 15). For example, an Edgar Wallace novel was passed "verbally" for serialisation in 1960 (G-588, 55/1: 127). Also, the Censorship Office was, in the words of Jerzy Łojek, only the final step in the "whole system of actual censorship, deeply rooted in the organisational structures of publishers, press, television, cinema and theatres". Zygmunt Hübner describes the censors he encountered before Mysia Street (the Main Censorship Office headquarters) as

> significantly more threatening. With Mysia Street I discuss details, individual sentences, but whether a play makes it to the stage at all is decided by someone else: the Voivodeship Committee [of the Party], which acts through the Culture Department of the Town Hall.

These comments, and Łojek's, date from around 1980 and are contained in an article that was to have appeared in a periodical called *Literatura*, but was banned and can now be found in the archives not of the censor, but of the Party's Central Committee (K-lvi863). One former censor tells of how he was admonished (during training, which lasted two weeks) for intervening too often in texts due for publication in *Forum* magazine. His supervisor told him the texts had already been selected and could go (Łopieńska 1981: 6). Czarnik, too, notes the existence of what he calls preliminary control: "This type of activity was the task of specified trusted persons, such as some editors in publishing houses and the press head offices, senior officials in scientific institutions, and some activists in literary and artistic organizations" (Czarnik 2001: 104-105). Another layer of control was the Writers' Union, which, at least in the early years, vetted books before they reached the censor (Kondek 1999: 124). Jacek Bocheński, co-founder of *Zapis* magazine, which was printed in London, away from the censor's attentions, described the Censorship Office as but "the bureaucratic transmitter of the political will of those who controlled everything, including the Censorship Office itself". He himself never saw a censor from the main office but was censored by them and "openly or secretly [by] politicians, editors, publishers and in a certain sense reviewers". He concludes that the Nazi-era term *Sprachregelung* better describes censorship (Bocheński 1995: 62).

The state tried bravely to ignore market forces. Under Stalinism, books with mass print runs were sometimes cheaper than the paper used to print them on (Jarosiński 1999: 20). Although the piles of unsold books did not go unnoticed, the authorities were still reluctant in the mid 1950s to pay attention to the actual reading preferences of the public (Kondek 1999: 173, 202), which are another restraint on the practices of producing literature.

Occasionally, also, the "final" verdict was not to permit publication but the book did, in fact, appear. It has often been said that lower-ranking censors were more zealous than their superiors (Żak 1999: 89), while Jadwiga Czachowska notes that mid-ranking editors were often more zealous than censors (Czachowska 1992, vol. 2: 228). In his study of the Poznań branch of the censorship office Piotr Nowak has found that the Head Office in Warsaw was often more liberal than the regional offices (Nowak 2012: 55). Claims of lower-rank zeal are substantiated by "K-62", the former censor interviewed in 1981. He told his interviewer that in principle if a rank and file censor passed something without comment no one else in the Censor's Office would read it before publication. This in turn meant that if a mistake was made it would only be discovered after publication, which was a more serious affair (Łopieńska 1981: 15). Low-ranking censors had an incentive to make changes and cuts: it meant sharing responsibility with a superior before publication. "And it is often the case that the higher up you go, the more liberal it gets: the censor crosses out and the boss lets it pass" (Łopieńska 1981: 15). As Mark Zaitsev observes: "For even when high officials may be inclined to overlook a transgression, it is an immutable fact of bureaucratic life that those further down the line do not dare do so, out of fear of eventual repercussions against themselves" (Zaitsev 1975: 121). It should be noted here that although the archives sometimes tell us unmistakeably that a particular change was made and even why, we cannot really know what the censor thought. All we can really be sure of is the difference between the cut and the uncut version and even this, in the case of translations, is not so obvious.

In addition, the Party could always override the censor – lowly or otherwise. Kondek reports that First Secretary Bierut took a personal interest in publishing plans (Kondek 1999: 43) and Gomułka too, in later years, had a baneful influence on who got published and in what form (Napiontkowa 1990: 230). A 1968 memorandum in the Central Committee's files complains that the necessity of consulting the Central Committee about publishing decisions was slowing things down (K-lvi859). Andrzej Krajewski describes the Culture Division of the Central Committee as another layer of censorship on top of the Main Office of Censorship. This institution continually monitored the Polish press and overall tendencies in literature and film as well as criticism. On the basis of such analyses it was decided which writers should be blacklisted (Krajewski 2004: 37).

To all these layers of control we must also add anticipatory self-censorship. Western writers were unlikely to watch their language on account of censorship in Poland but Polish editors, publishers and translators knew – or had to guess – what would be permitted. In Polish literature, the existence of censorship encouraged authors to use various tricks to get what they wanted to say into print. When a dangerous allusion was detected by the censor the author sometimes feigned naïveté. Another technique was to distract the censor by overloading the work in question with objectionable material in the hope that the important bits would get through (Hubner 1992: 63). This was a technique also used by Mae West (Gilbert 2012: 551). If translators tried to do this – which seems unlikely since they would not know which bits they added to the source text would be cut – I have found almost no evidence of it. Polish authors used Aesopian language in an attempt to smuggle subversive ideas into print but the effects of censorship on translated literature were different. Weizman and Blum-Kulka argue that the identification of a text as a translation "implies that deviations from cultural norms are not judged as intentional, and therefore are not assigned any 'hidden' meaning" (qtd. in Toury 1995: 28) and even in the Soviet Union itself there were periods when western literature was treated less severely by censors than Soviet literature (Blium, qtd. by Witt 2011: 154). An illustration of this in the Polish context may be John Updike's short story "Jesus on Honshu", which contains the line *"Jesus is said to have escaped and come back to Japan after wandering through the wastes of Siberia"* (Updike 1973: 216). Had this been written by a Polish author there is a good chance it would not have made it into print in this form. The censor would have thought – or would have thought readers would have thought – that this was a reference to Polish-Russian or Polish-Soviet relations. Nineteenth century Polish romantic poet Adam Mickiewicz called Poland the Christ of nations. A Christ (i.e. Poland) wandering the wastes (i.e. purgatory) of Siberia (i.e. the Gulag Archipelago) – this would be just too readable an allusion to pass the censor's watchful eyes. However, it was translated into Polish in 1978 and it *did* pass the censors, probably because Updike was American. Western writers did not have to use Aesopian language – or at least not for the same purposes as Poles – meaning the Polish censor did not have to strain to find allusions.

Translators had an incentive to try to rescue books by choosing safe, uncontroversial language. It is easy to demonise the censors but they may have been motivated by a desire to ensure the book appeared in *some* form at least. This has been advanced as the reason for removing the word "nigger" from the NewSouth editions of *Tom Sawyer* and *Huckleberry Finn*.[9] James Ferman, secretary of the British Board of Film Censors, argued that cuts made by British distributors to a film (*Hooper*) "made a delightful comedy available to a great many children" (Ferman 1980: 4). According to Wacław Sadkowski, Polish editors often asked foreign writers and publishers to put up with cuts in order that something, at least, of the books in question be made available to Polish readers. Such requests were usually acceded to (Sadkowski 2002: 114).

---

[1] Masculine and feminine pronouns will be used interchangeably in contexts such as this.

[2] The official name of Poland immediately after the war was The Republic of Poland. Its name was changed in 1952 to the People's Republic of Poland. Throughout this book "post-war Poland" and "People's Poland" will be used to refer to the country from 1945 to 1989. Similarly, where the term "the Party" appears it refers to the ruling party or coalition of the time. From late 1948 on, this was the Polish United Workers' Party (PZPR), which formed from the merger of the Polish Workers' Party (PPR, the communists) and the Polish Socialist Party (PPS), which had between them dominated the country.

[3] All translations are mine unless otherwise noted.

[4] The first letter denotes the collection and is followed by the call number. This is followed by the number of the individual file, where applicable. If the pages of the file are numbered, the page number comes after a colon. The abbreviations used are explained in the bibliography.

[5] See Kamila Budrowska (2009: 17-26). Marta Fik explored the archives in the 1990s and concluded that getting to grips with it was an almost unmanageable task (Fik 1996: 134). Also, some material seems to have gone missing *after* 1989 (Bates 2004b: 142).

[6] Data concerning the publication of books is taken from the Polish National Library's online catalogue. It is far more complete than the censors' archives but a few books may have escaped their attention.

[7] There is very seldom any reference in the archives to the original, source texts and it seems unlikely that the censor routinely compared translations to originals. The quality of translations is sometimes mentioned in reviews but without reference to the original.

[8] Decisions to remove books from libraries because their authors had fallen out of favour were usually transmitted by telephone (Białkowska 1991: 61).

[9] "The editor thus hopes to introduce both books to a wider readership than they can currently enjoy", from Alan Gribben's introduction to the 2011 NewSouth edition, http://www.newsouthbooks.com/twain/introduction-alan-gribben-mark-twain-tom-sawyer-huckleberry-finn-newsouth-books.html Accessed January 9th 2014.

Chapter 2
Progressives

Walter Rideout defines the radical novel as "one which demonstrates, either explicitly or implicitly, that its author objects to the human suffering imposed by some socioeconomic system and *advocates that the system be fundamentally changed*". Similarly, he divides protesters against social divisions into reformers and radicals (Rideout 1956: 12). If the socio-economic system in question is capitalism, it is not difficult to surmise that radical-minded novelists enjoyed more state patronage in People's Poland, at least in the early years. "Radical" is the term chosen by Rideout for his corpus of US novels published from 1900 to 1954, a corpus broken down into the socialist novel (1900-1919), novels of the twenties, the proletarian novel (1930-1939) and novels of the forties and fifties, and including writers such as Howard Fast, Myra Page, Lloyd Brown, Alexander Saxton, Albert Maltz, Richard Wright, Albert Halper, Clara Weatherwax and Henry Roth – most of them somewhat forgotten now but all translated into Polish in their day. "Radical" is also the term used in the title of the series in which Saxton's *The Great Midland* was re-issued in 1997: the Radical Novel Reconsidered. Daniel Aaron's work on the subject is entitled *Writers on the Left* and "left wing" might seem, at least in the American or capitalist context, the obvious word to describe such novelists. Aaron widens his scope to include "fellow travellers", liberals and "nonparty" radicals (Aaron 1977: xvii) but, as will be seen, western writers who were far enough left to get published in Poland were rarely radical enough to truly satisfy the censors in the early years of People's Poland.

Rideout further divides the radical novel of the thirties into four important types: strike stories, stories of personal conversions to radical politics, "bottom dog" novels and depictions of middle class decay (Rideout 1956: 171). Proletarian novels about strikes and the conversion of a character to the cause, he writes, tend to have an explicit message, often communist (Rideout 1956: 185) though such works are to be found among the socialist novels of the early twentieth century too, like I.K. Friedman's 1901 novel *By Bread Alone* (Rideout 1956: 13-18). Also, Steinbeck's *In Dubious Battle* is, in Rideout's understanding, a strike novel but not a proletarian novel (Rideout 1956: 325n). Bottom dog novels (the label comes from Edward

Dahlberg's 1930 book of the same name) depict life in the lower depths and here the message is usually implicit (Rideout 1956: 185). In Henry Roth's *Call it Sleep* the message is so implicit that it met with poor reviews in the radical *New Masses* (Rideout 1956: 189).

The difficulty of relating some tales of down-and-outs to any radical political agenda may account for Rideout's exclusion from his corpus of Erskine Caldwell, whose short story "Daughter" is included in *Proletarian Literature in the United States*, a 1935 anthology edited by Granville Hicks among others. Whether tales of middle class decay can also be classed among radical novels may also cause some controversy. Mary McCarthy's *The Group* follows the lives of a group of Vassar graduates in the Depression, some of whom flirt with left wing causes, but is that enough to make it radical, as opposed to merely critical of the status quo? Similarly, Raymond Chandler and Dashiell Hammett are rarely considered radical even though Hammett was imprisoned for his political beliefs and both writers expose the brutal mix of capitalism and gangsterism that was prized in one Polish review of the now forgotten *Tucker's People* by Ira Wolfert (Dudziński 1950: 11). On the left, Rideout points out, there was some disagreement about what constituted a "proletarian" novel: is it one set in a proletarian milieu, written by a working class author, or can it be any novel written with a Marxist point of view? (Rideout 1956: 166-169).

Arguments over labels such as Marxist, radical, revolutionary, left wing, communist and proletarian can largely be set aside when we turn to the Polish translations of – for want of a better word – radical fiction. Publishing policy became so strict under Stalinism that if a contemporary western novel appeared at all that meant it was considered at the very least "progressive". This was the word favoured in Polish ("postępowy") for writers who, being from the wrong side of the Iron Curtain, could not reasonably be expected to be truly revolutionary. Thus, the censor writes in 1952 of the character of Gideon Jackson in Howard Fast's novel of the American reconstruction period, *Freedom Road*, that "it should be stressed that Gideon's revolutionary nature is essentially bourgeois, not socialist, which is entirely understandable, given the period" (G-386, 31/123: 130). "Progressive" was a suitably vague and suitably tepid term. The publisher's note at the beginning of the Polish translation of Katharine Prichard's *Winged Seeds*, reads: "[The trilogy of books] presents the struggle of the Australian working class for progress, peace and human rights as well as the struggle with the fascist government of the Australian bourgeoisie and with British capital" (Prichard 1951: 5). For writers who were less explicitly radical there was another much-loved adjective in public discourse in Poland: "demaskatorski" ("revealing, exposing"). Books were often praised for exposing the true face of capitalism or racism in the United States, for example.

"Progressive" and "progress" were key words in the public sphere too, in time becoming the target of parody by, for example, Sławomir Mrożek. An advertisement for PIW (State Publishing Institute) publishers appearing in the October edition of *Nowe Książki* in 1949 presents its books under four headings, the second of which is "Contemporary works by Polish, Soviet and progressive western writers" ('Nowości...' 1949: n. pag.). The following number of the same periodical describes Anna Seghers as a well-known German progressive writer (Rev. of *Umarli* 1949: 10). The anonymous *Nowe Książki* review of Priestley's *Bright Day* begins: "A novel by one of the most popular progressive English writers of today..." (Rev. of *Jasny dzień* 1949: 10). A review in 1950 in the same publication of Howard Fast's *Unvanquished* refers to his jailing and describes him as "one of the most outstanding and progressive American writers" (Rev. of *Niezwyciężony* 1950: 24). The review of *Conceived in Liberty* does not use the word "progressive" but we do learn that it is a book of great literary and *ideological* value (Rev. of *Bitwa...* 1950: 13). Theodore Dreiser, on the same page, is labelled "progressive" (Rev. of *Siostra Carrie* 1950: 13) while a review elsewhere of part four of his *The Financier* (called "Money and Betrayal" in Polish) reads as follows: "The author paints, in a realistic manner, a picture of the moral poverty, hypocrisy and incredible corruption of the leading strata of the allegedly democratic republic [i.e. the USA]" (Rev. of *Pieniądz i zdrada* 1949: 9). Albert Halper is also described as progressive in the same periodical's review of his *The Foundry* (Rev. of *Dom...* 1950: 24).

The very first few years of People's Poland saw relative freedom, as publishing had not yet been taken over by the state. Nor was there anything to suggest that socialist realism in literature would become obligatory (Jarosiński 1999: 13). For example, Max Brand, a writer of westerns, was popular, with seven titles published from 1945 to 1947 (Szkup 1972). Also published up until 1949 were writers such as Walt Disney (an adaptation of *Three Little Pigs*, for example), Fannie Hurst, and Margaret Mitchell (*Gone With the Wind*) – as well as left-leaning writers such as Jack London (22 titles), Albert Maltz, John Steinbeck (one book, *Of Mice and Men*) and Ira Wolfert (*Tucker's People*). This freedom was short-lived. In 1951, Max Brand found himself ("all works") on a list of books for "immediate withdrawal" from circulation (*Cenzura PRL...*2002). Various reasons can be proposed for the presence of some books and authors on this list. One is undoubtedly didactic. Many of the authors on the list are low-brow or writers of genre fiction, for example, Rex Beach ("all works"), a writer of adventure stories, E.M. Dell ("all works"), a writer of popular romances, and Edgar Wallace ("all works"), a detective fiction writer. Romances, sensational novels, detective fiction and fantasy were "loudly condemned" after 1948

(Kondek 2006: 25). Agatha Christie ("all works") was also withdrawn but later permitted to return.[1] The authorities were trying to break and, especially in the case of children, make the habits of the Polish reading public. Max Brand had over a dozen titles translated in Poland before the war, Rex Beach seven, E.M. Dell over 40, and Edgar Wallace over 60 (Wnęk 2006). Once 1948 came, Max Brand had to wait until 1984 for a re-edition in Poland. Beach did not appear in Poland in book form between the years 1939 and 1990. Nor did Dell, while only one Wallace book appeared after the war, in 1947. Zane Grey is another writer that dropped out of sight in post-war Poland. Once the 1990s came, "the market for popular Anglo-American literature opened up and hundreds of thousands of books by authors such as Ludlum, Forsyth and MacLean were printed" (Kitrasiewicz and Gołębiewski 2005: 277). Forsyth (*Day of the Jackal*) and MacLean (*Guns of Navarone*), though not Ludlum, had been published in People's Poland but evidently not in sufficient quantities.

Gone With the Wind was also marked down for withdrawal and one censor wrote of Fannie Hurst's *Wielki uśmiech* (presumably *Great Laughter* of 1936) that it might rob the masses of their energy ("demobilizować") and "instil in them lack of faith in their strength. [...] In the Poland of 1949 there is no place for this book. It should not be published" (G-173c, 32/44: 109). Such was the zeal that some western writers were rejected even though they revealed the harsh realities of life in the West (Kondek 1999: 35).

In the early post-war years, non-progressive writers were still occasionally published in Poland. Hemingway's *To Have and Have Not* re-appeared in 1948 and Dorothy Parker and William Saroyan also had pieces published in periodicals in the 1940s but the times were changing. In her memoirs, publisher and translator Irena Szymańska recalls Jerzy Borejsza of Czytelnik publishers returning from America in 1947 with the rights to Hemingway, Faulkner, Caldwell and Saroyan but he could not use them (Szymańska 2001: 43). None of them were published in book form from 1950 to 1955 – not even Caldwell, with his excoriation of the depression-era American South. The lead here had been given by the USSR: Hemingway, Caldwell and Steinbeck were denounced in the late 1940s (Rev. of *A Guide...* 1955: 271). After *For Whom the Bell Tolls*, with its unflattering portrayal of Communists, Hemingway went unpublished in the USSR until 1955 (Sherry 2012: 95).

The pages of *Literatura Radziecka* (*Soviet Literature*), a Moscow periodical that appeared in several languages, give some clues as to which writers were ruled in and which were ruled out. In particular, a 1950 article attacking Henry Miller was probably responsible for keeping Miller off Polish publishing plans until the 1960s. The same article also attacks Huxley, Orwell and, by extension, Lawrence Durrell, who had expressed his admiration for Henry Miller (Jakowlew 1950: 162). Other articles in the late 40s and early 50s praise Theodore Dreiser, Mike Gold, Ira Wolfert, Howard Fast, Albert Maltz and Alexander Saxton. Norman Mailer was also praised for *The Naked and the Dead*, although unfortunately it lacked a "warrior hero" ("bohater-bojownik") (Romanow 1949: 166).

Szymańska's account of her years in publishing show attempts to run Czytelnik like an ordinary publishing house, with occasional mass-market hits subsidising more ambitious but loss-making books (Szymańska 2001: 39). However, publishers in the 1950s were directed to read a weekly digest of new books in the USSR for ideas and to produce monthly reports in Russian concerning the propositions therein (Kondek 1999: 121). Szymańska dates the beginning of the authoritarian turn to First Secretary Bierut's address to the Party, "On right-wing and nationalist deviation in the leadership of the party" at the plenary session of the communist Polish Workers' Party in 1948 (Szymańska 2001: 47). It was in 1948, too, that Jerzy Borejsza, who had edited *Odrodzenie*, in which excerpts from Faulkner had appeared, underwent self-criticism for indulging petit bourgeois culture (Fik 1989: 104). Michał Głowiński dates the beginnings of enforced socialist realism to a speech given by First Secretary Bierut in November 1947 on the occasion of the opening of a radio station, although the term "socialist realism" does not appear in the speech (Głowiński 1996: 116-117). By 1948, the stated publishing policy was not to meet readers' current tastes but to shape their future tastes (Kondek 1999: 9-10).

There is some debate over the starting point of Stalinism in Poland, with some dating its beginnings to 1944. However, Andrzej Werblan (who in 1958 was head of the propaganda division of the Party's Central Committee) argues that until the formation in 1947 of the Cominform (Information Bureau of Communist and Workers' Parties) Poland and other countries in the eastern bloc seemed to be following a socialist path somewhat independent of the Soviet Union. He accepts 1948 as a key year in the full Stalinisation of Poland, allowing that Stalinist politico-legal repressions started earlier (Werblan 2009: 53-55). In the realm of public discourse, the change that came about in 1948 was particularly marked. Political language

> became pompous, stiff – in essence primitive and impoverished. Ever more areas of life fell under the heading of state secrets and were closed off to public opinion, resulting in a propaganda consisting solely of generalisations and magic formulas [zaklęcia]. It is enough to flick through the pages of one year's worth (1948) of daily newspapers and, in particular, weeklies, including Marxist publications – not long previously excellently produced – to see how sudden the change was. It got so bad that old periodicals had to be closed down and new ones started up (Werblan 2009: 58).

An ominous sign of the direction Polish translation and publishing was to take was the call in 1949, at a censors' meeting, for permission for publication to be given to books even if they were artistically weak "if there is a guarantee that the author will in the future become a progressive, militant, useful writer" (Nałęcz 1994: 24; see also Bates 2004: 20). Such pronouncements were directed more at Polish authors, and in this case at beginners, but the implications for translation should be clear: more Maltz, less Waugh; more Fast, less Faulkner.

In the case of the radical novel, the most insistent form of censorship was censorship by selection: the promotion of politically correct work with little or no regard for its artistic merits, particularly evident in the years from 1949 to 1955.[2] A review from roughly 1950 of Jack London's autobiographical sketches *The Road* in the files of the Ministry for Culture and Art describes the book as artistically mediocre. "However", the reviewer (not, at least nominally, a censor) continues, "given its simplicity and the author's negative relationship to the American bourgeoisie it should not provoke objections" (M-709, Departament Twórczości Artystycznej; Wydział Wydawniczy: 225). The reference to the book's "simplicity" indicates the concern of the authorities with reaching the "new reader"; that is, people who had never belonged to the intelligentsia and were only just, on the heels of a literacy campaign, turning to books. Another document, drawn up by the committee on belles lettres attached to the Party's Central Committee and dating from 1959, contains a list of things to be done. Under the sub-heading of translated literature it is proposed that a list of works by "left wing and progressive writers" and outstanding writers be drawn up (as if unintentionally distinguishing between good writers and progressive writers) (K-237/viii-466: 43).

In the years 1950 to 1955, progressives really start to make their mark – in terms of raw numbers, if not of being taken to heart by Polish readers. Howard Fast has 13 entries from this period in Jerzy Szkup's bibliography of American (that is, US) literature in translation in Poland, with *The Last Frontier* going through five editions. In publishers' lists from 1950 to 1955, there was room for Lloyd Brown's *Iron City* and Alexander Saxton's *The Great Midland* (both of which were also published in the USSR), Theodore Dreiser, Jack London (consistently popular in Poland before and after the war), Albert Maltz, Robert Mende, Myra Page, and Clara Weatherwax, but not for Ernest Hemingway, William Faulkner or even John Steinbeck. It is apparent that progressive writers were favoured. The numbers of their books published attests to this, as does the obvious weakness of some of them. While the ardour may have worn off over time, one still finds in the late 1970s enthusiasm – real or feigned – for progressive writers or writers who were (or could be) perceived as progressive. One publisher's draft "Basic

Directions and Tendencies" for the period 1976-1980 undertakes to translate from western literature such books as show political and social problems (K-lvi474).

Official approval of progressive western literature may have put the likes of Jane Austen in the shade, at least for a time, but the fact is that *all* western literature was, under Stalinism (that is, roughly 1949 to 1955), overshadowed by the promotion of fiction from politically correct countries: the USSR and the eastern bloc.

From 1944 to 1948 just 90 titles were translated from Russian and Soviet (i.e. from countries belonging to the Soviet Union) literature. In 1948 less than 10% of belles lettres in Poland were translations of Soviet and Russian literature (Bromberg 1966: 152; diagram VI, n. pag.). However, a browse through the back numbers of *Nowe Książki* in the late 1940s and early 1950s shows the growing imbalance between East and West. This quick subjective impression is borne out by more thorough, empirical studies. The Soviet Union came to dominate not only translated literature – it also rivalled Polish belles lettres. From 1944/5 to 1955, 680 titles were translated from English into Polish. The figure for Russian and other languages of the USSR was 2,257 (French accounted for 504 titles, German 307). The total print run in this period for English translations (of belles lettres) was just under 15 million. For Russian and other languages of the USSR it was nearly 50 million. In 1950, Soviet literature accounted for 35% of *all* belles lettres titles while Polish accounted for 40%. Over time – and with occasional reversals – Soviet literature's position weakened while that of English language literature strengthened. Nevertheless, by 1980, 3,056 books (belles lettres) had been translated from the English language, while the corresponding figure for Russian and other languages of the USSR was 4,353 (Czarnik 1993: 240-241). In 1989, the figures were 4,019 and 5,047, respectively, but the total print run for English language translations was, at 159.5 million, higher than that of USSR translations, 145.5 million (*Ruch Wydawniczy* 1990: 95).[3]

Just as enthusiasm for progressive western writers with at least slightly revolutionary values wears off over the years following the thaw of 1956, so too does the enthusiasm for Soviet literature. In 1956, Soviet literature's share of the 109 contemporary foreign prose titles was 43. By 1958 there were 21 Soviet books among the 137 contemporary foreign prose titles (K-237/viii-466: 55). The archives of the Party's Central Committee have numerous documents in which concern is expressed at the low number of translations from Russian or Soviet languages. In a 1952 information bulletin from the censors' archives, for example, a section on the Czytelnik publishing house notes the lack of certain kinds of translation, nearly always with the words "especially Soviet" added (G-420, 165/1: 211-220). A 1973 document from the Party's Central Committee files headed "Decisions and Conclusions", and also concerning Czytelnik publishers, notes that more translations from – in particular – Romania, Hungary and the USSR must be published (K-lvi783). The Association of Polish Translators noted in the 1980s that the number of translations from Russian and from Soviet languages had been in decline for twenty years (K-lvi1307: 6). An internal party document covering publishing plans for 1983-1984 complains that there are not enough books about the working class, the political organisation of society, the socialist way of life, or the workers' movement in Poland; nor is there enough literature from socialist countries, the third world or by progressive writers from the West (K-lvi885).

In Stalinist Poland the trend towards "progressive" contemporary prose concerning such matters as trade union activity and the growing class consciousness of a socialist realist hero is to be found not just in translated literature but also in home grown literary production. That is, translations did not move to fill a gap in the Polish literary market since Polish writers were already writing "to order" – to satisfy a demand created by the state. A concise description of recurring motifs in so-called "production novels" in Poland is provided by Alicja Lisiecka: the hero gives inspirational speeches at meetings of workers; work brigades start to work as teams; shirkers mend their ways or are exposed as foreign agents; saboteurs are caught. In addition, Lisiecka also mentions a spirit of competition among workers turning selfish types who live only for the moment into socialist heroes (Lisiecka 1964: 81). Tadeusz Konwicki's *Przy budowie* ("On the Building Site") – and many more books of the period – concerns a "random group of people" transformed into a proper team of dedicated workers (Lisiecka 1964: 115). The steering of Polish literature in the post-war years, and especially after the turn away from formalism and the official adaptation of socialist realism at the Writers' Union congress in Szczecin in 1949, has been well-documented (see, e.g., Bates 2004, Miłosz 1983: 453-458) but a quick comparison of reviews published in *Nowe Książki* is still instructive. Andrzej Braun's *Lewanty* ("Freighters") is reviewed as follows:

> One of the first contemporary novels about the Gdańsk shipyards and the founders and heroes of the Polish shipbuilding industry. From the very beginning the author leads us into the tense atmosphere of sharp class struggle in which the enemy aims at and strikes every weak link of our young but ever so important shipbuilding industry. [...] The struggle with the enemy – inextricably bound up with the struggle to complete the [six-year] plan and raise production to a higher level – becomes the measure of people's character... (Rev. of *Lewanty* 1953: 152).

The same issue carries a review of Clara Weatherwax's *Marching! Marching!* It runs:

> A novel by a contemporary American writer who took an active part in the workers'
> movement and learned at first hand the work of the labourer and the clerk in large
> corporations. The novel is set in the 1930s and presents the struggle of sawmill workers,
> lumberjacks and clam diggers on the Pacific coast against capitalists seeking to prevent
> the establishment of a strong trade union movement (Rev. of *Będzie...* 1953: 154).

The problems of the post-war Polish working class are not quite those of the
pre-war American working class but both books can safely be called
"progressive". The translation of Clara Weatherwax fills a gap in Polish
literature only insofar as Polish readers were eager for any information at all
about the US (it seems unlikely that Poles were crying out for novels about
strikes *per se*, even if their own literature concentrated on reactionary
saboteurs rather than striking workers). American books were very popular in
post-war Poland, sometimes selling out before any review even appeared and
often sold under the counter or in second hand shops at twice the cover price
(Lyra 1989: 201). However, there were limits to Polish readers' desire for
information about the USA. In 1955 Czytelnik publishers produced a list of
books to be pulped or given away due to poor sales. It includes Howard
Fast's *Peekskill USA* (the Polish title translates as "The Attack on Paul
Robeson"), while *Murzyni w USA. Pisarze amerykańscy o rasizmie w
Stanach Zjednoczonych* ("Black People in the USA: American Writers on
Racism in the United States") was on the pulping list of another publisher,
Książka i Wiedza (C-74: 113, 177).

Home-grown Polish literature was not in dire need of an injection
from the West of "conversion" novels either, although the emphasis is a little
different in the Polish context. *Nowe Książki* reviews Aleksander
Jackiewicz's *Wiedeńska wiosna* ("Viennese Spring"), which is about an
Austrian writer's conversion from political passivity (Rev. of *Wiedeńska
wiosna* 1953: 152). The targets of conversion in home-grown progressive
novels of the fifties were usually members of the old intelligentsia. Such
stock characters were usually mistrustful of the new Poland at first. Some of
them never become "engaged" (another favourite watchword of the times) in
the process of building a better future and become "tools in the hands of the
class enemy" but others are converted (Jarosiński 1999: 79). Although these
"hesitant intellectuals" are usually secondary characters they are, according
to Jarosiński, very important because the intelligentsia were books' target
readers (Jarosiński 1999: 80).

To look at the censorship archives, however, one would think at times
that the path of progressive western writers was not, in fact, strewn with
roses. Because they were radicals, Communists or fellow travellers they had
much more to say about subjects like Stalin and the Molotov-Ribbentrop pact
than, say, Henry Miller or William Faulkner. But because they wrote in freer
societies there was a greater risk that they would come out with unacceptable

deviations from the party line. As a general rule the Polish censor was far more concerned with interpretations of recent Polish history – and military secrets – than just about anything else. Hence, his or her attention was focused first and foremost on Polish writers who might, for example, have the temerity to refer to the Soviet invasion of Poland in September 1939 as an invasion. Few English language writers dwelled on such subjects but those who did were more likely to be progressives or radicals than navel-gazing formalist experimenters. Although official policy strongly favoured *littérature engagée*, the practice of censorship encouraged books that did not broach touchy subjects like comparisons between communism and fascism. Michał Głowiński commented privately in 1981 that "Communism can never, under any circumstances, be compared with Fascism" (Głowiński 1993: 318).

A recurring complaint of the censors is that so-and-so's book is progressive but not progressive enough, or perhaps not quite the right *kind* of progressive. This may be an occupational hazard for left wing writers in general. For example, Upton Sinclair had a similar reception in Poland before the war, never being "fully accepted" by the left; for communist critics his "exposure of social relations" was not enough (Kieniewicz 1977: 68). One critic, Markowicz, wrote in a left wing publication called *Lewar* in 1935:

> 'as well as the realistic element in Sinclair's work there has (always) been a utopian and reactionary element [...] the method of dialectic materialism has always been foreign to him and he expects social liberation to come from a powerful, self-sacrificing individual, not from a mass movement of workers' (qtd. Kieniewicz 1977: 68).

This is similar to critical practice of the Stalinist period in Poland. Nearly every new Polish novel was accused of not keeping pace with the times. Critics complained about "political faults, failure to notice socially important phenomena, relics of the old way of thinking..." (Jarosiński 1999: 62). This attempt by critics to show that they, at least, were keeping up with the times, is mirrored in the censorship archives. Of J.B. Priestley's *Daylight on Saturday* one censor writes that it is "very progressive, for England" (G-145, 31/22: 100). A review of the same writer's *Bright Day* reads in part, "Ideologically, it is a progressive novel but this progress is understood very naïvely" (G-145, 31/23: 412) and John Bates has shown how censors' reviews of this book got cooler as time went on, until a critical mention of him in *Soviet Literature* put an end to his publishing career in Poland until 1957 (Bates 2011: 67). Priestley's entry in the *Polish Literary Bibliography* was also censored (Tokarzówna 1992, vol. 2: 243).

Reviewers at ministry level expressed unhappiness at Jack London's *Tales of the Fish Patrol* (Polish title: *Przygody w zatoce San Francisco*) because although London mentions that some people fish illegally because of poverty, he does not develop the issue, instead showing all poachers as villains (M-709, Departament Twórczości Artystycznej; Wydział Wydawniczy: 220). A batch of reviews of Jack London's books dating from 1949 can be found in the archives of the Ministry for Culture and Art, where his path did not run as smoothly as might be expected for an avowed socialist. The problem was that he was also considered a racist. Among the reasons given for not publishing *The Sea Wolf* in Poland was racism, the book's defence of idealism, and its religious and metaphysical elements. The reviewer also mentions the poor quality of the translation, by J.B. Rychliński (M-705, Departament Twórczości Artystycznej; Wydział Wydawniczy). *The Sea Wolf* was published eventually, in 1955. London seems to have been unfortunate with his translators. One of them was Stanisława Kuszelewska, and although a ministry reviewer praises her work on a book of Klondike stories to be entitled *Prawo białego człowieka* ("The White Man's Law"), the book's reissue was not allowed because Kuszelewska had "signed a declaration on non-publication in the country". This last comment is added in red under the otherwise favourable review, which noted that London was a "progressive" (at that time these ministerial review sheets had a heading "Socio-political views suggested by the author") (M-705, Departament Twórczości Artystycznej; Wydział Wydawniczy). Kuszelewska was out of political favour. Her name was cut from the yearbooks of the *Polish Literary Bibliography* (Czachowska 1992, vol. 2: 223-224) and her translation of *White Fang* was replaced in the 1950s by Anna Przedpełska-Trzeciakowska's. By the 1980s, however, her translation of London's *A Daughter of the Snows*, was back in print, having last appeared in 1948.

Myra Page's *With Sun in our Blood* was welcomed by the censors, but one of them notes among its weaknesses a failure to clearly show the class struggle (G-145, 31/26: 594). Another censor writes that the miners in the book show no reaction to their exploitation even though it is just before the First World War. What rebellion there is, is anaemic: the miners have no broader vision and are interested only in material improvements (G-145, 31/26: 597). The same complaint is made of Robert Mende's *Spit and the Stars*: one has the impression that the struggle of American workers is steered not by class consciousness but by the chase for the dollar (G-386, 31/122: 374). Katharine Prichard, as a founder member of the Australian Communist Party, might be expected to get these things right – that is, to show the workers' movement in the correct, communist perspective – but she too runs afoul of politics. Although her *Winged Seeds* is good, one of the censors writes, it does not show the opportunism of the Australian Labour Party and the Australian trade unions. Nor does it give full credit for the USSR's role in World War Two, and there is no socialist realist hero (G-375, 31/28: 256).

These are not criticisms that would or could be levelled at, say, *Brideshead Revisited.*

Commenting on Stephen Crane's *Red Badge of Courage*, the censor writes:

> Of course *the concept of just and unjust wars, which was born in the age of imperialist wars, proletarian revolutions and national liberation struggles, was alien to this classic of nineteenth* century America and it is therefore essential that these matters be dealt with in Zieliński's introduction [to the book] (G-375, 31/35: 485; emphasis in original).

Crane's book, it seems, was anti-war but not exactly anti-the-right-war. Also in need of a good, Marxist introduction was Alexander Saxton's *The Great Midland* (G-386, 31/122: 84).

However, the books the censors sniffed at did generally get published – at least until their authors started to complain about Soviet cold war aggression. Not only did progressive writers get published despite tut-tutting from the censors, but the complaints were often overridden. No doubt censors sometimes strove to impress their superiors by pointing out ideological deficiencies in the books they were given to examine. In this way they could demonstrate their vigilance without necessarily blocking the publication of western progressives. Also, since "reactionary" translations seldom even came before the censors, there was only progressives to complain about and behind some of the ideological carping we might detect censors trying to justify their jobs. For all the censors' fervour, progressives did have the advantage of official patronage, as seen in the case of Jack London. Traven's *Das Totenschiff* was permitted publication (albeit during the thaw, in 1957), despite the criticism of Russian Communists contained in it, because the book and its author were progressive, according to one censor's report (G-424, 31/7: 143). Left wing writer Frank Hardy's *Power Without Glory* passes muster despite being artistically weak. His language – or maybe it is the translator's fault, the censor acknowledges – is "impoverished, flat and devoid of style" but there are no "political reservations" concerning the book (G-375, 31/28: 664). Likewise, Alexander Saxton's *The Great Midland*, despite its flaws, is "progressive" and therefore makes the grade in one censor's review (G-386, 31/122: 86-92). In early 1956, one censor acknowledged that a play called *The Travellers*, attributed to Ewan MacColl, was not very good but given its politics was good enough (G-424, 31/36: 10). The second reviewer praised its value as propaganda (G-424, 31/36: 10) and the translation appeared in 1956.

A particularly good example of politics trumping (perceived) quality is Sean O'Casey's autobiographical *I Knock at the Door*, which may have been saved by its author's reputed membership of the Communist Party. One censor panned it for presenting no "social values", accusing it of being bad literature too (boring, garrulous), and recommending that it not be published (G-771, 132/106). However, another censor intervened, pointing out, among other things, that "according to the publisher the author is an active member of the Irish Communist Party. Also, he is published in the Soviet Union. Obviously this is no argument for this particular book but an explanation of what kind of a writer we are dealing with here" (G-771, 132/106). The translation's flyleaf states that O'Casey was never actually a Communist Party member. This example comes from 1963, well after the end of Stalinism in Poland.

Four censor's reports on *Kipps* by H.G. Wells can be found in the archives, all in favour of publication "without changes" (G-145, 31/25: 168-175). But changes were made to the book and they were quite clearly politically motivated, suggesting again that the censors' job was largely done even before they read the manuscript. The changes mostly concern Masterman, the ailing socialist who lectures the newly wealthy Kipps of the title. Gone is the following passage:

> 'Man is a social animal with a mind nowadays that goes around the globe, and a community cannot be happy in one part and unhappy in another. It's all or nothing, no patching any more for ever. It is the standing mistake of the world not to understand that. Consequently people think there is a class or order somewhere just above them or just below them, or a country or place somewhere that is really safe and happy' (Wells 1941: 239-240).

Although *Kipps* was first published before the Russian Revolution, it does not do to suggest there is a no safe and happy country. Also, Wells is not permitted to make as much fun of the socialist Masterman and his beliefs in Polish as he is in English. This may explain why his name is untranslated, unlike Nietzsche's "Overman", which is. There is quite a clear instance of manipulation of the translation of Kipps's response to Masterman's "case against property and the property class":

> Kipps was completely carried away, and never thought of asking for a clear vision of the thing that would fill the void this abolition might create. For a time he quite forgot his own private opulence (Wells 1941: 242).

In back translation this reads: "Kipps felt entirely convinced and even forgot about his 'private property'" (Wells 1950: 289). The issue has been narrowed down to Kipps himself, ignoring the broader question posed in the original. And yet the translation remains true enough to the original for the follow-up review, which in this case is an altogether sterner piece of work, to complain of Masterman's "pseudo-socialist" views. The censor notes that Masterman is the only representative of the working class and the book, then, "demands of the reader a certain sophistication and is not suitable for the masses" (G-145,

31/25: 175). Another censor writes: "No reservation, especially as the publisher's editor removed a few statements characteristic of petit bourgeois anarchism", supplying the page numbers that correspond to the excised passages given above (G-145, 31/25: 171).

A sign of the times is the removal of the word "Russian" in the translation of the following line: "And then, and more in the manner of a Russian prince than any common count, Chitterlow bowed and withdrew" (Wells 1941: 194). The book predates the Russian revolution and yet the publishers baulked at mentioning the existence of such a thing as a Russian nobleman (Wells 1950: 234).

One censor considered Alexander Saxton's *The Great Midland*, a tale of trade unionism in the Chicago railways, a weak book and although he or she recommended permission to publish, it was after "interventions" were made. The censor was dismayed that the Communist Party only has one representative in the book, Dave Spaas (actually there is also Pledger McAdams), and that the communist angle is in any case just background to the psychological love story between Dave and Stephanie Koviak (G-386, 31/122: 84). The first edition of the novel did not get the good Marxist review called for but the accompanying footnotes (credited to the editor, not the translator) are very pointed. The clearest example is probably the note explaining what the Congress of Industrial Organisations (CIO) was – and when:

> ...a professional organisation with six million American workers. The CIO, founded in 1935 by J. Lewis, stands in opposition to the American Federation of Labour (AFL). Before the war it was politically radical and led important strikes. Currently, the leadership of the CIO is reactionary (Saxton 1951: 116n).

The AFL is described in another footnote as "opportunist" and its leadership "entirely reactionary and linked with the bourgeoisie" (Saxton 1951: 10n).[4]

Radicals were more likely to tread on thin ice but in this case it was probably coincidence that Saxton exposed himself to censorious displeasure by briefly mentioning a picture of Józef Piłsudski, the pre-war Polish soldier, politician and one-time socialist, hanging in a bar. This was "unnecessary", the censor wrote, and should be cut. It was not cut. Nor were the words, "'Do you think there is any essential difference between the Nazi and Soviet forms of government?'" (Saxton 1997: 297). The censor was concerned that although spoken by a "muddle-head", which detracts from its seriousness, the question is left unanswered (G-386, 31/122: 85). Nor is this the only occasion in the book when the unpleasant association is brought up. "'What's scientific dogma?'" Stephanie asks at one point. "'Communism,' Marguerite said. 'Fascism. Utopias based on a faulty understanding of science...'" (Saxton 1997: 203). This is largely intact in translation, though Stephanie asks "what kind of scientific dogmas" ("–Co za naukowe dogmaty?") (Saxton 1951: 272). This time, at least, the veiled criticism of communism does not go unchallenged: Stephanie says: "'As a matter of fact [...] I'm considering seriously joining the Communist Party. And I'll match my understanding of science against yours – or Victor's either – any day of the week'" (Saxton 1997: 203). The translation is not quite exact: "'or Victor's either'" becomes "or rather Victor's?" (Saxton 1951: 273). Victor is the "muddle-head" referred to earlier, while Marguerite may be identified with Walter Rideout's "middle class decay". This, and the translator's accentuation of Victor's role in spreading confused ideas about science, may soften the criticism but not all writers could get away with drawing such parallels, as will be seen.

Saxton again sails close to the wind in chapter 23 when Dave debates with Red (a fellow trade unionist, but not a Communist) about Soviet diplomacy during World War Two: "'You ask me how come the communists change their position about the war. [...] Because the war changed, that's why'" (Saxton 1997: 305). This exchange of views is largely present and correct in translation. The only real difference is that there is less flippancy and rudeness. Red says, "'I'm all for you, boy, but I think you commies got caught with your pants down'" (Saxton 1997: 306). In Polish it is, in back translation, "I'm of the same opinion as you but I think you were unpleasantly surprised" (Saxton 1951: 407), avoiding the unflattering "commie". When Red says, "'You bastards always got your own answers'" (Saxton 1997: 306) the translation here and elsewhere in the exchange omits "bastards" even though it almost qualifies as a term of endearment. Dave and Red's argument is heated – Red baits red, one might say – but they remain friends. In the following example the task of the editor (or translator or censor) was admittedly made easier by Saxton's own evasion tactics – in this case evading the Polish question: "Dave told him [Pledger McAdams] the Russians were retreating, the Nazis had crossed the Soviet frontier from Poland" (Saxton 1997: 324).[5] There is some obfuscation in the original: the Nazi-Soviet frontier ran *through* Poland, not along the country's border. This means the translator can translate straightforwardly without giving offence to the USSR. It is notable that the translator does not intervene to correct or clarify.

The translation also gives a stronger impression than the original that the Russian retreat is a "plan" to defeat the Germans. The original has:

> 'They'll hold them,' Pledger said. 'They'll drop back and then they'll hold 'em.'
>
> Dave nodded. He understood what was in Pledger's mind. It wasn't that anyone knew for sure they could; but now it was useless thinking any different (Saxton 1997: 324).

In Polish, in back translation, the last sentence is "No one was sure if the Soviet Army's plan would succeed but there was no point thinking about the opposite eventuality" (Saxton 1951: 433). Calling the Soviet Union's catastrophic retreat before the Nazis a "plan" might be understood as a sly attempt by the translator to ridicule Dave's and Pledger's faith in the USSR. If this *was* an act of passive resistance by the translator it is isolated in this book and seems unlikely to have registered very strongly with readers. Publishers (or printers) did sometimes make mistakes that appear to have been deliberate but they were usually a little more obvious. Irena Szymańska in her memoirs recalls changing by hand the entire print run (19,000 copies) of a book in which Karl Marx was accidentally described as a "tyrant of work" instead of a "titan of work" ("tyran/tytan" in Polish). The mistake (if it was a mistake – Szymańska does not say it was deliberate) had gone unnoticed by the censors (Szymańska 2001: 43). Another, more readable attack can be found, much later, in the translation of Dashiell Hammett's story "The Scorched Face" where January 13th, the date on which "Mrs Dorothy Sawdon, a young widow, had shot herself" (Hammett 2005: 86), is changed to December 13th – the date martial law was imposed in Poland in 1981 (Hammett 1988: 20).

In *The Great Midland* some criticism of communism and the USSR could pass, especially if it was tainted by association with undesirables, but not if it was too disrespectful. A reference in the original to "Joe Stalin in Moscow" (Saxton 1997: 202) is changed to "Joseph Stalin and Moscow" (Saxton 1951: 270), and "'Joe Stalin got his ass in the hot water'" (Saxton 1997: 304) is changed to "'Joseph Stalin got caught up in this whole mess'" (Saxton 1951: 405).

A follow-up review has also survived in the archives. The censor does not rate the novel highly but it is – for America – "progressive" and the verdict is that the book may be renewed with certain corrections. The censor notes the lack of "revolutionary spirit" in the Communist Party of the USA, which will come as a surprise to Polish readers (G-386, 31/122: 89). Also, the opening parts of the book are grist to the mill of reactionaries as they show some workers with telephones and their own cars (G-386, 31/122: 90). This was indeed something the translator had "overlooked": all the source text's references to the material wealth of US workers are present in the translation (as are references to poverty, unemployment, exploitation and racial discrimination). Pledger McAdams holds his "railroad watch on its square-linked gold chain" (Saxton 1997: 207) in the original. The translation substitutes "old" for "railroad" (Saxton 1951: 278). Apart from this, which may be a stylistic change (it is 1940 and Pledger has been a railwayman off and on since before World War One so it probably is an "old" watch) there is no attempt made by the translator or censor to hide the wealth of workers in capitalist America from Polish eyes. Even in later, more lenient years authors could run into trouble for excessive displays of wealth and luxury in America. The film *The Swimmer*, with Burt Lancaster, was banned for this reason (Fik 1993: 184).

A committed communist translator seeking to play up the poverty and hardship experienced by US industrial workers in Albert Maltz's *The Underground Stream* for propaganda purposes would not have had much work to do. Saxton's *The Great Midland*, over the span of some 20 years, covers periods of unemployment and real hardship during the depression but there are also scenes in which Dave goes for a beer with workmates and even goes to a hotel with Stephanie, where they drink whiskey. *Underground Stream* covers three days in the lives of workers employed in the automobile industry in 1936 but this novel paints a much darker picture of the life of the American industrial worker. In *The Great Midland* the workers appear able to lead family lives and do things outside of working hours; here workers seem to have only a scant few hours to themselves a week. It is a hard life in Maltz's fiction. For example, there is this brief socialist realist passage: "...out of the sweat, the exploitation, the spiritual hungers that are the companions of a worker at the bottom of the industrial pit..." (Maltz 1940: 19), which is reproduced in the Polish minus the last seven words, widening the scope of the passage to *all* workers, not just those at the bottom (Maltz 1949: 26). In short, the living conditions in both *The Great Midland* and *Underground Stream* are faithfully rendered, even if a little over zealously in the latter, which in general is a worse translation.

The censors responded favourably to this exposition of the seamy side of American capitalism, showing none of the reservations they had towards *The Great Midland*:

> A very good novel, presenting the heroic struggle of American communists to establish trade unions (CIO). The barbaric methods of capital used in the struggle against activist workers with the friendly 'neutrality' of the police lay bare the entire hypocrisy of American 'democracy' (G-145, 31/23: 235).[6]

The only sour note in this censor's review is a handwritten addendum concerning the CIO's "metamorphosis" (G-145, 31/23: 235). References to the CIO are cut from the translation, and in one case changed to the Federation of Trade Unions (Maltz 1949: 93), though one did survive (Maltz 1949: 55). Another review is more descriptive and less ideological but also enthusiastic about the book's counterattack on "the remnants of Anglo-Saxon propaganda about the alleged wealth of society in capitalist countries" (G-145, 31/23: 237). A follow-up review says it is of great literary and ideological value (G-145, 31/23: 241).

The translation is, however, much weaker than Ewa Fiszer's of *The Great Midland*, with numerous misunderstandings and what seem to be elisions of the hard parts. Harvey Kellog, in the source text, is "a striking-looking man" (Maltz 1940: 4). In translation he "looks old" (Maltz 1949: 9). "What on earth made this thug tick?" (Maltz 1940: 181) is mistranslated as "What had made this animal fat?" (Maltz 1949: 186) and "'Why do you interrupt to lecture me on baby stuff?'" (Maltz 1940: 49) becomes "Why have you stopped talking about [having] a child?" (Maltz 1949: 55) in what seems to be a variation on the well-known English learner's confusion about stopping doing something and stopping to do something. A car that looks "as though it had just rolled off the assembly" (Maltz 1940: 149) is transformed into a car such as can be seen in front of government buildings (Maltz 1949: 157: the translator seems to have mistaken assembly line for parliamentary assembly). A "righteous, holier-than-thou smirk" (Maltz 1940: 235) is changed into a "polite smile" (Maltz 1949: 235). Examples could be adduced at length. They include instances where the translation says the exact opposite of the original but there is nothing to suggest deliberate sabotage of the pro-communist message of the original book. That is, there is no pattern of mistakes. *Underground Stream* cannot be counted among the successes of post-war translation.

The translation is quite free with the text, humanising Jeffry Grebb in the opening pages of the book, cutting or modifying disrespectful references to the Catholic Church and other religions, cutting bits out of political debates, removing most sex scenes and toning down the occasionally strong language. The book opens with Jeffry Grebb, who has a solidly working class background, and the translator seems to have thought he was going to be a positive character. Grebb, a "hunter of women" who feels "a need for possession" for Adelaide Kellog (Maltz 1940: 7), is in Polish a "lover" of women who "desires" Adelaide Kellog (Maltz 1949: 12). Again, Grebb is prone to "imperious desire" for "possession" of women (Maltz 1940: 15). In Polish he has a "strong desire" with no mention of possession (Maltz 1949: 21). Missing from the Polish are the following lines:

> A man was a composite of various appetites, he knew that; some psychological, some physical, all needing satisfaction! There was nothing beyond this truth, no creed, no reality. Anything else was pretence or religious nonsense. Yet why did the satisfaction of those appetites so often involve defeat? (Maltz 1940: 28).

As a result of such changes and omissions, Grebb comes across at the start of the book as more of a victim of his desire for Adelaide Kellog. She, for her part, cannot "help responding to the flattery of his instant, bold pursuit" (Maltz 1940: 8) whereas in Polish she cannot resist his "brash adoration" (Maltz 1949: 13). Grebb is less imperious, less possessive and less materialist in translation. This Polish Grebb does not dismiss organised religion out of hand. When he thinks about the man-made barriers between himself and Adelaide, one of them is the church (Maltz 1940: 21) – but it is not among the barriers in the Polish translation (Maltz 1949: 27).

The translation's sensitivity to matters religious is especially noticeable in the scene in which Grebb is inducted into the Iron Guard of the Black Legion, a slightly ridiculous, fascist, anti-labour secret organisation. The rhetoric here is strongly anti-Catholic (and anti-Jewish) and although the speakers are clearly evil (if not actually demented) their words are censored as if for fear that they might be taken seriously. The oath Grebb takes runs (in part – it is very long): "*I will exert every possible means in my power for the extermination* [...] *of the anarchists, Communists, the Roman Hierarchy and their abettors*'" (Maltz 1940: 82). The anarchists and the Roman hierarchy are missing from the Polish version of the pledge (Maltz 1949: 88). Further on, the words "*Would you oppose by ballot, and if necessary by force of arms, any attempt to place any portion of the public tax money in the hands of the Roman Catholic Church?*'" (Maltz 1940: 85) are cut from the Polish version (Maltz 1949: 91). *Not* cut, however, is the sentence from the pledge that follows immediately after: "*Will you do all in your power to place only white Protestant Americans in public office?*'" (Maltz 1940: 85). This means that the anti-Catholicism of the Iron Guard remains, if implicitly, in the Polish. The translator or editor behaved as if the words themselves, not their meanings or implications, were the important things. Jan Błoński has drawn attention to this in the context of the theatre: the censor does not see the big picture but rather weeds out allusions (Błoński 1995: 271-272). This crude approach is quite common and sometimes backfires. For example, the translation of "craw-thumpers" as a more respectful "priests" in a translation of an Edna O'Brien novel actually widens the scope of abuse – from craw-thumpers to all priests (Looby 2013: 162).

Once the oath has been taken the Iron Guard gets down to business. A proposal to burn down a communist bookshop is made and dutifully translated; the proposal to "'bomb every Cathlick Church in town'" (Maltz 1940: 92) is not (Maltz 1949: 99). A full two and a half pages of deranged bigotry is missing from the Polish. This is the speech made by Harvey Kellog, "intoxicated with his triumph" (Maltz 1940: 98), railing at Catholics, Communists, black people, Jews, Stalin, Trotsky and "'long-haired comrades'" (Maltz 1940: 99). As is often the case (see chapter five), this translation avoids repeating derogatory words for black people, Jews and others. It even goes so far as to rename the manager of the party bookshop (which the Black Legion bomb). Instead of Jack Cohn (Maltz 1940: 281) he is Jack Conny in Polish (Maltz 1949: 279). Although it could be simply an oversight (Cohn only appears once, briefly, in the book), it could also be that someone in the translation, editing, censorship and publication process did not want to suggest connections between communism and Jews. As for the excision of attacks on the Catholic Church, it may be that someone bridled at *any* fictive attack on the Church, no matter how ridiculous or despicable the source.

Other jibes at religion are missing too. In a more sober discussion between Grebb and Kellog after the initiation (Grebb is highly sarcastic about this "'idea of a beer hall *putsch*'" (Maltz 1940: 137)), the latter is still talking about freedom from, among others, "'Papists'" (Maltz 1940: 137), who are absent from the Polish (Maltz 1949: 143). When Grebb tries to persuade Princey, the Communist organiser, to join him he says men who are not "'bogged down in Christian sentiment'" (Maltz 1940: 302) can go a long way. In the Polish version what allegedly holds people back is "prejudices and mawkish morality" (Maltz 1949: 301). In the same scene, which has quite a few cuts in Polish, Grebb's expression of disdain for "'Christian sentimentalists with their tongues out for a taste of the Lord's Body'" (Maltz 1940: 305) is also missing from the Polish (Maltz 1949: 303-304), as is his reference to the nonsense of "'Christian cant'" and the "'brand of weak tea'" that Jesus started (Maltz 1940: 339, 340; Maltz 1949: 337, 338). The big questions of self-respect, revolution, socialism and faith are central in this great debate between Grebb and the unbreakable Party man but elsewhere in the book even passing references to religion show evidence of timidity on the Polish side. Non-Christian references to crucifixion are changed: Kellog, after going bankrupt, thinks, "'Life is a crucifixion'" in English (Maltz 1940: 65) but that it is "'permanent bankruptcy'" in Polish (Maltz 1949: 71). He refers to "'the whole groaning, crucified world!'" (Maltz 1940: 75) in conversation with his daughter but the crucifixion reference is not there in the Polish (Maltz 1949: 81). Kellog – a villain if ever there was one – reminds Grebb of the "portrait of a God-possessed anchorite he had once seen – the martyred priest enraptured by pain" (Maltz 1940: 136). In Polish, Kellog reminds him of, in back translation, a "fanatical hermit and the faces of martyrs twisted in pain and simultaneously bathed in faith" (Maltz 1949: 143).

The translation also, on occasion, cloaks references in the source text to Marxism and Communism: Grebb "had read widely, particularly in radical and Marxist literature" (Maltz 1940: 87). In Polish he has read "literature from the socialist movement" (Maltz 1949: 94). It may be that the translator (or censor) thought "socialism" would be more palatable than Marxism to Polish audiences, who had, after all, enjoyed the work of such socialist writers as Upton Sinclair and Jack London before the war. Jesse Vandermill, who seems to perform the role of comic relief in the novel, repeats a "Party truism" at one point, adding, "'Without real Marxist knowledge, the danger is you will become oppor-oppor-opportunist'" (Maltz 1940: 106). In Polish there is no mention of the Party or Marxism (Maltz 1949: 111). Similarly, Paul Turner is described as a "Communist" in English (Maltz 1940: 107) but an "old comrade" in Polish (Maltz 1949: 113). Turner is also referred to as a Communist Party functionary in the original (Maltz 1940: 108) but as "an old labour activist" in the Polish (Maltz 1949: 114). "Professional revolutionaries" (Maltz 1940: 115) are changed to "professional trade union activists" in Polish (Maltz 1949: 121). Even Lenin's name is left out, twice, from Grebb's argument with Princey (Maltz 1940: 296), replaced with "'the greatest revolutionaries and theorists of Marxism'" (Maltz 1949: 295). As can be seen, Marx does creep back into the translation and indeed any attempts to make this book over into a simple story of trade union activism so as not to lose readers antipathetic to communism seem futile: *Underground Stream* is not a subtle piece of work and only a wholesale re-write could hide its communist credentials. This might have been feasible – though difficult – with *The Great Midland*, a less propagandistic work, but not with Maltz's novel.

If the translator – and it could well have been the censor too – seems at times embarrassed by the overt Communist Party sympathies, that does not mean he is as willing to criticise the Party as freely as Maltz permits himself or his characters to. As in *The Great Midland*, opponents are allowed to voice some criticism of communism but disrespectful joking and banter directed at the movement is not readily tolerated in the translation. Princey, during a political discussion with his wife Betsy says, "'Now you're pulling Communist statistics on me. You can't trust those Reds, don't you know that?'" (Maltz 1940: 47) and this is permitted in the Polish version, perhaps in the spirit of constructive self-criticism or to show that Communists have a sense of humour, but when Betsy says the Party is, and has to be, a "'cannibal'" (Maltz 1940: 56) this is cut (Maltz 1949: 62). However, so too is the succeeding paragraph about how the Party places the working class above the needs of its individual members. This may have been cut for "over-glorifying" the Party (see Fik 1996: 137). Cut, too, is Princey's joking suggestion that Party Central Committee meetings "'end up with a strip-tease'" (Maltz 1940: 113). In Polish he bets Turner they end up with a "minority report" ("'votum separatum'") (Maltz 1940: 119). When Turner proposes that Princey attend a Party school and get a "'thorough grasp of Marxist-Leninist writings'", Princey enquires "humorously": "'What? No Stalin texts too? […] No Engels?'" (Maltz 1940: 117). This levity with the name of Stalin is not permitted in the Polish, where Princey says – albeit still "humorously" – that he will end up knowing Marx by heart (Maltz 1949: 122). Stalin's name is taboo also in the passages concerning Princey's imprisonment. One of his captors nicknames him Stalin (Maltz 1940: 189,

265, 266) but in the Polish it is either left out (Maltz 1949: 194) or changed to "revolutionary" (Maltz 1949: 261, 262). Other flippant references to Stalin are also cut. You just could not make fun of or about Stalin.

As might be expected, much of the more serious criticism of communism comes not from the hired thugs but from their boss, Grebb himself, during the climactic confrontation between himself and Princey. His claim that the Comintern has failed (Maltz 1940: 295) is missing from the translation, as is quite a lengthy passage about, among other things, how Stalin has made "'a puppet out of the Russian Trade Union Movement'" (Maltz 1940: 298) and betrayed socialism by making a pact with France (Maltz 1940: 299). It is hardly surprising that this heresy was cut. Interestingly, though, the censor makes no mention of it, suggesting verbal instructions or that it was cut before the manuscript ever made its way to the censor's office. Criticism of communism could be voiced, especially by negative characters – which by now Grebb clearly is – but censors generally did not like it to go unanswered, as the example of *The Great Midland* shows. Princey is in a position to answer Grebb but it cannot be said that he shows his opponent is wrong. His answer is merely that he has unshakeable faith. Rideout identifies Princey's recourse to mere self-discipline in answer to Grebb as a major weakness of the novel (Rideout 1956: 265), but even if Princey had offered a devastating, energetic rebuttal of Grebb's arguments it seems unlikely that the criticism of Stalin would have passed the censor. Stalin, like the pope in modern day Poland, was simply taboo.

Maltz describes *Underground Stream* as "an historical novel", claiming, "The facts which underlie the main event of this book are historical" (Maltz 1940: n. pag.). Nonetheless, the characters and events do not always ring true: Princey and Betsy's soul-searching debates about the Party are unconvincing; Princey's faults seem tacked on simply to show that despite his good, communist convictions and iron will he is, after all, a human being. Grebb's whole plan to convert Princey – to what, precisely, is not as clear as it might be – by kidnapping him instead of, say, summoning him to his office in the factory where they both work, is frankly ludicrous. Despite all this, Maltz seems, as his prefatory words suggest, to have been aiming for realism. At times this realism is too gritty for Polish tastes. Maltz is quite risqué for his times. When Princey is kidnapped his thoughts are presented thus: "Was Ambrose carrying his party book? That would bollix everything up" (Maltz 1940: 155). This is changed to "all their excuses would be in vain" in the Polish (Maltz 1949: 163). As is often, but not always, the case in Polish translations, especially in the early post-war years, words like "son-of-a-bitch" and "bastard" (Maltz 1940: 209, 318) are translated with "drań" (Maltz 1949: 209, 317), which is less rude. The Polish also removes a reference to Princey's captor breaking wind in reply to his offer of a bribe to set him free (Maltz 1940: 190; Maltz 1949: 194).

If words like "ass", "damn" and "constipation" (Maltz 1940: 3, 10, 108) are cut – and they are – it should come as no surprise that Princey's "'Frig you, Turner! You can't talk to me like that'" (Maltz 1940: 119) is changed to "Comrade! How can you talk to me like that?" (Maltz 1949: 125) as befits an earnest, though heartfelt discussion between two Party members. Similarly, Princey says, "'All right, you're so damn wise, tell me what the reason is'" (Maltz 1940: 119) in English but in Polish he says, "Since you already know everything, tell me what I'm hiding from you" (Maltz 1949: 125).[7] While the previous examples may, at a pinch, be written off as harmless adaptations to Polish norms, these shifts towards greater delicacy have some impact on how the scene is read. In the course of this conversation it emerges that Princey is not yet ready to become a "'full time functionary'" (Maltz 1940: 120) but the Polish Princey is calmer: one would think that he *was* mature enough to take the next step on his communist path. The Polish version does translate sentences like "Princey blazed fiercely" (Maltz 1940: 119) but without his strong language the portrayal of his recalcitrance is less effective. Princey is like Pavel Korchagin in Nikolai Ostrovsky's *How the Steel was Tempered* (translated into Polish in 1950): his conversion consists in the subordination of his impetuous, "anarchic spontaneity" (Günther 1990: 203) to the party. It is, then, quite an important element of the novel. In the Polish socialist realist novel of the early 1950s conflict between the hero and the Party was not permitted (Jarosiński 1999: 56) so in this respect the translation – or choice of book – is a little daring.

Also victim of Polish sensibilities are the novel's sex scenes. The cuts here are quite extensive and unremarked by the censor, although one of them did note that the translation was very poor (G-145, 31/22: 29). A few lines are cut when Grebb summons his housekeeper Shirley for sex. The English is as yet quite circumspect and little damage is done as it is still obvious to the Polish reader what is going on between the two of them. The two-page bed scene itself consists mostly of Grebb undressing Shirley and dialogue – actually mostly monologue, with Shirley saying little more than "yes". It is not particularly explicit but it is all cut, though once again it remains clear what has happened from the lines following the sex – "Drowsily, Shirley asked, 'Do you want me to leave you now?'" (Maltz 1940: 27) – which are reproduced in Polish. The relationship of Grebb and his housekeeper is fairly obviously in contrast with that of Princey and his wife. When the latter engage in pillow talk it is a dialogue, with differences of opinion. Cuts are made to the Princey and Betsy sex scene but it is, at least, present in the Polish, as is nearly all the (lengthy) dialogue.

The cutting from the Polish of lines like "They [Princey and Betsy] embraced with passionate love and forgiveness" (Maltz 1940: 58) and "He [Grebb] captured her finally, and with his kiss she yielded passionately, flinging her arms about him" (Maltz 1940: 27) may seem like a small loss – a blessing, even – but the novel loses more than just some "dirty bits" as these lines are artistically motivated. The sex is not gratuitous. The removal of the Grebb sex scene and the predatory adjectives describing him personally means that the contrast between the capitalist Grebb's treatment of people like objects and the Communist Princey's treatment of people like equals is gone from, or at any rate significantly weakened, in the Polish. One could argue that this actually improves the book: Grebb has sex with his servant, Princey with his wife; Grebb hardly speaks to his sexual partner while Princey and Betsy talk and talk (for some 20 pages). The contrast is still present in Polish but it is not bludgeoned home in the same way that it is by Maltz in the original. Nevertheless, it seems the change, whether for the better or the worse, was motivated purely by a desire to avoid mention of things like "His hardness against her" (Maltz 1940: 35 – cut from the Polish (Maltz 1949: 41)) rather than a desire to improve on the original: there are many other opportunities to make the novel more subtle and understated that are not taken.

Physiology – especially matters gynaecological – seems to make the translator uncomfortable, a feature of some translations into at least the 1970s. A paragraph in which Betsy casts her mind back to her first period and to sex education in general (Maltz 1940: 168-9) goes missing from the Polish (Maltz 1949: 174).[8] Reference to "'the curse'" (Maltz 1940: 216) is removed once again, later in the book (Maltz 1949: 216), and a mention of breastfeeding (Maltz 1940: 227-8) is obfuscated in translation (Maltz 1949: 227) in such a way as to obscure the fact that the mother feeds her child in the presence of other people, albeit in "a corner of the room" (Maltz 1940: 227). Not all mentions of unmentionables are removed. One of Princey's captors describes his frame-up for the rape of a 14-year-old and it is translated but even here we are not told in the Polish (Maltz 1949: 263-264) that the victim "'flipped her fanny'" (Maltz 1940: 267). Perhaps because this is illustrative of the criminal, immoral underbelly of the United States it was allowed to remain mostly complete in translation. However, the general tendency in the novel is definitely towards bowdlerisation.

If the discussion here of *The Underground Stream* is long it is because the translation shows with exaggerated clarity so many traits common to the Polish translations of English language literature which will be returned to in the subsequent chapters. To begin with, Maltz, as a progressive, is just the candidate for translation. As a free-speaking American he also presents the censor (translator, editor) with quite a few problems. The swearing, the use by some characters of words like "nigger", the sex scenes, the scandalising mentions of periods and semi-public breastfeeding, jocular references to Stalin and open criticism, even if mouthed by capitalist tools, of the USSR – . all of these elements fell victim to censorship broadly understood. While Stalin jokes were no doubt removed for fear of reprisals, menstruation was probably removed because in Polish literature it was still considered unseemly, despite its use as a plot device in a Stefan Żeromski novel from 1912. This was still being used as a reference point many years later in Dorota Masłowska's *White and Red* (*Wojna polsko-ruska pod flagą biało-czerwoną*), a novel controversial, and even shocking for some, precisely for its unseemliness. Brodzki's translation of *The Underground Stream* demonstrates in a number of places how a strongly conservative (despite all official proclamations of progress) target culture can distort the translated text, changing the emphasis of certain scenes in a novel that would seem to fit right into the political and literary landscape of the times.

As seen, some of the censors were sceptical about the political merits of Myra Page's *With Sun in our Blood*, the tale of a Cumberlands, Tennessee mining community. Although among the book's strengths is its demonstration that only by fighting capitalism can one's lot be improved (G-145, 31/26: 593), the miners are just not radical enough. One censor recommended that the last chapter, concerning the laying of the cornerstone for a first aid station, be removed entirely as it was typically social-democratic and might even sap readers' energy. The problem seems to be that the station is built in agreement with, rather than, say, open defiance of, the mining company, which even, in the same chapter, provides beer to celebrate the installation of a water pump. An insight is given into the informal means of control in this censor's report, where he or she proposes discussing the chapter's removal with the publisher's "political editor" (G-145, 31/26: 597). In the event the book was published with the last chapter mostly intact and this may be an example of a censor concerned more with demonstrating zeal than actually censoring a book. The same censor praises the book's literary values and the quality of its translation.

The few changes that seem to be ideologically motivated in the target text are greatly outnumbered by artistically motivated changes. The original tries to capture the peculiarities of Cumberlands English in both dialogue and narrative. The narrator, Dolly Hawkins, is of Irish descent, which may account for constructions such as "The music kept on, and we dancing", a calque from Irish, and "'I can't be making you out. I'll not be urging you to dance…'" (Page 1950a: 68, 69) – though the latter is actually spoken by John Cooper, who is from Kentucky. The former is rendered in standard literary Polish: "Muzyka nie milkła, a my tańczyliśmy" (Page 1950b: 64). Cooper's words are also "standardised". In Polish they are "–Nie mogę tego zrozumieć. Przecież jeśli nie chcesz, nie będę cię zapraszał do tańca..." (Page 1950b: 65). Page also uses archaic-sounding constructions and occasionally vocabulary, such as "My hair ablowing free" or "I had hearkened to them since a child and took a kind of pleasuring in it..." (Page 1950a: 1, 2). These are translated into standard Polish while "'I got rats in me belly'", for example, and "'I could eat a bear fried in spit'" (Page 1950a: 14, 15) are translated with standard Polish idioms for hunger. Whether or not the speech of Dolly Hawkins and other characters in the novel is an accurate reflection of how people spoke in mining camps in Tennessee is beyond the scope of this book but it is certain that the translator made no real attempt to capture their linguistic otherness. This also applies to the speech of characters whose first language is not English. For example, "'For why they give no men to feex?' Jake's voice rose. 'Dirty *svollich!* Them prop fall. Cavein. Meester T.S.I. Big Boss, not him back broke. You, Johneey. Me. Eh?'" (Page 1950a: 164) is translated into standard Polish. That Jake speaks broken English is mentioned a few pages earlier (in both source and target text) and this was evidently considered enough.

This practice is quite common in the translations surveyed here but in this case the translator goes further, correcting passages in the original that range from the obscure to the badly written: "Like a storm, I knew my fear was passing from me, and what I lost with my Dad's going, my joy in the rightness of things, acoming back" (Page 1950a: 84) is greatly clarified in Polish. Similarly, "I began hurrying supper, trying to drive off the cold going through me, thinking the sooner the meal done, the sooner Clyde and Old Harry home, their noses aquiver for a draught of my stew" (Page 1950a: 7), is much clearer in translation: "it seemed to me that the sooner the meal was ready, the sooner Clyde and uncle Harry would appear, sniffing delightedly the smell of stewing meat from the threshold" ("Wydawało mi się, że im wcześniej posiłek będzie gotowy, tym prędzej zjawią się Clyde i wuj Harry, od progu już wciągając z rozkoszą zapach duszonego mięsa") (Page 1950b: 11). The tense progression in "A question kept running through my head, but I daren't ask it" (Page 1950a: 52) is clarified in the translation.

Myra Page is lax with inverted commas, sometimes just ignoring them, as in "There'll be a downpour tomorrow, he [Harry] said. Then the dancing must end" (Page 1950a: 56), which leaves the reader uncertain if "then the dancing must end" are Harry's spoken words or the narrator's thoughts. Quotation marks are used in the Polish (Page 1950b: 54). Another example is: "'Leave the Hollow?' I took his arm. Do it the proper way, let Pop McFever and the pit committee handle it? And before the week was spent, Pop had John back on his regular shift" (Page 1950a: 133). The second sentence seems to be what Dolly said, belonging, along with the first sentence, in inverted commas – though the question mark seems out of place.

The third sentence is definitely narrative but all three sentences are in one block of running text. The Polish is far clearer. The second sentence is in quotation marks and the question mark is gone (Page 1950b: 120). If the translators thought they were dealing with some kind of avant garde free indirect discourse technique they chose not to pass the formal experimentation on the Polish reader.[9]

Chapter five ends "I had known pride in my Dad, and the way our hills stood by him. There was danger well met, and meaning. Once more I would draw on them..." (Page 1950a: 72; ellipsis in the original). It is not clear how Dolly can "draw on" danger and meaning, or what drawing on meaning even means, though it is also possible that she means she will "draw on" the hills. The troublesome lines are cut from the Polish, which ends the chapter thus: "Mogłam być dumna z mego ojca i z tego, w jaki sposób nasze góry go poparły" ("I could be proud of my father and the way our mountains had supported him") (Page 1950b: 68).

"Correcting" mistakes is a risky business and the translators were arguably over-zealous in turning some passages into standard Polish, such as "It was a magic woods I passed through: the same I'd known since barely able to crawl along its pine-needle sweet-giving floor" and "Look like with all John and I had said and shared together, we'd hardly begun" (Page 1950a: 96, 99). In both these cases the folksy quality of the original is gone from the Polish.[10] And yet, folksy or not, it seems the following sentence is just bad English: "'Unc, there'll be no end of nail and hammering to do!' I broke in, for we never talked money before Unc Harry, put it to keep a few coppers by him" (Page 1950a: 105). Its translation is not bad Polish (Page 1950b: 95).

The translators also felt obliged to correct some logical or stylistic mistakes, as when "Clyde had the cart waiting" is stated twice in less than ten lines in the original (Page 1950a: 224, 225) but only once in the Polish (Page 1950b: 197). Perhaps the most blatant example comes when "my brother Alec" (Page 1950a: 73) is changed to "Caleb" (Page 1950b: 68), presumably because there is no mention of an "Alec" when Dolly enumerates her family on page 11 of the original.

Such changes, whether one considers them detrimental to the original or improvements, can hardly be laid at the door of institutional censorship, though one may blame the "general drift of society". There is even one report, dating from around 1950, on file from the Ministry for Culture and Art complaining about the polishing of the language of simple people in a translation of a Ukrainian play (M-709, Departament Twórczości Artystycznej; Wydział Wydawniczy: 285). However, the tendency is to produce standard Polish, with one censor's review complaining about what are evidently calques from the source language in the translation of Frank Hardy's *Power without Glory* (G-375, 31/28: 665). Critics also complained sometimes about attempts to capture varieties of English in Polish translations. Jan Kott complains that Hemingway's Venetian characters are made to speak the "language of Warsaw louts" in one translation by Bronisław Zieliński, who was otherwise a very highly regarded translator (Kott 1961: 8).

After publication of *With Sun in Our Blood* the censors considered the possibility of a second edition (with a print run of 50,000, as compared to the original run of a typical 10,000 copies). Once again, the censors complain that the miners are not class conscious. The capitalists, bourgeoisie and mine administrators come across as "kindly uncles" according to one censor, who concludes that one edition was enough (G-375, 31/17: 181). Another censor says there is too much religion and the proposed print run would be too large even if the religious bits were cut (G-375, 31/17: 182). Even though these reviews were written a full year and more *after* publication, religion is played down, though only slightly, and mining is denigrated less in the translation than in the original. It appears, then, that the translators anticipated the censor's objections but did not cut enough to head off those objections, though it is also possible that the objections were made known verbally to the translators before publication of the first edition.

So, for example, the words "Seth hearkened back to another saying in our hills: God made all critters and breathed in life, and when all said and done [sic], human is human" (Page 1950a: 157) are removed from the Polish. In particular, what the translators or their editors cut were references to "the Good Book". Examples are dotted around the novel but one very prominently placed instance is the very last sentence, "He would dig deep and long, with others searching out as the Good Book told, the truth to set men free" (Page 1950a: 245), which in back translation is "He would search far and wide with others for the truth that would bring people freedom" (Page 1950b: 214). Although the novel is not strikingly religious there are plenty of passing mentions of God. However, the number of cuts of such mentions increases as the book progresses, as if the translators realised around chapter seven that there might be too much religion. Another possibility is that references to the good book were perceived as particularly Protestant and therefore cutting them came easier in Catholic Poland.

The key sentence concerning mining's undesirability as a way of life, as it happens, also contains a reference to God: "And I fell to wondering if there might be a living for my men to be made above ground, hunting fish and game and making things grow, out in the open like God intended, not burrowing like moles in the dark earth" (Page 1950a: 140). This is missing from the Polish, although Dolly's dreams of saving up for a farm and getting out of mining, a few pages earlier, are left unchanged (Page 1950a: 132). However, John's reference to mines as "'hellholes'" (Page 1950a: 133) is softened to "holes" (Page 1950b: 120). The translators had to walk a fine line here. They had to convey the exploitation of American miners, display their bad working conditions and portray the dangers to life and limb, but they guessed correctly that they could not be too harsh on mining as such: coal was very important to Poland's economy.[11] They nearly got it right: one of the first censors approved of the book's depiction of the lack of safety in mines (G-145, 31/26: 593) but one of the later censors thought it might dissuade Poles from a career underground (G-375, 31/17: 182). The book did not run to a second edition.

The miners who are the main characters of Katharine Prichard's *Winged Seeds* could not be accused of not being ideological as they seem to spend most of their time debating world affairs of the 1930s and 1940s through the prism of Marxist-Leninism. One of them, Bill (actually he is a mining engineer), addresses a public meeting in chapter three: "'Just consider for a moment what the stranglehold of these monopolies means to our right to organise for a commonwealth – for social ownership, which is scientific socialism'" (Prichard 1984: 44-45). Another example is that of Pam and Pat, the glamorous visitors to the area, who turn out to be rather unlikely communist sympathisers. On being shown the workshops of a goldmine, Pat exclaims:

> 'And to think all that energy and ingenuity is devoted to chasing the tiniest specks of gold! That the miracle of this place is subservient to the skill of a few workers operating the controls, and to the will of men behind the scenes whose wealth and power it serves!'

to which Pam responds, "'Why can't as much tenacity and genius be used to clean up the mess of the world?'" (Prichard 1984: 145). Such passages are faithfully reproduced in the translation, as is the sense of the following exchange:

> 'Fascism and communism, there's nowt of a difference between two of 'em, far as I can see,' Eli piped up.
> 'Then y'r blind as a bat,' Blunt Pick shouted.
> 'Only the difference between night and day,' Dinny said dryly. 'Fascism spits on the workers, turns them into machines for makin' profits and wars. Communism says the world and everything in it belongs to the workers, and organises for peace' (Prichard 1984: 246-247).

Again we see a radical novelist getting away with airing criticisms of communism thanks, at least in part, to the fact that this criticism comes from an unsavoury character and meets a swift response. Even the criticism voiced by Sally Gough, a very positive character, is permitted in the translation: "'If the Soviet Union hadn't changed their tune about Germany maybe there'd've

been no war'" (Prichard 1984: 252). Dinny moves quickly to instruct her on
the correct line to take:

> 'Now, now, missus, […] you don't want to do your block. All along the Soviet's [sic]
> been askin' for an agreement with the Allies, and they've been shilly-shallyin' over the
> proposition. The Soviet Government's got its own people and country to think of, and if
> a non-aggression pact with Germany'll keep them out of the war, they've got a right to
> make it' (Prichard 1984: 252).

In line with official nomenclature, "Soviet" is translated not as "sowiecki"
but as "radziecki" but apart from this the entire exchange is captured in
translation, as is the final, crushing blow to the validity of Sally's doubts:
"Sally, in her frantic resentment of every move which precipitated the war,
was prepared to blame anybody and everybody responsible for its outbreak"
(Prichard 1984: 252). It is the same when Dick, the black sheep of the
otherwise left wing family, delivers his tirade against the workers shortly
after the burial of his communist father:

> 'But I'm not going to waste my life for a mob who'd rather swill beer and bust up their
> pay at the two-up, than try to better themselves and live as well as they could. I've got
> no confidence in the workers, I tell you straight, Bill. I don't believe they ought to have
> the power to run the state. I don't believe they care a bloody damn for what you call
> their democratic rights – not the crowd working on the mines these days. I've heard
> them shout dad down when he talked about a fair deal for the Soviet Union. Do they
> want to hear the truth about Spain? Not on your life! They take the line of least
> resistance, siding with the priests and the bosses, when it's a question of putting up a
> fight for anything that doesn't touch their pockets' (Prichard 1984: 105-106).

All of this is kept in translation and, like the previous examples, did not even
merit a comment from most of the censors. Bill, an ideologically sound
character, makes a counterattack and, although it is a lot less spirited and
persuasive than Dick's words, this – along with Prichard's membership of the
Communist Party – seems to have been enough to save the passage.

Once can find more transgressions that survived the transition from
English to Polish. Sally Gough, an old comrade, encourages "Frisco" to play
the stock market in both source and target text; the workers never seem to be
short of money, with cars, motorbikes and formal balls seeming at times to
crowd token references of poverty and hardship off the pages of both original
and translation. Saxton got a slap on the wrist for this, but not Prichard. And
where Myra Page was criticised for denigrating mining, Prichard can have
her characters think: "The mines had broken two generations of men. How
many more would they destroy before life became of more value than
profits?" (Prichard 1984: 101). This goes uncut and uncommented in Polish,
although this may be because Prichard was careful enough to tie the hardship
to profit as well as mining itself. The story of a miner who dynamites his

head off to spare his family the burden of caring for him throughout his terminal illness, an apparently inevitable consequence of long years of mining (Prichard 1984: 100), is also present in the Polish.

But the censors did find fault, as mentioned above. The leading role allegedly played by the Communist Party of Australia is not stressed, one notes (G-375, 31/28: 256). Another censor's remarks hint, perhaps, at the difficulties of keeping up with the twists and turns of official policy: the censor did not approve of the mention of Yugoslavians at a political meeting (although she or he claims it is because they do not reappear in the book). Also, the source text contains some praise of US soldiers, equipment, efficiency and bravery. This may have been permissible in Australia but in the Poland of 1951 the censor recommended it be cut before permitting publication (G-375, 31/28: 254).[12] Bolesław Zagała had been censured in 1949 for praising English and American technology in his *Na przełaj przez świat* (Kondek 1999: 20-21) and much later *2001: A Space Odyssey* was banned for glorifying US technology (G-848, 86/3: 223). The censor also wanted the removal from *Winged Seeds* of a passage about Sir Isaac Isaacs, since he would have been unknown to Polish readers, who might think him a "'good' capitalist" (G-375, 31/28: 254). None of these changes were made. In fact, the translation even refers to Germans as Germans, rather than Hitlerites ("Hitlerowcy"), the word preferred in post-war Poland, apparently as a way of distinguishing between "good" Germans (the German Democratic Republic) and "bad" Germans (the Federal Republic of Germany) (see Bates 2004a: 16; Nowak 2012: 137).

It may be that Prichard and her translator just "slipped through the cracks" but it is probably of some significance that her first two books about the Australian goldfields, *The Roaring Nineties* and *Golden Miles*, had already been successful. Drusilla Modjeska, in her introduction to the 1984 edition of *Winged Seeds*, admits it is not a great book (Modjeska 1984: xi) but *The Roaring Nineties* had received good reviews (Modjeska 1984: vii) and been translated into nine languages (Modjeska 1984: v). This book was published in Poland in 1950, a year before *Winged Seeds*. Three censors' reviews of *Golden Miles* were positive, with no demands for changes (G-375, 31/17: 33-36). Another reads: "It shows capitalist exploitation and oppression as well as the forms of class struggle at a certain stage of development and in a certain place" (G-145, 31/26: 442). Prichard was a more highly placed Communist than, for example, Saxton or Maltz. She was a founder member of the Communist Party of Australia and joined its Central Committee in 1943. The Polish translation of *Winged Seeds* came out very soon after the original and the same translator (Tadeusz Dehnel) did *Golden Miles*, also published in 1951. Although the translation is meticulous, with no signs of haste, it seems possible that a desire to get the second two books of the trilogy out quickly may have softened the censors' cough. Evidence of haste is in the six pages left blank in the Polish translation, which one finds occasionally with Polish books.

Censors' reports on Howard Fast's books are usually glowing to say the least: *The Passion of Sacco and Venzetti* is written straightforwardly and movingly and "the book deserves a massive print run". The censor and his or her supervisor recommended no changes (G-375, 31/34: 381). The actual print run was an unspectacular 10,176. *Freedom Road*, which was for a time on school reading lists (Czarnik 1993: 286), is a "beautiful novel of great artistic and educational value" (G-386, 31/123: 128). *Conceived in Liberty: a novel of Valley Forge* is educationally and artistically very good (G-145, 31/24: 143-144) and, another censor writes, "very topical" (G-145, 31/24: 145-146). The censors have no reservations, suggest no alterations (G-145, 31/24: 141-148).

But even before Fast's break with the Communist Party it was not the case that he could do no wrong. While most of the censors' complaints were not acted on, cuts were demanded. Not all of Fast's work was politically engaged enough to satisfy the censors in Poland. This can be seen in their reception of his short story collection, *Departure*. One review remarks on the love of humanity and indictment of imperialism that characterise the stories but, the censor writes, their political value is uneven. The title story is among the best in the collection but "Thirty Pieces of Silver" (not to be confused with Fast's play of the same name) is questionable and it is difficult to draw conclusions from the symbolism of the letter (the story consists of a letter from a follower of Christ to a friend about Judas). The censor also has difficulties making out "An Epitaph for Sidney" (G-145, 31/26: 552), a straightforward reminiscence about a labour organiser and freedom fighter which presents no comprehension problems, even if "Thirty Pieces of Silver" is a little opaque. A second review also complains that the stories are uneven and recommends cutting "Thirty Pieces of Silver", although the conclusion seems to be to leave the decision to the editor (G-145, 31-26: 554). In the end, "Epitaph" was published in the translation, but not "Thirty Pieces of Silver". The follow-up review recommends cutting three stories because of their weak connection with social issues (G-375, 31/17: 215) but there was no second edition from which to cut them. In fact, another three stories, unmentioned by the censor, had been left out of the Polish edition, including "Who is He?" a story about a young Jewish boy's experience of anti-Semitism in the United States. If a second edition had appeared and the censor's advice been taken, it would have had 12 stories, down from the original's 19.

One censor objected to the cursing in one of the stories (G-145, 31/26: 552). Fast does not go as far as Maltz ("frig"), Norman Mailer ("fug"), or

Brendan Behan ("fugh") but he does attempt to capture everyday speech, warts and all. Strong language is generally attenuated although the translator is not entirely consistent, perhaps having taken the view that what counts is the absolute number of swear words. The soldierly "'They crap on you with niceness'" (Fast 1949: 107) becomes "'They make you want to puke with their niceness'" ("Rzygać się chce od ich sympatyczności") (Fast 1950: 72), a small adjustment, but an adjustment nonetheless. "'You horse's ass'" (Fast 1949: 114) goes missing and "'pissed-off'" (Fast 1949: 115) is simply "angry" in translation (Fast 1950: 78). And yet "'You, my friend, are a dirty second-rate son of a bitch – an upstanding pile of crap, if you follow me'" (Fast 1949: 114) is kept, while the not exactly shocking "'bloody'" and "'damn well'" (Fast 1949: 217) go missing in translation. Also, little attempt is made to render the variety of different voices in Fast's fiction. The stories range across the years and the archaic "'Then I be sorry'", the vernacular "'I ain't askin' yet'" and "'I been in Normandy'", the Scottish-American "'Ye been a woodsy man these twenty year'", and the very British English "'I should not think it would be so'" (Fast 1949: 84, 25, 51, 82, 85) all come out in standard literary Polish.

Walter Rideout criticises the language of Fast's novel *Freedom Road*, which is "a pseudo-Biblical, pseudo-'folksy' diction, [that] ends by blurring all the characters rather than illuminating any of them sharply" (Rideout 1956: 278). Given this, it would not seem to matter that the translation is in standard Polish, also blurring any linguistic markers of differences between characters. "Brother Peter" advises the hero, Gideon, to learn how to read and how to talk like a white man: "'Words match up, white folks call that grammar. Man with a head on his shoulders, he talks the words right, old nigger like me, he don't'" (Fast 1979: 15). The Polish is perfectly grammatical, though the sentences are, presumably as a concession to Brother Peter's way of talking, a little shorter than is usual in written Polish (Fast 1952: 25; "nigger" is translated "Murzyn", the neutral word). Gideon, a former slave, does learn to speak "like a white man". At the start of the novel he says things like "'How you figure this here Convention?'" (Fast 1979: 16). At the end he addresses a white man, Sheriff Bentley, thus:

'I think you're alive at this moment, Bentley, because we are civilised and law abiding people. I think you knew that. It's a quality of your kind to have an instinctive if primitive understanding of what constitutes civilisation. Do you follow me?' (Fast 1979: 232).

In both cases in the translation Gideon speaks perfect Polish.[13] The characters may not be as undifferentiated – at least over time – as Rideout claims but his remarks do apply to the Polish translation, where obedience to the strong cultural norm of "good" Polish means that an important dimension of

Gideon's development is significantly weakened. We know, because Fast tells us, that Gideon learns to read, learns for example, that "'A gentleman will avoid contractions when possible and will never, under any circumstances, use "ain't"'" (Fast 1979: 53) but the English reader "hears", as it were, the effects of this learning. The Polish reader does not. Polish does not use contractions as much as English but they do exist – in spoken Polish if very seldom in the written language. "Powiedziałem" ("I said") is very often pronounced "pojedziałem" or "podziałem" and "trzeba" ("one must") is often shortened in speech to "trza". Rather than substitute, say, "trza" for "ain't" the translator of the above passage actually uses the English words, explaining rules of English usage to Polish readers (Fast 1952: 68-69). The first letter Gideon ever writes in his life is, in its Polish incarnation, a remarkable achievement. Halting and ungrammatical in English, it is nearly perfect in translation, although the sentences are a little shorter than usual.

It would be tempting to read politics into this. By deliberately omitting such a fundamental distinguishing feature as language variety, the translator is associating Fast with an element of socialist realism that even ideologues admitted was a weak point: the fact that the characters were all very alike. For example, the review of *Lewanty* ("Freighters") quoted above takes the trouble to stress that all the characters are different (Rev. of *Lewanty* 1953: 152). However, the fact is that Polish translations are generally conservative when it comes to linguistic variation, regardless of the author's politics. In neither *Departure* nor *Freedom Road* can one see any attempt to ridicule a Communist author by turning the book into a parody of socialist realist literature. Nor is there a tendency to "improve" the books by toning down any socialist flights of fancy.[14] *Freedom Road* contains some very exalted descriptions of its hero, Gideon Jackson, who remains just as idealised in the Polish. "Gideon was a quantity of man, built like a bull [...] He was himself, and there was a reason why people turned to him" (Fast 1979: 7). Likewise, his family is wonderful:

> Gideon thought with pride that there were few men who had all this, a wife like Rachel, two strong sons, and a pretty little daughter like Jenny. The boys were wild and headstrong, but so had he been in his time; and on his back were the scars of more than a hundred lashes to show just how headstrong he had been (Fast 1979: 13).

This is all present and correct in the Polish, which also gives the impression that Gideon's faults are token attempts to humanise him: "It was true that he moved slowly, both his body and his brain, but if he had a need to, he could move fast" (Fast 1979: 7).

The appeal of such books as those studied above to communist ideologues is clear enough, but the authorities in Poland also favoured less explicitly ideological fiction if it showed the USA in a bad light. However, excessive "naturalism" in such stories could be an obstacle. *Przekrój* magazine tried to publish a translation-adaptation of an American crime story in 1951, stating in the introduction that the book drew attention to the capitalist morass, but it was discontinued after the intervention of a higher-up in the Czytelnik publishing house. The magazine published a self-criticism, claiming that the naturalism in fact hid the essence of the depravity of the United States and distracted readers from that country's social problems (Matras-Mastelarz 2012: 203). To the category of bottom dog fiction belongs "Season of Celebration", a long short story in Albert Maltz's collection *The Way Things Are*, published in Poland under the title of *Człowiek na drodze* ("Man on a Road", the last story in the collection), with a large print run, 50,475. Politics plays a smaller role in this slice of flophouse life, and the most notable modifications are to the strong language and sexual references of the original. The men in the story talk of sex and prostitutes, and one of them has pornographic pictures for trade. These details are preserved in the story but the more graphic parts are cut or modified. "'You wanna celebrate – get in bed'n have a good time with yourself – but shut your hole'" (Maltz 1938: 37) is translated as "You can celebrate alright – lie in bed and relax – but shut your trap [jadaczka]" (Maltz 1951: 29). "'Sounds like crabs to me'" (Maltz 1938: 46) is changed to "Sounds like rubbish to me" (Maltz 1951: 39), though this could have been a misunderstanding: the translation is a little inexpert. Words like "grease ball" (Maltz 1938: 35) are cut and "'bums from Idaho'" (Maltz 1938: 41) is replaced with "boys from Idaho" (Maltz 1951: 33, 34). The speaker is not really insulting people from Idaho and this may be why "bums" is changed to "boys". Also, the reference to a "grease ball", despite the absence of inverted commas, is probably not an authorial comment. The full quotation is "Benson interrupted his solitaire. He glared over at the hymn-singing grease ball with savage contempt". The translator either decided this was not free indirect discourse or that the readers would not realise that it was.

Maltz did bring politics into "A Letter From the Country", in the same collection, which describes the suppression by a vigilante mob of farmers' union activity. One of the reactionaries is quoted in the story saying, "'Well we don't like this red socialist and anarchist union of yours and we're gone [sic] to bust it up'" (Maltz 1938: 127). In the translation this is "your red union" (Maltz 1951: 125): even provincial American reactionaries must know and observe the difference between socialism and anarchism.

Erskine Caldwell was highly praised for exposing the evils of the USA, especially racial discrimination, and *Tobacco Road* and *Trouble in July* were published in a single volume in Poland under the telling title *Druga Ameryka* ("The Other America") in 1949. The censor commends 1961's *Tragic Ground* for revealing the true face of America and for pointing an accusatory finger. He or she is less enthusiastic about the vulgar language but this is not a "censorial" objection and the book should be published without changes (G-710, 68/93: 240). An earlier review, of *Trouble in July*, reads: "A very sharp satire of American relations. [...] The book undermines the myth of the wonderful America, shows the 'other side of the coin' and has a clearly class-oriented approach to the subject matter" (G-145, 31/22: 340). The follow-up review continues in the same vein: the book shows a less well-known side of America, with people reduced to the level of animals. It often seems, the censor writes, that Caldwell is exaggerating but there is humanity in the two tales that make up *Druga Ameryka* and the author shows that economics are to blame (G-145, 31/23: 165). A review of *Tobacco Road* on file in the archives is also positive about this portrayal of the other side of the "promised land" (G-145, 31/22: 285). The inverted commas used by the censor were a favourite device of critics of the USA and one brought to a frenzy on the pages of *Literatura Radziecka*.[15]

The translations of *Tobacco Road* and *Trouble in July* show no signs of ideological interference apart from the replacement of derogatory words for black people with the neutral "Murzyn", although on a handful of occasions in *Trouble in July* the word used was "Negr", which *was* pejorative. Readers not favourably disposed to Erskine Caldwell might argue that the translation's scrupulous adherence to the source text of *Tobacco Road* results in a book which is anti-poor people rather than anti-poverty or anti-share-cropping. Calder Willingham argues in the introduction to *Tragic Ground* and *Trouble in July* that the Lesters in *Tobacco Road* are "truly 'mythic' and legendary" (Willingham 1979: xiii). Perhaps: when Jeeter Lester's imbecilic son drives over Jeeter's mother in a car that cost roughly three years' pay but he ruined in two days, Jeeter does not even bother to see if his own mother is seriously hurt. All of this is faithfully reproduced in the translation. There is no telling if Polish readers saw the brutalisation of the Lesters as a result of US capitalism or Caldwell's overheated myth-making or something else entirely. Whatever their opinion, *Tobacco Road* enjoyed a better career in the US, with millions of copies sold, than in Poland, where it was not reissued.

Caldwell's position in post-war Poland might be described as transitional, in that he stayed the course, with his books continuing to appear when the Saxtons, Maltzes and Pages had been forgotten. A collection of 44 short stories was published under the title of *Szarlatan* (after the story "The Medicine Man") in 1957 with a print run of 20,250 and a volume of collected stories came out in 1984. The stories, too, show little evidence of interference. The most noticeable change is that derogatory words for black people are nearly always neutralised, with exceptions in Jan Zakrzewski's translations of "Return to Lavinia" and "Kneel to the Rising Sun" (Caldwell 1984).

Georgia Boy went through several editions, the third of which, in 1971, had a run of 50,290. The stories that make up this book are much less drastic than the novels, treating poverty and race relations in a more light-hearted way. From the point of view of a censor, they are politically unobjectionable and were it not for the jacket notes the reader probably would not guess that Caldwell had a "liberal and progressive" worldview. Here too there is little evidence of interference, apart from the general use of standard literary Polish, meaning that Handsome Brown, the black character in the stories, is linguistically undifferentiated from the white people in the household.

Zarzecki's translation of *Tragic Ground* is exceptional in this respect. Jan Kott criticised his attempts to render Caldwell's style with a mixture of peasant Polish and the style of Warsaw writer Stefan "Wiech" Wiechecki, who used the slang of inter-war Warsaw (Kott 1961: 5). Zarzecki does try to capture the non-standard English, although he backs off from most of the explicit vocabulary, such as, in particular, Spence Douthit's trademark expression, "'Dogbite my pecker'" (Caldwell 1979: 7), which becomes "'ale niech mi psy'" (Caldwell 1961: 8) (literally: "let dogs...me"). "'Like a rabbit with his balls caught in a sewing machine'" (Caldwell 1979: 15) is translated using ellipsis to indicate the Polish word for "balls" (Caldwell 1961: 22). It is the vocabulary that causes problems: the translator does not back away from the drastic situations described, such as the near-automatic prostitution of all girls almost immediately after reaching puberty. Nor does Zarzecki or any editor try to rescue the book from its absurdity or brutality, as when a child climbs into bed with Spence Douthit to warm himself: "he hit the child as hard as he could with both knees and shoved him down under the quilt to the foot of the bed". Douthit then starts trying to make love to Jessica in the same bed (Caldwell 1979: 123-124). If this book is propaganda, it is not left wing propaganda: the poor are portrayed as lazy, feckless, shiftless, moronic alcoholics, in both the English and the Polish versions.

A comparison of the finished translations with the censors' records sometimes gives the impression that publishers simply ignored the censors. This is misleading: the translations were altered, and altered in the spirit of the Censorship Office at that. A great deal of the censor's work was done by telephone, as indicated by Krzysztof Kozłowski:

> By the way, not so long ago I realised that in a few years a historian might discover there was no censorship. He'll dig out the first proofs of *Tygodnik* [newspaper] and see that all the crossings out were made by the same hand. From there it's only a short step to finding out whose hand. How will he know that the censor dictated all the changes to

me over the telephone? It was I who physically crossed out everything so the question might someday arise: why did Krzysztof Kozłowski do it? (Kozłowski 2013: 29).

If the cutting of Stalin's ass is all arranged informally, the censor is left with grouching in his or her written review about less important things – or at any rate more debatable issues – such as portraits of Piłsudski hanging in American diners, or whether Yugoslavians should be renamed "Slavs". Even if such informal discussions were held with editors, rather than the translators themselves, the translators would have quickly learned what was expected of them as information filtered down from their publishers. Although they may never have seen the Censorship Office's internal reviews, they could read reviews in *Nowe Książki* and *Nowa Kultura* which, though usually more enthusiastic, do not differ greatly from what we find in the censors' archives in Stalinist Poland. Forewarned about publishing policy and the original author's progressive pedigree, translators and editors could forestall some of the censors' objections. Objections raised by censors, even if not always acted on, would have had a chilling effect.

The changes made to the radical fiction imposed on Polish readers, particularly in the early 1950s, are similar to those made all through the duration of People's Poland. The translations tend to be prudish, with less explicit sex, fewer references to bodily functions and less cursing. There are fewer pejorative references to ethnic and racial groups. The Roman Catholic Church is treated slightly more respectfully. These are Polish norms that asserted themselves despite communism's avowed and at times active atheism. The translated literature of the period may have been – politically if not formally – radical but it was accompanied by no break with translational norms of correct and decorous Polish. Radical writers were permitted more leeway in criticising communist dogma, especially if such criticism was answered by communist characters, which it usually was. However, even the most radical, dyed in the wool western Communist could not, in translation, be too flippant about communism or, especially, Stalin.

What one does not find in this period is any serious attempt at passive resistance to communism on the part of translators. On the contrary, one censor wrote in his 1949 review of Fanny Hurst's *Wielki uśmiech* (*Great Laughter*):

> It is not, however, free from prejudice against the Soviet Union. [Abbey Neal's decision to go to the USSR] is made under the influence of disappointment with her personal life and national life. The translator, or rather the publisher, 'polished' the part of the book concerning this episode, crossing out many words. As a result, this event acquires a different, more positive character (G-173c, 32/44: 108).

The translations do not undermine the central message of the novels by, say, an unflattering choice of adjectives for the positive, socialist realist hero. Nor do the translators, notwithstanding the above example, usually demonstrate great communist zeal: they do not paint the "kindly uncles" of capitalism any blacker than the original authors did, for example. There are no attempts (beyond domestication) to drastically re-write the translations, as happened with the Estonian version of *For Whom the Bell Tolls*, which was changed to make Communist and Russian characters look morally better (Monticelli and Lange 2014: 103). In the Polish archives there is a 1967 document reproducing an entire story with a new ending as demanded by the censor (G-833: 125-138). But it is a Polish story and I have found no such gross interference in translations. Another example is the requirement, in Polish socialist realist novels, to openly evaluate characters when they were first introduced to the reader (Tomasik 1988: 113; see also Głowiński (1990: 8-12) for the importance of evaluation in propaganda). This does not happen in Polish translations but it seems to have been a feature of at least some translations in the Soviet Union. The Russian version of *Catch-22* "often has Heller reproving his hero" (Leighton 1991: 31) and Samantha Sherry has shown how the Russian translation of Howard Fast's *The Passion of Sacco and Vanzetti* moved the tale closer to socialist realism (Sherry 2010).

One does not see much political sabotage on the part of translators. There is, however, one important argument to be made on this point: the refusal to improve on source texts that are often of inferior quality could in itself be seen as an act of resistance. The artificial dialogue at the start of *Winged Seeds* is a case in point: "'This is the place, I'm sure, Pam,' one of them exclaimed. 'I believe it is,' the other cried. 'There's the ramshackle old house like a broken concertina, and the creeper with masses of creamy blossom over the veranda!'" (Prichard 1984: 11). In the Polish too, this reads like clumsy exposition, properly belonging to narrative rather than dialogue in what is, after all, supposed to be a realistic novel. Precisely by being faithful, the Polish translator sends a message to the reader that this book is not worth reading, even if it is translated into standard, literary Polish. Translators did sometimes improve on the originals described here, particularly Myra Page's *With Sun in our Blood*, but usually they translate "as is", restricting themselves to some linguistic polishing. For example, in *The Great Midland* (a far better book than *With Sun in Our Blood* or *Winged Seeds*) there is a scene at the end of the novel (1942) in which Eddie Spaas, Dave's uncle, goes away to work in Arizona. On the train, "Eddie unlimbered his guitar and he and the harmonica player cranked out all the songs they could think of" (Saxton 1997: 347). In 1920, however, Eddie's left arm is cut off at the elbow in an accident. Both of these incidents are faithfully preserved in the translation.

[1] The Communist Manifesto also made the list.

[2] See Michelle Woods (2010) for a selection process in the West that favoured translations of Václav Havel – but only after he became a dissident.

[3] Figures for 1944-5 are "partly estimated data". This proviso applies also to Czarnik's figures.

[4] The footnotes to *Marching! Marching!* are similar in tone. The AFL "has rejected the principle of class struggle", and the IWW is described as follows: "Until the rise of communist parties this organisation represented progressive thought but from World War One on anarcho-syndicalist tendencies emerged" (Weatherwax 1952: 67n, 112n).

[5] "Dave opowiedział, że Rosjanie wycofują się, a hitlerowcy ruszywszy z terytorium Polski przeszli już granicę Związku Radzieckiego" (Saxton 1951: 433).

[6] Another complaint made of *Great Midland* was that in it the US communist party was not suppressed by the police and capitalists (G-386, 31/122: 90).

[7] Here the translation uses the second person plural form of address (favoured by communists), which means that the ambiguity ("you" could mean the Party or it could mean Paul Turner) is preserved in translation.

[8] The excision of her subsequent thoughts on "the irreplaceable thing about marriage" (Maltz 1940: 169) may have been for stylistic reasons. Having cut the previous paragraph it is difficult to make the transition from her memory of work in a car factory, which prompted her thoughts on sex, to the marriage question.

[9] In *Marching! Marching!* Clara Weatherwax abandoned punctuation but the Polish version has been "normalised".

[10] "Las, którym szłam, wydawał mi się zaczarowany, mimo że był to ten sam las, który znałam od czasu, kiedy uczyłam się pełzać po jego pachnącym podszyciu, okrytym igłami sosen" and "Choć tak wiele już powiedzieliśmy sobie, choć tyle razem przeżyliśmy – wydawało się jednak, że dopiero teraz wszystko się zaczyna" (Page 1950b: 88, 91).

[11] A Polish book about mining was rejected by the censors in 1948 because, among other things, it portrayed coal mining as hellish. True, the mines in the book were French and capitalist but "harmful analogies" might suggest themselves (Nowak 2012: 140).

[12] The censor also recommended removing a description of the American army in World War One as soldiers of freedom in *The Great Midland* (G-386, 31/122:85). This change was not made.

[13] "–Jak sobie wyobrażasz ten Konwent?'" and "–Zaraz panu odpowiem, Bentley – zaczął Gedeon. – Myślę, że pan dlatego jeszcze żyje, że jesteśmy cywilizowanymi ludźmi i szanujemy prawo. Myślę, że pan o tym wiedział. Jest to właściwość takich ludzi jak pan, że instynktownie, chociaż prymitywnie, rozumiecie, na czym polega cywilizacja. Czy pan mnie słucha?" (Fast 1952: 25, 275).

[14] "K-62", the former censor interviewed in 1981, claimed that texts which were too positive (about socialism) were sometimes toned down by the censors but only if it was thought they had been written with the intent to ridicule. If the author wrote in good faith the praise was allowed to stand (Łopieńska 1981: 15).

[15] See also Klemperer (2006: 67-68).

Chapter 3
Others

Under Stalinism, the most obvious sign that a book was considered reactionary was its absence from the marketplace but signs of displeasure can also be found in the censors' archives. In 1949, one censor wrote of Strickland in Somerset Maugham's *The Moon and Sixpence* that his conception of art is "exceptionally asocial and reactionary". Worse, since Maugham does not criticise Strickland the tone of the book as a whole is reactionary. The recommendation was to deny the publisher paper for the book (G-173c, 32/44: 280). Another censor declares a total absence of "social values" in the book (G-173c, 32/44: 281). A third censor is more favourable (daring?), describing the novel as "'good' escapist literature", which is also needed (G-173c, 32/44: 282). The novel was eventually published, after the thaw, in 1959. In 1955 a libraries committee attached to the Ministry for Culture and Art directed that Maugham's *Up at the Villa* be excluded from libraries, along with Tarzan books, which were deemed rubbish – so much for escapism (M-167, Centralny Zarząd Bibliotek; Wydział Bibliotek Powszechnych: 70-71). Maugham, many of whose books had been translated in pre-war Poland, continued to have problems in Poland after Stalinism had passed.

A translation of a Mr. Bunting novel by Robert Greenwood was stopped in 1950 at the level of the ministry for its "problematic" ideological value. The English in the book are all "egotistical members of the bourgeoisie for whom the ideal is Roosevelt and a quiet life" (M-709, Departament Twórczości Artystycznej; Wydział Wydawniczy: 25). The author's occasional irony directed at the characters is outweighed by his sympathy for them. More interestingly, perhaps, the ministry official in the Department of the Arts, Publishing Division, writes, "I see no reason to be more indulgent of translations than of original Polish work. Under the present circumstances [this book] does not deserve to be published" (M-709, Departament Twórczości Artystycznej; Wydział Wydawniczy: 26). There are three reviews of Greenwood's work in the same file. All say "no" because of the lack of progressive ideology. Greenwood went unpublished in People's Poland. The censors also came out against reissuing a novel by Florence Barclay called *Through the Postern Gate* in 1949 for similar reasons. Though it might be a "nice read" it was petit bourgeois and had no "social values" (Nowak 2012: 62). It was not published after the war. Graham Greene's *Heart of the Matter* did get published during this period but the ministry officials were not happy with its concentration on the inner life of its characters, claiming that the external environment only impinges on the novel's characters because their lives are in turmoil (M-709, Departament Twórczości Artystycznej; Wydział Wydawniczy: 40).

With contemporary non-radical or progressive fiction largely out of bounds under Stalinism, publishers turned to the classics and to well-established authors of western literature. Of the 71 novels from the USA that appeared from 1950 to 1955, as listed in Jerzy Szkup's bibliography, 13 are by Jack London, seven by Mark Twain and four by Fenimore Cooper (all of them very late in the period). The policy, not always adhered to, was not to censor the classics. Piotr Nowak quotes a 1946 circular from the Head Office to the regional branches to the effect that classics, if printed in full, should not be interfered with without first consulting Head Office in Warsaw. Where excerpts are to be published, only politically correct ones should be chosen for publication (Nowak 2012: 53).

A 1952 training bulletin for censors reads, "'Interventions in classic literary works are in principle not advisable except where the works of little known authors are involved and the proposals concern minor deletions'" (qtd. in Bates 2011: 65) but this does not mean they had a free and easy passage. *Wuthering Heights*, though it did get published, in 1950, met with a cool reception. One censor complained:

> the relationships [...] are entirely isolated from any kind of social background. [...] Considering its melodrama, its harmful social tone and the downright sick isolation of the novel's action from the [main] stream of life in England, I believe publishing the book would be harmful (G-145, 31/24: 448-449; see also Bates 2011).

The brief, anonymous introduction to the 1950 edition is somewhat apologetic, saying, "This novel is no record of truth about the world. This novel only shows us how writers of the time perceived the world and how they portrayed it" ('Wstęp' 1950: vii). Thackeray's *The Book of Snobs* also made it past the censors but the writer of the follow-up review in 1951 was not so easily fooled. He or she admits that the book does have some value in that it shows up the bourgeoisie but this was not the intention of Thackeray, who did not see the class divisions in English society. His satire is not sharp enough and does not go beyond anecdotes (G-386, 31/122: 293). Not all censors were so eager to condemn, though, and a second edition did appear, in 1953. *Lovel the Widower* was assessed very favourably in 1951 (Thackeray's sympathies lie with the ordinary people (G-386, 31/122: 482)), although the follow-up review writes it off as a typical, banal, bourgeois book with no trace of social problems, which should not be re-issued (G-386, 31/122: 484). Among the classics, Charles Dickens enjoyed patronage from the authorities, with many editions of his books appearing throughout the years of People's Poland. A sign of the times from the Stalinist period, though, is the censor's 1952 report, not on *Dombey and Son* itself, but on its foreword, which "correctly stresses the limits of the novelistic realism of the author who did not muster up the courage to show the whole truth about the capitalist enterprise" (G-375, 31/29: 60).

Conspicuously absent under Stalinism were Elizabeth Gaskell (see Bates 2011: 65), Jane Austen and Charlotte Brontë. The authorities seem to have treated Austen with some reserve right up until 1989. *Mansfield Park* was not published at all (it had been translated in 1867), *Pride and Prejudice* had just two editions, and *Emma, Northanger Abbey* and *Sense and Sensibility* just one each. The years after 1989 brought many, many more editions. The same is true of Frances Hodgson Burnett, though to a lesser extent: nothing at all under Stalinism, a steady stream of titles afterwards, and a flood after 1989.

It is not hard to see why the censors would prefer not to intervene in translated classics: cuts and alterations were most likely to be noticed in books with which ordinary readers were familiar from before the war. Also, the originals were on the shelves of many scholars, waiting to be compared with new Polish translations. In addition, there were scholarly works on classic fiction. In short, the truth was already out and the censor therefore ran a greater risk of detection. This applies, though to a lesser extent, to translations of contemporary literature too and partly accounts for the easier passage through censorship of translations than of original Polish works. The critical reception in Poland of Steinbeck and Faulkner, for example, began before they were translated into Polish (Szkup 1972: 28). Additionally, in the 1950s the Catholic periodicals carried quite extensive reports on new books by Evelyn Waugh and Graham Greene before they were translated into Polish. In such circumstances censorship is harder to conduct in secret.

Searching through the translations of classics for evidence of censorship is a thankless task. The translation of Elizabeth Gaskell's *Cranford* might even be described as, in parts, "de-censored". The original's "'D—n Dr. Johnson'" (Gaskell s.d.: 14) is rendered without ellipsis in Polish (Gaskell 1970: 18). Thackeray's delicacy, which leads him sometimes to use ellipsis instead of the word "God" (presumably), is not matched in the Polish translation. So, for example, the original's "'By G— he shall'" (Thackeray 1983: 278) is, in back translation, "as I love God" (Thackeray 1960, vol. 1: 358). Similarly with Dickens's *Great Expectations*: when Magwitch says, "'By G—, it's Death!'" (Dickens 1992: 307), the Polish tells spells out "God" (Dickens 1951: 325).

This lenient treatment of classics sometimes meant fairly subversive sentiments made it into Polish print. In "Politics vs. Literature" George Orwell draws our attention to the anti-totalitarian character of part three, and in particular chapter six, of *Gulliver's Travels*. In Langden,

> the Bulk of the People consisted wholly of Discoverers, Witnesses, Informers, Accusers, Prosecutors, Evidences, Swearers; together with their several subservient and subaltern Instruments; all under the Colours, the Conduct, and pay of Ministers and their Deputies (Swift 1986: 191).

With a passage like "It is first agreed and settled among them, what suspected Persons shall be accused of a Plot..." (Swift 1986: 191), Orwell says, "we seem to be positively in the middle of the Russian purges" (Orwell 1998, vol. 18: 423). Two translations of the novel were in circulation in People's Poland. The first is an anonymous one dating from 1784, which translated the whole chapter with its allusions to totalitarianism fully present and correct (Swift 1971: 213-219). The second, by Maciej Słomczyński, was published in 1979 and also shows no signs of censorship (Swift 1979: 202-207). To leave out the chapter or to alter it could not have gone unnoticed. The 1949 edition of *Gulliver's Travels* has an introduction by Jan Kott but far from evading the issue, he chooses precisely that passage to quote as evidence of the sharpness of Swift's satire of eighteenth century British corruption and exploitation. It is hardly surprising that he does not draw an analogy with the USSR or, for that matter, with the West (Kott 1949: vii-viii). The new translation from 1979 includes an afterword by Juliusz Kydryński, who writes that Swift foresaw not totalitarianism but surrealism, and stresses the novel's universality and timelessness (Kydryński 1979: 323).

There were, however, occasions on which the censor did intervene in the classics. An example is *Moby-Dick*, from which goes missing Melville's praise of white people: "though this pre-eminence in it [the colour white] applies to the human race itself, giving the white man ideal mastership over every dusky tribe..." (Melville 1994: 189). Even though this lengthy song of praise ends with "there yet lurks an elusive something in the innermost idea of this hue, which strikes more of panic to the soul than that redness which affrights in blood" (Melville 1994: 190) the racism of the passage was too much for the Polish version (Melville 1971, vol. 1: 286). A little further on, Melville is still discussing whiteness:

> But there are other instances where this whiteness loses all that accessory and strange glory which invests it in the White Steed and Albatross.
> What is it that in the Albino man so peculiarly repels and often shocks the eye, as that sometimes he is loathed by his own kith and kin! It is that whiteness which invests him, a thing expressed by the name he bears. The Albino is as well made as other men – has no substantive deformity – and yet this mere aspect of all-pervading

whiteness makes him more strangely hideous than the ugliest abortion. Why should this be so? (Melville 1950: 190).

This is cut from the Polish (Melville 1971, vol. 1: 289-290), although "'Some old darkey's wedding ring'" (Melville 1994: 414) was translated with racism intact (Melville 1971, vol. 2: 227). The publishers (censors, etc.) may have been emboldened by the fact that *Moby-Dick* was not that well known in Poland – certainly not as well-known as *Gulliver's Travels*. A 1949 version, for example, omitted a lot of the text, leaving mostly the exotic and exciting bits. The translator was uncredited but may have been Janina Sujkowska, who translated the book in 1929 ('Dwaj amerykańscy klasycy' 1949: 9). The admittedly much less fulsome praise of white skin in *Gulliver's Travels* ("I am as fair as most of my Sex and Country, and very little Sunburnt by all my Travels" (Swift 1986: 82-83)) is left to stand in both Polish versions (Swift 1971: 104; 1979: 100).

In the censors' archives one finds a suggestion that a reference in Fielding's *Joseph Andrews* to Gypsies kidnapping a child be changed to "a band of vagrants/tramps" ("włóczędzy") (G-386, 31/124: 299). This instruction was ignored or overridden. Despite concerns about ethnic tensions, "Wicked travelling People whom they call *Gipsies*" (Fielding 1980: 195) is translated as "ten podły naród włóczęgów, których nazywają Cyganami" ("that miserable race of travellers they call Gypsies") (Fielding 1953: 278). The Polish version of *Barnaby Rudge* also preserves the sometimes slighting references to Gypsies and the same is true of the translation of *The Mill on the Floss* when Maggie runs away to join the Gypsies. Lines such as "Everything would be quite charming when she had taught the gypsies to use a washing-basin", and "indulging him with a bite of excellent stolen hay" (Eliot, s.d.: 120) are preserved in the translation.

Nineteenth century classics were also allowed more latitude in stereotyping Jews. In *The Mill on the Floss* the lawyer, Wakem, is described in what might reasonably be called a passage of free indirect discourse as a "hook-nosed glib fellow" and elsewhere Bob Jakin refers to someone getting "'as rich as a Jew'" (Eliot s.d.: 173, 346). These are accurately translated into Polish (Eliot 1960: 187, 382-3). One could read the novel closely (and conclude that Wakem is not such a bad person after all) and study nineteenth century anti-Semitism and general xenophobia in order to tease out the precise views of the author or, if one prefers, the implied author but, as will be shown in chapter five, when it came to contemporary literature Polish censors and translators were usually not so subtle, removing pejorative words "to be on the safe side", regardless of the author's motivation or the motivation of the characters. There was a different standard for classics. Dickens, in *Great Expectations*, mentions "a red-eyed little Jew" (Dickens

1992: 156) while Thackeray, in *Vanity Fair*, has "a little pink-eyed Jewboy" (Thackeray 1983: 668). The translations use the word "Żydek" (Dickens 1951: 164; Thackeray 1960, vol. 2: 283), the diminutive of "Jew", usually perceived as derogatory. Mary Shelley's reference to "slothful Asiatics" (Shelley 1994: 115) is allowed to pass into Polish (Shelley 1989: 103).

The authorities tried to combat any possible "misunderstandings" with afterwords and prefaces but this does not always mean a hectoring from a commissar. "It is difficult", Jan Kott writes in his introduction to *Robinson Crusoe*, "to defend the morality of his [Defoe's] behaviour but he cannot be measured in our categories" (Kott 1953, vol.1: 10). Jan Kott wrote distinctly Marxist introductions to *Robinson Crusoe* and *Gulliver's Travels* but he was also a respected literary critic. It was seen fit to translate his *Shakespeare, Our Contemporary* into the language of Shakespeare. In addition, many classics passed into Polish without any critical apparatus, even under Stalinism. Thackeray's *Henry Esmond* (1957), *Lovel the Widower* (1951), and *Vanity Fair* (1950), Brontë's *Jane Eyre* (1959), Hardy's *Far From the Madding Crowd* (1957), *The Mayor of Casterbridge* (1959), and *Under the Greenwood Tree* (1957), and Dickens's *Oliver Twist* (1953) and *Our Mutual Friend* (1949) all appeared without instruction.

The advantage of a Marxist introduction for translators and readers is that it takes care of any perceived necessity to put an ideological slant on the translation. The 1978 Russian translation of Studs Terkel's *Working*, for example, used Marxist terminology such as "bourgeois public, the so-called middle class" instead of the original's "middle class" (Tax-Choldin 1986: 345). This does not seem to have happened with Polish translations of classics. It might be argued that these paratexts were added to already completed translations and could have no influence on the translator. No doubt this was sometimes the case but there is evidence that translator, editor, and paratext writer worked together. For instance, Jan Kott not only wrote the introduction to *Gulliver's Travels*; he also adapted the existing, anonymous translation from 1784. This version was made from Desfontaines' French translation. Kott removed the moralising additions left over from Desfontaines and in places simplified the syntax (Kott 1949: xix). Witold Chwalewik wrote the preface to *Tristram Shandy* but was also involved in the editing (Chwalewik 1958, vol. 1: 43). Prefaces would have had an indirect influence on translators as well. That is: Kott's comments on Defoe and Swift were a marker for *all* translators of classic novels.

There is no need for the translator of *Crusoe* to distort the text by over-emphasising Crusoe's bourgeois mentality: Kott has already hammered the point home in the introduction, citing Lenin and Marx and declaring that *Robinson Crusoe* is a "chapter in the history of England, social history, and the history of the bourgeoisie" (Kott 1953, vol. 1: 17). The word bourgeoisie does not appear in the novel and thanks to the introduction it was not necessary – even at the height of Stalinism – to introduce it, anachronistically, into the Polish translation. Nor need the translator feel obliged to mention capitalism – another word absent from the book – because Kott has already claimed Defoe is a spokesman for early capitalism (Kott 1953, vol. 1: 11). Kott was aware of the problem of manipulation in translation. He points out that of the dozen or more Polish translations of the book not one had correctly translated the 32,800 pieces of eight the narrator receives from a remittance of 33,000. It was obvious to Defoe that 200 would be deducted as a commission but for a translator to miss this is to miss the point that Crusoe is a merchant right up to the last page of the book (Kott 1953, vol. 1: 18, 19). Over the centuries, the novel had been traduced, Kott continues, reduced to children's reading and banned, for example in the Northern states of the USA during the Civil War because Crusoe is a slave trader. Now, he finishes, it and *Gulliver's Travels* were being restored to their former glory so that "in these two wonderful books of the early bourgeoisie a great lesson in history and in realism could be found" (Kott 1953, vol. 1: 40). The ideological burden has been taken from the translation (not, strictly speaking, the translator, since it is a pre-war version) and shouldered by Kott.

Similarly with *Gulliver's Travels*: there is no need for the translation to force "capitalism", "bourgeoisie" or even "feudalism" (words all absent from the original) into the book as that has been done in the introduction, again by Kott, who writes that the book satirises feudalism and is the first "historical criticism of capitalism" (Kott 1949: vi). Nor does the translation need to take pains to highlight (or invent) any exploitation of the poor in the book. Kott's sketch of Swift's times has plenty to say about peasants turned into wage slaves and about the plunder of Ireland, Scotland and India (Kott 1949: v).

Włodzimierz Lewik's 1953 afterword to *Joseph Andrews* is distinctly Marxist, also mentioning the transformation of free peasants into a proletariat, and the "primitive accumulation" of the eighteenth century (Lewik 1953: 437-438). Just as Kott did not fight shy of passages in Swift reminiscent of the purges in Soviet Russia, so too does Lewik tackle the censorship question head on: "So we have English theatre censorship to thank for the birth of Fielding the novelist" (Fielding 1953: 437). Lewik also quotes George Bernard Shaw's words to the effect that the 1737 Licensing Act still censors English theatre (Fielding 1953: 437). There is no hint of embarrassment, even if the afterword does at times resemble a censor's review:

> Fielding cannot bring himself to openly criticise the political system. He confines himself to portraying the private flaws of his heroes and yet even this method allows us

> without difficulty to read the causes of those flaws: causes arising from the particular
> political system of the times (Fielding 1953: 444).

This at least saves the translator the bother of trying to make the private faults of Joseph Andrews somehow seem relevant to the bourgeois government of England.

George Bidwell sketches the historical background to Smollett's *Roderick Random* in similar terms: the Restoration was a compromise between urban upper classes and landowners; there was fraud and exploitation in the eighteenth century; capitalism was becoming more vicious; and the English proletariat was in its infancy. "We must keep this in mind when reading Smollett and remember that his portrait [of the times] is incomplete because there is no wider analysis of the epoch" (Bidwell 1955, vol. 2: 271).

Zygmunt Bauman supplied the afterword to Elizabeth Gaskell's *Mary Barton* in 1956, when the thaw was setting in. By now some of its themes will be familiar (proletarianisation of peasants, exploitation of workers during the industrial revolution). Gaskell pities the proletariat and vividly portrays their poverty but she cannot see that this poverty is caused by the "development of the capitalist industry which she praises" (Bauman 1956: 467). Gaskell's belief that by curbing excesses things could be improved within the existing framework was, *at that time*, forgivable: by the late nineteenth century it would not have been a view an honest person could hold (Bauman 1956: 467). The translator need not fear to convey the author's praise of capitalism: it has been explained away. Nor need the translator have worried too much about the depiction of trade unionism or the condemnation of violence against manufacturers: readers are warned that Gaskell had only a vague idea of trade unionism (Bauman 1956: 469).

Roman Karst's 1954 introduction to *Dombey and Son* is, not to put too fine a point on it, more of the same: the bourgeois revolution, accumulation of capital, Chartism (also mentioned by Bauman), and exploitation of the workers (Karst 1954, vol. 1: 6-7). Karst mentions *Gulliver's Travels* and *Robinson Crusoe* and his debt to Kott is very clear, though it might be more accurate to talk of their debt to Marx. Like Elizabeth Gaskell, Charles Dickens is a better observer than reformer. Like Gaskell, he has a "limited field of vision" and it is only thanks to his gifts of observation and description that we get a feel for the inhumanity of the English bourgeoisie (Karst 1954, vol. 1: 8). Dickens's criticism is sentimental, with no philosophical framework: he wanted to improve the system, not radically change it. He was afraid of revolution and posed no threat to the oppressors (Karst 1954, vol. 1: 9). As seen in censors' reviews in general, a problem here is that no great social processes lie behind – in this case – Dombey's fall, which is brought about by the personal failing of pride (Karst 1954, vol. 1: 12).

Janusz Wilhelmi, faced with the task of writing an afterword to *A Tale of Two Cities*, evidently decided to brazen it out. He tells readers that Dickens's obvious horror of the guillotine should not fool us into thinking that he was against the revolution (Wilhelmi 1960: 439). No, Dickens understood and praised revolution, knew it was "necessary, the natural order of things, irrevocable" (Wilhelmi 1960: 441). Strained as the argument may seem, it did give the translator a free hand in dealing with Dickens's horror of revolution. Wilhelmi, meanwhile, went on to become minister for arts and culture.

Australian writer Jack Lindsay is the author of the 1950 introduction to *Hard Times* in Polish. He describes Dickens as politically a kind of anarchist. Although he hated the bourgeois state, Dickens never expressed his rebellion in political terms (Lindsay 1950: 7). Lindsay's discussion of Carlyle's influence on Dickens has an interesting example of the kind of license extended to the classics. Some of Carlyle's theses, he writes, led to fascism, and some to socialism, "but in his day the historical process had not yet crystallised these opposites" (Lindsay 1950: 11). To suggest similarities between communism and fascism was usually the kiss of death.

Walter Scott was in even greater need of a dispensation for his sins. He was a Tory snob – writes Stanisław Helsztyński in the 1949 preface to *Kenilworth* – whose disapproval of even the watered down Reform Act of 1832 was decidedly "anti-democratic and anti-progressive" (Helsztyński 1949: 12, 13). Scott, looking 100 years back over his shoulder, failed to see the social and economic changes taking place in his own times, i.e. industrialisation and the activity of Robert Owen (Helsztyński 1949: 12). Balzac has stood the test of time better than Scott because he could think in socio-economical terms (Helsztyński 1949: 15). The 1948 preface to *Ivanhoe* (by "S.D.", presumably the translator) tries harder than Helsztyński to claim Scott for the cause of progress: Scott understands, as few others do, that history is made by ordinary people and in his descriptions of these people he is objective and democratic. Much as Scott – a true blue Englishman, after all – disliked Napoleon, he agreed with him on many points and this comes across in the books (Draczko 1948: 6-7). The two prefaces take a different tack but both serve to excuse the translation for the author's failings.

Butler's *The Way of All Flesh* is, in Czesław Ferens's 1960 afterword, a story of inter-generation conflict whose real cause is not people but the system, which is based on exploitation of the weak by the strong and the young by the old (Ferens 1960: 641). The satire is sharp and well-aimed but Butler – inevitably, one wearily feels – misses the "wider social problems, class conflict, and the mechanisms of social oppression" (Ferens 1960: 642).

This afterword comes from a little later than most of the ones given above and while the concern with wider (underlying, real etc.) social processes is clear to see, there is by now, no mention of Marx, Engels or Lenin, as is true of Wilhelmi's essay on *A Tale of Two Cities* from the same year. Sometimes a certain amount of detective work has to be done to even find the ideology (if, indeed it *is* ideology) in these paratexts. For example, Bronisława Bałutowa's afterword to *The House of the Seven Gables* claims Hawthorne as a realist because the "hidden conflicts of the age" come through in his fantastic stories. Marx is not mentioned but hidden conflicts might be understood as code for class struggle (Bałutowa 1959: 315). In 1963 Thomas Hardy escapes accusations of missing the bigger picture of class struggle in Irena Dobrzycka's afterword to *Jude the Obscure* (Dobrzycka 1963: 480). Once Stalinism had passed, critics can even be found smuggling references to touchy subjects past the censor in paratexts. For example, Henryk Krzeczkowski, in the afterword to *The Ambassadors*, discusses the question of expatriate writers. He writes, "Turgenev could live and work for years abroad and Polish writers – for entirely different reasons – could spend their entire lives abroad and that had no effect on their ties with their own literature and culture" (Krzeczkowski 1960, vol. 2: 360). The authorities were particularly sensitive about Polish writers living in the West, such as Witold Gombrowicz, and Krzeczkowski seems to be making a reference to modern day Poland in his discussion of Henry James's relationship with Britain and the USA.

It is often argued that such critical paratexts are a way of steering the reader to ideologically desirable conclusions. Perhaps so, if readers are interested enough to read them, but they also give translators and editors valuable breathing space. The classics are absolved of their sins in afterwords and forewords, meaning the editor can use an already existing translation without worrying too much about its politics. If a fresh translation be commissioned, the translator does not have to strive to make the book politically acceptable. If Robinson Crusoe is a mercantile enslaver of his fellow human beings then so be it. Czesław Ferens even explains why the translator of *The Way of All Flesh* used the words "rasa" and "rasowy" ("race" and "racial"). Butler, he explains, is an elitist, perhaps, but no racist, and the words are used to translate "breeding" and "well bred" (Ferens 1960: 642-643). It will be seen in chapter five that the race question was a very touchy one and translators often censored themselves or were censored when it arose.

These paratexts not only excused authors and by extension translators for their class politics; they also, on occasion, apologised for the boring bits and the coarse language in classic literature. Despite the tendency for Polish translations to be more prim than their source texts, Swift, to take one example, in both Polish versions is just as faecal and obscene: the episode from book three, chapter five recounting the awful experiment with an enema on dogs is given in full in Polish. Kott wrote in his introduction to the book that within a hundred years of its publication it had been cut and castrated (Kott 1949: v) and, as seen, he boasted that it had now been re-issued in full (Kott 1953, vol. 1: 40).

Witold Chwalewik, in his lengthy preface to *Tristram Shandy*, writes that the twentieth century is better able to appreciate the humour of writers such as Chaucer and Sterne but – he warns – the latter is a difficult writer, not for the young or the unsophisticated (Chwalewik 1958, vol. 1: 6). Much use is made in *Tristram Shandy* of the phallic motif, although Sterne, unlike Swift, never uses rude words. The current practice (not just in Poland) is not to cut coarse language from translations (Chwalewik 1958, vol. 1: 12, 16). Chwalewik also refers to boring passages in the novel and argues that the book's lengthy, overburdened sentences and even bad grammar are artistically justified. He quotes (in Polish) a sentence which breaks down under its own weight, ending with the narrator admitting that he himself is lost, thus giving the translator license (if not instructions) to break the cultural norm of writing correct Polish (Chwalewik 1958, vol. 1: 36).

George Bidwell also signals to the translator that he need not censor the gory bits in *Roderick Random*: what seems to be Smollett's "sadistic pleasure in descriptions of horror and suffering is actually a manifestation of the author's deep revulsion" at the inhumanity of the ruling classes in eighteenth century England (Bidwell 1955, vol. 2: 269). Lest the translator still feel shy of naturalist depictions of suffering, Maxim Gorky is quoted: "'England is the mother of realism'" (Bidwell 1955, vol. 2: 270). Irena Dobrzycka's afterword to Thackeray's *The Newcomes* might even be read as a message to readers that yes, there is censorship but no, it was not the fault of your Polish translator. Both Thackeray and Dickens, she writes, were either silent on certain subjects or else they idealised love. "Physical love was taboo", she explains (Dobrzycka 1955, vol. 2: 537). The idealisation of love was a feature of socialist realist literature so this serves to reassure readers that in the case of Thackeray and Dickens it was there in the original. The same critic prepares readers of *Jude the Obscure* for frankness on sexual and marital matters by pointing out that Hardy was attacked for precisely this by non-progressive critics at a time when prudery was strangling English literature (Dobrzycka 1963: 479).

A review written by an employee of the GUKPPiW could prevent the publication of the book: that was the point of the institution after all. Newspaper reviews appearing after the fact did not have such power. John Bates, in his article on the censorship of Polish literature under Stalinism, argues that the Party determined each work's reception. By dominating the literary and non-literary press, which also came under censorship office supervision, and by setting up 'creative sections' in the Writers' Union, which subjected a colleague's latest endeavour to sometimes astringent criticism, the Party ensured its decisive voice in the agencies of reception (Bates 2004a: 13).

The Propaganda and Agitation Section of the Party's Central Committee, in a 1955 internal document, decided that criticism in *Trybuna Ludu* (the Party's organ) and *Nowe Drogi* should be tightened up because criticism "should become an important instrument of the Party leadership and should effect the activity of writers". However, the system of indoctrination was not watertight: this document complains that the two papers had practically ignored the publication of 21 volumes of Lenin's works (K-237/viii-212: 5, 1). Later, too, the Party interfered with the critical reception of various works. For example, the Censorship Office directed that reviews of an encyclopaedia not be too positive (Karpiński 1978: 96). Yet Poles remained loyal to their own tastes in literature. They continued to prefer Henryk Sienkiewicz's *Trilogy* to Witold Zalewski's *Traktory zdobędą wiosnę* (*Tractors will Win Spring*). A 1984 report from Rzeszów's public library ("for internal use") to the Party Central Committee places John Steinbeck on the list of much-read authors: so much for the official condemnation of the author for his stance on the Vietnam war (K-lvi1452).

Bad reviews might hit sales and deter the publisher from issuing a second edition of the book or another book by the same writer, and under Stalinism many reviewers tried to enforce socialist realism. However, there was still some pluralism, although the range of translated books that could be reviewed had been drastically narrowed. There were critics who welcomed and reinforced this narrowing of the selection of books for publishing. For example, Krystyna Michalik-Nedelković dropped a heavy hint for publishing houses in a 1949 article in which she declared that Steinbeck had started out as a progressive but had reconciled himself to American capitalism. Meanwhile American critics, she continued, had falsified their interpretations of Dreiser, a progressive through and through (Michalik-Nedelković 1949: 7). This kind of message may have discouraged a translator from working on Steinbeck but its effect on how the same translator might have translated Dreiser is hard to measure.

Reviews of Dickens attempt to claim him for the socialist cause in the early 1950s, although critics are usually a little more cautious than, for example, Wilhelmi was in his afterword to *A Tale of Two Cities*. Jadwiga Żylińska accuses bourgeois criticism of claiming Dickens had no politics, only, at most, certain sympathies. In fact he was "against monarchy, the church, the power and privilege of the aristocracy and sinecures and rent taking", but he is easily dismissed as apolitical because "he expressed his protest not in political categories but in terms of morality and ethics" (Żylińska 1953: 6). Żylińska admits it would be going too far to call Dickens a socialist but although he would not join the trade union movement Dickens was always ready to storm the Bastille (Żylińska 1953: 7). The note of pride sounded by Kott in Poland's restoration of classics is also to be heard in Żylińska's review: she writes that Poles could be forgiven for thinking Dickens was just the nice guy who wrote the *Pickwick Papers* (Żylińska 1953: 6). People's Poland was making great strides in bringing all of Dickens to the public. A reviewer signing him or herself "A.W." also mentions that up until the war Polish readers often knew Dickens in abridged forms, for children, with some of the more serious, grown-up books untranslated. A.W. also refers to Dickens's fear of trade unionism and his lack of real radicalism ('Dickens, jakiego nie znamy' 1950: 12). Roman Karst's article on Dickens is much like his introduction to *Dombey and Son*. Dickens did not question the political order and is at his best as a realist and worst as a reforming thinker: he had no philosophy and his relationship to evil is an emotional one (Karst 1950: 5).

Daniela Bielecka, following George Orwell, attributes Dickens's exceptional success in Poland after the war to the fact that he

> proved worth stealing also for the supporters of different doctrines and tendencies prevailing in Polish post-war literary criticism. The earliest contributions made in the period of a considerable ideological liberalism, continued the tradition of a comparative analysis (Bielecka 1989: 130).

Later, Dickens "was easily fitted into the pattern of a 'progressive,' realistically depicting the excesses and perversities of the capitalistic system" (Bielecka 1989: 131). In the 1960s, Bielecka continues,

> the dogmatic approach was rejected and Marxist criteria were reappraised. Dickens emerged again as the novelist not simply ideologically safe and acceptable but also artistically satisfying and illuminating in his approach to problems and people (Bielecka 1989: 132).

In fact, Bielecka's survey of the reception of Dickens in Poland shows that throughout the years all kinds of literary groupings tried to claim Dickens for themselves.

Wojciech Tomasik writes that book reviews in the early 1950s were often very similar to each other (Tomasik 1988: 185). It is true, also, that the tone of these reviews was remarkably similar to that of the internal reviews written by censors and often to the introductions accompanying classic novels. It has often been suggested that censors also wrote reviews of books for the press and in reviews from the 1950s you occasionally find conclusions that sound as if they were written by someone accustomed to wielding more power than the typical book reviewer. For example, "b.d.", the reviewer of a translation of O. Henry stories, writes that it was not worth translating and publishing. The translation is good, he or she writes, and it is a shame that incomparably more valuable books are often given to poorly qualified translators ('Wśród książek' 1950: 11).

A person signing him or herself "WISZ" reviewed *The Great Midland* in 1953 in terms familiar from the censors' archives: *The Great Midland* is "not just an attempt to expose the methods of exploitation used by the great railway societies of America. It is also an attempt to show the shared struggle by the railway workers on the tracks and in the stations against exploitation". The Dave and Stephanie story is not the most important thing in the novel. Through their fate Saxton shows the real social and political state of America in a novel that is realistic and ideologically mature ('Amerykański przyjaciel' 1953: 6). The same familiarity greets us in a 1951 review of the novel written by W.K. Oesterloef, who takes the trouble to tell us that the Congress of Industrial Organisations is now eaten through with opportunism (as a footnote in the novel says). The novel is outstandingly political but avoids "verbalism" by having fully fleshed out and differentiated characters. Like one of the censors, Oesterloef was worried that there might be a bit too much about Dave's and Stephanie's marital problems. An important ideological mistake is the failure, typical of some American communists, to see the unity of theory (represented in the book by Stephanie) and action (represented by Dave) (Oesterloef 1951: 11). Presumably it would have improved the book if Dave and Stephanie had married happily.

Grzeniewski's 1955 discussion of Fast's progressive *Freedom Road* is predictably favourable and also takes the opportunity to hit out at, among others, *Gone With the Wind*. Contemporary American literature, the critic claims, longs for plantation residences from 100 years ago, just as the Polish aristocracy and bourgeoisie – especially between the wars – longed for the estates of feudal Poland. *Gone with the Wind* is a classic example of the type but Fast is immune to the lure of the plantation house on the hill and its residents. *Freedom Road* is more than just a fictionalised history lecture, as Fast the writer beats Fast the historian (Grzeniewski 1955: 5). Grzeniewski goes to bat for what might be perceived as a weakness of the book: the speed with which the main character, Gideon, learns. Grzeniewski claims that this speed of learning is explained by the historical circumstances. In this respect Fast was no doubt under the influence of Jack London's *Martin Eden* (Grzeniewski 1955: 5).

A 1951 review of story collections by Albert Maltz (*Człowiek na drodze*) and Howard Fast (*Departure*) describes progressive literature as "an expression of the consciousness of the working masses", showing that there is a second America, one of patriots "harshly, critically and justly evaluating the alleged paradise of America". Fast and Maltz are firmly in this group of writers, exposing the "merciless exploitation of workers and small farmers" in America ('Dwie Ameryki' 1951: 17). Maltz's "A Letter From the Country" reveals the "fascist face of America in its imperial phase" and the treatment meted out to the progressive organisers resembles Gestapo tactics ('Dwie Ameryki' 1951: 18). As in many such reviews of progressive novels, there is more about the evils of America than the merits of the book being reviewed. However, Howard Fast is commended for showing not just the "tragic situation of the working masses in a capitalist country" but also the causes of and the solutions to that tragic state of affairs ('Dwie Ameryki' 1951: 19). This is particularly high praise, since the alleged fault of so many western writers was that they only observed injustice, without understanding its causes or advocating a class-based struggle. Failure to see this was noted by the reviewer of *The Ragged Trousered Philanthropists*. Dudziński writes that the novel's Frank Owen, like its author, Robert Tressall, was a loner and this lone struggle inevitably led to pessimism, breakdown, despair and destruction. So the failure is Owen's fault as well. It is realistic and detailed, a good exposé but – the implication is – it does not show the way forward (Dudziński 1952: 2). Similarly, Stanisław Mędelski praises Ira Wolfert's *Tucker's People* because it shows the process of the concentration of capital, the moral decay brought by imperialism and the "hideousness, moral rot and degeneracy of the contemporary American bourgeoisie". The novel's murderer is driven, not by some internal need, but by the dictates of the imperialist system (Mędelski 1950: 5). This is all to the good but, Mędelski cautions, the reader leaves the book pessimistic and "helpless" because Wolfert only shows the evils and apart from an occasional mention of trade unions, does not show how the working class pulling together can bring about change (Mędelski 1950: 5). Albert Halper meets the same criticism for his *Foundry*: class consciousness does not develop and the ending is pessimistic. This suggestion that class solidarity is impossible, the critic writes, is a serious charge against Halper. He concludes that despite the mistaken ending and the minimalist plan for improving the workers' lot (i.e. incremental change rather than revolution) the book is good (Wallicht 1950: 7). A 1951 review in *Nowa Kultura*, signed by "b.d.", gives a less favourable verdict. The book has too little "social class based analysis" and too much naturalism. True, there is a radical character in the book, Heitman, but he suffers the ignominious fate of having his radicalism put in inverted commas by the critic. He is not a radical. He is a "radical" ('Wśród książek' 1951: 11). Groten-Sonecka also complains of Maltz that his collection of stories, *Człowiek na drodze*, is not always free of the extreme naturalism typical of American literature (Groten-Sonecka 1950: 8).

As well as this kind of qualified praise for western progressives, the critics also dealt out reprimands to non-progressive writers. In a review of *The Heart of the Matter* George Bidwell tells us that Graham Greene does not know "the people" ("lud"). He only knows "officials, blackmailers, opportunist priests – tools for exploitation in the hands of the ruling class". Greene never criticises capitalism because he is up to his neck in it and "cannot perceive its causes, its essence" (Bidwell 1952: 10). Tadeusz Myślik discusses A.J. Cronin more sympathetically than Bidwell does Greene but some of the Stalinist uniformity can nevertheless be seen. *The Stars Look Down* exposes the futility of the "third force", i.e. "democratic" socialism, using the Labour Party as an example, but Cronin is helpless in the face of this evil. He does not see the solution and when the novel's hero loses the election he just goes back to work in the mine, even though Cronin must know the hopelessness of parliamentary democracy. Cronin "cannot overcome the mistakes of social evolutionism" (Myślik 1954: 3). Once again the writer is progressive but not radical.

Myślik was writing in *Dziś i Jutro*, a Catholic periodical, but there were periodicals more closely aligned with the government, whose critics were made of sterner stuff. Ludwik Grzeniewski savaged Bruce Marshall's *All Glorious Within* in *Nowa Kultura* in 1950. Marshall's main thesis is that God sent us to save our souls and nothing else matters. No wonder, the critic comments, that the novel's Father Smith, "absorbed by this medieval maxim and apologia", does not know what to make of the striking workers. Marshall's book is "regressive and harmful". It is in praise of capitalism (Grzeniewski 1950: 6).

What makes this last review interesting is the response to it by Paweł Jasienica that was published in *Dziś i Jutro*. Jasienica states quite baldly that of course Grzeniewski did not like the book: he's a Marxist so what would you expect? Grzeniewski's article is purely political (Jasienica 1950a: 2). In the same year Jasienica also took up the cudgels in defence of Graham Greene's *Heart of the Matter* – or rather against Tadeusz Borowski's criticism of it. Borowski attacked the book, Jasienica argued, in exactly the same way Grzeniewski attacked Marshall: without a word about artistic merits. Jasienica disputes Borowski's claim that the book is a defence of imperialism and questions his comparison of the book to Kipling's *Jungle Book* (specifically, "Toomai of the Elephants" and "Her Majesty's Servants"). He asks rhetorically if a tendency away from old fashioned imperialism is not visible here (Jasienica 1950b: 7).

Thus, even under Stalinism in Poland it was possible to engage in polemics with socialist realist criticism. Alternative points of view were to be found in *Dziś i Jutro* and *Tygodnik Powszechny*, Catholic newspapers. Both of them reviewed *The Great Midland*. Wincenty Kos in *Tygodnik*

Powszechny devotes a lot of space to Dave and Stephanie's marriage. Saxton, he says – in a favourable but not excessively or slavishly favourable review – does a good job of showing the larger picture through the lives of Dave and Stephanie and their friends (Kos 1954: 14). *Dziś i Jutro* reviewed the book in 1951, saying it would interest Polish readers with its description of an unknown milieu – like Halper's *The Foundry*. In Halper, though, there is a better balance between plot and socio-political elements. Saxton's book has a sometimes boring overload of ideology but this is overcome by the good characterisation ('Kolejarze z Chicago' 1951: 9). This is a review that could have been written yesterday. Ewa Szonert, in the same newspaper, reviewed Katharine Prichard's gold fields trilogy. There is a dose of ideology in the comment that "the author has not shown clearly enough that the entire working class is engaged in the class struggle, not just individuals" but the review also contains criticism that goes beyond the expected charges of naturalism or pessimism. For example, Dinny Quin's transformation into a trade unionist is rather abrupt and it seems unconvincing that Cavan's capitalist stepdaughters (Pam and Pat, from *Winged Seeds*) initiate the aid for the Spanish Civil War. The books' non-ideological faults are questioned too: Morris Gough's life story is told three times in *The Roaring Nineties* (Szonert 1952: 11).

Adam Weber manages to slip into a review of a Stefan Heym novel some implicit criticism of – if not Maltz and Fast themselves – then certainly their slavish admirers in the Polish press. Heym's *Hostages* was weak and sensationalist with "pseudo-ideological" pretensions but *The Crusaders* is top-notch, as if by a different writer. In it Heym remembers to let his characters and the story do the talking. It is an indictment – but subtle, not demagogic – of US government policy towards Germany (Weber 1950: 9). Subtlety was not always and everywhere so highly esteemed.

One would be hard put to find the narrow ideology-based criticism that preaches to readers – and potential translators – in Maria Morstin-Górska's reviews in *Tygodnik Powszechny*, where she criticised Sinclair Lewis's *Cass Timberlane* not because it was too radical or not radical enough or the wrong kind of radical but simply because she thought it was "insipid and banal". In the same article's review of *Daylight on Saturday*, she attacks Priestley for writing books soaked in "social didactics" – the very thing a committed communist critic would applaud (Morstin-Górska 1949: 9). It will be recalled that the censors thought this book "very progressive, for England" (G-145, 31/22: 100).

It was not just Catholic periodicals either. *Życie Literackie* published a review of Ralph de Boissiere's *Jewel in The Crown* whose modest amount of ideological content is justified by the contents of the book (that is, de Boissiere really did write about the social hierarchy and workers' organisation). Also, there is some non-ideological criticism of the author, who is accused of trying to pack too much into the book. All the discussions and descriptions of "actions" and strikes gathered in the book's main storyline – the organisation of a Marxist trade union – begin to bore as they resemble each other and do not always add anything new to the plot (Urbańczyk 1953: 14). Dudziński's review of Dreiser's *The Bulwark* does contain much about issues such as the accumulation of capital and creation of monopolies but it also admits that the novel is not Dreiser's best: it is sketchy in parts and has longueurs (Dudziński 1951: 10).

However, just as reviews in more government-aligned papers concentrated on the admirable or sometimes questionable ideological position of the Fasts, Maltzes and Saxtons, so too, on occasion, did the more independent, Catholic papers concentrate on the doctrinal position of their Greenes, Chestertons, Waughs and Cronins. Anna Iwaszkiewiczowa, for example, wonders why Greene's *Heart of the Matter* is considered a "'Catholic novel'". She argues that it is an act of sabotage "because its effects can only be in conflict with the task of Catholic literature", which is to show how much even a weak person can achieve with love. The word she uses here, "dywersyjna" ("sabotage", adj.), is typical of communist propaganda (Iwaszkiewiczowa 1951: 6). This interpenetration of ideologies can be seen also in Witold Ostrowski's 1953 discussion of Cronin. *Citadel* does not attack the whole system, only the citadel of the title, in which doctors have locked themselves, eaten away by "the spirit of comfort and capitalism". *The Keys of the Kingdom* is the only one of Cronin's books in which religion is central. The other novels are "undoubtedly socially progressive and are also imbued with Christian humanism". However, Chisholm misunderstands the essence of doctrinal points such as not eating meat on Fridays (Ostrowski 1953: 1). Stefan Lichański, a year later, describes the book as a hagiography, in which everything and everyone is secondary to Chisholm: either with him or against him (Lichański 1954: 4).

This concentration on the religious or political questions raised by the books is often at the expense of the language in which they were written and translated and it means that reviews are less helpful than they might otherwise have been in telling us how the translations were perceived, which in turn would tell us more about the norms applied to language. Wacław Sadkowski's comments on translations from the 1950s of nineteenth century classic realist novels were made long after the fact, although he was involved in publishing in the 1950s. He writes that the translations are poised between a light "patina" of archaism and a degree of modernisation, which gave very good results. He singles out Tadeusz Dehnel's translation of *Vanity Fair* for special praise: Dehnel uses a style modelled on nineteenth century Polish writer Bolesław Prus but with "delicately modernised" syntax (Sadkowski

2002: 119). In her study of the post-war Polish reception of Ibero-American literature, Gaszyńska-Magiera examines several hundred reviews and shows that their authors usually prized "easy to receive", "transparent" translations, in which the translator remains invisible (Gaszyńska-Magiera 2011: 106-107).

The "pane of glass" metaphor is used, for example, by Zofia Starowieyska-Morstinowa in her review of *The Heart of the Matter*. The translation is good, giving a full view of the original and letting the reader forget it is a translation. At the same time, she says, a good translation should preserve the source text's originality and roughness (Starowieyska-Morstinowa 1950: 3). Maria Morstin-Górska seems to argue for this kind of domestication in her comments on the translation of a Harry Reasoner novel: it too often follows the English syntax, which is not a good idea in Polish. The favouring of correct Polish is apparent in her review of Lehmann's *The Ballad and the Source*. The critic takes the trouble to note that it is "grammatically correct" but it is stiff, without the author's style. In this group review she praises Maria Wisłowska's translation of Priestley, one of the best in recent years and standing out against a whole lot of mistakes (Morstin-Górska 1949: 9). Elsewhere, the same reviewer criticised the translation of a Cronin novel for its tendency to follow foreign syntax. The result is a stiff, even if grammatically impeccable, translation. Morstin-Górska goes on to point out that the word "zabulgotać" ("bubble, gurgle") can be applied to water but not to people; for them we must use "bełkotać" ("mumble, gabble") (Morstin-Górska 1948: 9). If this was an attempt by the translator to introduce a metaphorical extension of the meaning of "zabulgotać" it was shot down mercilessly by Morstin-Górska. One may interpret this as an act of post-publication censorship but no doubt Morstin-Górska would say she was merely doing her job of protecting Polish against barbarisms.

A similar concern for linguistic hygiene can be seen in the 1952 review of *The Spit and the Stars*. The review is politically very orthodox (claiming, for example, that not much has changed for working Americans since 1935 – the depth of the depression) but it also finds space to attack the translation itself for its mistakes and general carelessness. Some of the mistakes appear to be calques from English, for example, "'chcesz dostać podwójnego zapalenia'" ("do you want to get double inflammation"; presumably from "double pneumonia". In colloquial Polish the distinction between single pneumonia, of one lung, and double pneumonia, of both lungs, is not made) ('Powszednie dni Brooklynu' 1952: 10).

Not all attempts at domestication were welcomed by critics. Alfred Liebfeld is taken to task by Antoni Szymanowski for his translation of a Howard Fast novel for correcting, explicating and prettifying Fast's simple style with his own "untrammelled caprices" ("bujna fantazja"). Where, for example, Fast simply wrote that it was still light, Liebfeld has "'Słońce wciąż jeszcze zalewało świat swym hojnym blaskiem'" ("The sun was still flooding the world with its generous glitter"). Where Fast has "'odpowiedział'" ("answered"), Liebfeld has "'zapewnił gorąco'" ("hotly assured") (Szymanowski 1952: 9). This last is an interesting example of a critic speaking out against Polish norms, for literary Polish does tend to use a much wider range of reporting verbs than English. Although the first example is a travesty of Fast's style, the second could more easily be justified as domestication.

A full survey of the critical reception of fiction translated from English is beyond the scope of this book and would take us a long way from the central practices of censorship and into peripheral phenomena (to use the "family resemblance" terminology proposed by Müller). This brief look at reviews from the most oppressive, Stalinist period is only feasible because so little English fiction was published in these years, meaning the number of reviews is correspondingly small. After the thaw of 1956, politics still sometimes find their way into reviews but there is no longer the same kind of uniformity (of censors' reviews, of paratexts and of critics' reviews) that might encourage or enforce conformity among translators. To suggest that what heavily ideological reviews there were dictated translation strategies is to presuppose extremely malleable translators.

It may be possible to discern a preference among reviewers and – more importantly – in the translations themselves for standard, domesticated literary Polish but translators did experiment and were reasonably free to do so. Anna Przedpełska-Trzeciakowska used archaic vocabulary in her translations of Jane Austen (Bystydzieńska 2005: 112). Bronisław Zieliński did not standardise the archaic English used by Hemingway in *For Whom the Bell Tolls*. Critics noted attempts made by translators to render regionalisms in Frank O'Connor's short stories (Szymańska 1972: 160) and in Caldwell's *House in the Uplands* (Wegner 1973: 9). Maciej Słomczyński admits that his 1972 translation of *Alice in Wonderland* is not written in "'the most beautiful Polish'" but that the language he used was, he believed, most suitable for his purpose, which was to preserve both the adult and the child addressee (Słomczyński 1972: 6). Słomczyński – like Zieliński – enjoyed an impressive reputation as a translator and the book had a print run of over 100,000. His refusal to conform to an ideal of "beautiful Polish" does not seem to have harmed him.

Furthermore, translators were subject to (or rather, a part of) the general milieu of Polish letters. Julian Rogoziński writes of the translation of a collection of Thomas Wolfe's stories entitled *Włóczędzy o zachodzie słońca* that it is over-ambitious, full of "gerunds, for which we should not really blame the translator, since this is a plague that has of late hit our own young original prose" (Rogoziński 1961: 6). While some critics may have expected and praised domesticating techniques, translators did not necessarily feel obliged to use them. It is difficult to label criticism of translation strategies censorship when texts were being cut and banned by government-employed censors.

An early sign in censorship of the thaw can be found in an Instruction Bulletin in the censors' archives from 1953. It grants the possibility that in scholarly editions with very long introductions those introductions may contain "debatable theses, even such as a censor might be doubtful about" (G-420, 165/2: 547). In 1954, an article appeared in *Nowa Kultura* calling for the publication of Caldwell, Steinbeck and Faulkner because their arguments about exploitation and poverty in the US were more convincing than the works of such establishment favourites as Howard Fast and Jack Lindsay (Kondek 1999: 188). Some date the beginnings of the thaw as far back as 1952 (see Łapiński and Tomasik 2004: 163) but the effects really only begin to make themselves felt in the publishing of translated books in 1956. That year alone saw books by Greene, Hemingway, Melville and Poe published, with Faulkner, Capote, Steinbeck, Sherwood Anderson, and William Saroyan following very soon afterwards. The ban on *Gone With the Wind* was lifted and the book appeared again in 1957.

An illustration of how much more liberal Polish publishing was during this period is provided by some book reviews from 1957 in *Przegląd Kulturalny* signed "B. Cz." (probably Bohdan Czeszko). The reviewer's criticism of the regime is nothing if not open. In one review he expresses disbelief that Caldwell is considered one of the "big four" of American literature (who the other three were is left unsaid but Steinbeck, Faulkner and Hemingway are likely candidates). Critics and publishers knew socialist realism was nonsense, the reviewer writes, but some western books were praised far above their merits simply because they were "forbidden fruit". Caldwell's stories, far from exposing the evils of capitalism in the United States, have "unconvincing cruelty, unconvincing eroticism and false psychological depths" ('Szarlatan i inne...' 1957: 3).[1] Also in 1957, Bohdan Czeszko claims – more to the point, is permitted to claim – that *The Grapes of Wrath* appeared only in October 1956 because Steinbeck was not the greatest friend of the USSR. The delay can only be explained by the immense stupidity of the "inquisitors of the index of forbidden books". Czeszko continues: "So what if there are so many among us who could faultlessly write in the margins of the book pre-prepared comments taught on Marxist training courses...?" (Czeszko 1957: 3). Censors and critics had, as seen, often complained that even in the fiction of progressive western writers, workers were preoccupied with their individual, immediate, material needs rather than the collective class struggle. Czeszko has a heretical comment on that score too: "So what if Steinbeck only calls for bread and freedom? Are such calls no longer necessary?" (Czeszko 1957: 3).

The thaw in Poland is usually considered (by Poles) short-lived. Krzysztof Kozłowski worked for many years with *Tygodnik Powszechny* and described his encounters with the censors in an interview in 2009:

> Two months after October [1956] everything was clear. The thaw ended quickest in censorship. They tightened the screws with every passing month. In July 1957 I spent the whole night on the telephone in the editorial room because they wouldn't let us publish a decree by the Primate of Poland, Wyszyński, forbidding priests from cooperating in any way with PAX [the establishment Catholic publishing house] (Kozłowski 2013: 29).

Jerzy Smulski dates the thaw proper from 1956 to the autumn of 1957 (Łapiński and Tomasik 2004: 165). In October 1957, the periodical *Po Prostu*, which had called for liberalisation in the arts, was closed down and a new periodical, to have been called *Europa*, was blocked. In 1958, there was criticism in the Party of the translation of western "pulp" fiction (Friszke 2003: 118) and in April of the same year the Party's Central Committee directed that books "o wymowie rozrachunkowej" (i.e. books that aimed to settle accounts with the "mistakes and deviations" of Stalinism) not be published (Łapiński and Tomasik 2004: 167). Although this was a blow more obviously aimed at Polish writers weighing up the failures of Stalinism, books like *The God That Failed*, first-hand accounts of western writers' abandonment of communism, would have come under the same heading. A Central Committee document from 1960 admits that a lot of artistically weak Soviet literature had been translated from 1949 to 1954 with too-high print runs (K-237/viii-466: 81). However, the counter reaction had been too strong and after 1956, because of pro-western snobbery, the works of existentialists had been published too numerously. Things had been set to rights, the report continues, in 1959 and 1960 by the Central Committee's Propaganda Section and the Ministry for Art and Culture: "The selection criteria for translations have been tightened up and are guided by the work's ideological message and artistic value. Titles that do not meet these criteria have been rejected" (K-237/viii-466: 87). The same document admits the possibility of publishing works by authors who are themselves not necessarily progressive (K-237/viii-466: 86). In 1963, *Nowa Kultura* and *Przegląd Kulturalny* ceased publishing. They were replaced by a pro-government periodical called *Kultura*, edited by Janusz Wilhelmi, which was boycotted by many writers for a number of years (Fik 1989: 352). In 1964, Gomułka was still criticising writers for trying to "settle accounts" with the Stalinist period, announcing also that such contestations of socialism "must be doomed to failure" (Gomułka 1967: 67).

And yet 1956 was a watershed, with Andrzej Walicki, among others, arguing that it marked the beginning of Poland's path away from Communism (Walicki 2013). Certainly for translations from English the post-1956 normalisation seems to have lasted longer than the scant year or two given it by Smulski, even if, as Andrzej Friszke writes, culture remained a part of the "ideological front" (Friszke 2003: 116). *Darkness at Noon, Animal Farm, The Spy Who Came in From the Cold* and *Brave New World* remained on or joined the list of banned books but once Hemingway, Faulkner, Maugham, Waugh and other objectionable types were permitted back into the fold, they remained, with their books re-issued over the years. *Wuthering Heights* went through at least six editions in People's Poland. The biggest exception is low-brow literature. Many writers of genre fiction (such as Edgar Wallace), consigned to oblivion under Stalinism, never really made it back into print in Polish. According to Wilczyński, it is hard to find political events – apart from October 1956 – that weighed on the fate of American writers' books in Poland (Wilczyński 1993: 134). There were, in fact, occasional hiccups in the careers of western writers. Graham Greene's *The Power and the Glory* was refused publication in 1958 and Steinbeck was punished for his stance on Vietnam but Wilczyński's assessment of the years 1956 to 1989 seems fair, even if First Secretary Gomułka did express displeasure in 1963 at the borrowings from American and French literature in the work of some young Polish writers (Mielczarek 2010: 223).

Progressives continued to find their way into print in Poland but did not dominate in the way they had before 1956. Dreiser and Caldwell continued to be published but the Polish National Library lists no entries for Myra Page after 1951, Alexander Saxton after 1953 (year of the second edition of *The Great Midland*), or Katharine Prichard after 1951. Lloyd Brown, Albert Halper, Clara Weatherwax and Ira Wolfert did not reappear. Albert Maltz's *The Cross and the Arrow* was published in 1960 and 1964, *The Journey of Simon McKeever* in 1962 and *The Happiest Man on Earth* in 1964 but there were no translations of his novels in the 70s or 80s. No books by Howard Fast were published after 1957, although this is probably because he left the Communist Party of the USA. Interestingly, he did make a comeback in post-1989 Poland. Attempts were still made to steer translators towards certain writers and works. A censors' report from 1974 notes that the following words (regarding Hungarian literature) were cut from a periodical called *Kierunki* ("Directions"): "Most so-called official recommendations are no good". Also withheld from the public was the mention of the fact that Conrad's *Works* had appeared in Polish without his political writings (G-1091, 175/18: 189). The disillusionment of intellectuals with First Secretary Gierek, who had come to power in 1970 and seemed to herald greater openness in Polish culture, is reflected in 1974's fourth quarter "main tendencies" report. It refers to a conviction at large that Polish culture was in crisis, that art had been politicised and literature channelled into certain subjects. Other subjects had become holy cows and there was a climate of self-censorship (G-1091, 175/18: 231).

In the Książka i Wiedza publishing house's plan for 1977, which is on file in the Party Central Committee archives, the translations planned for release are briefly described. One gets the impression that the publishers tried to play up the socialist/progressive credentials of at least some books. The descriptions of Willa Cather's and Katherine Mansfield's short stories show little evidence of this kind of prettifying but the note on V.S. Naipaul's *The Suffrage of Elvira* refers to the grotesqueness of an "American-style" election campaign in Trinidad; Anthony Quinn's autobiography *The Original Sin* "expresses [the author's] humanist position and progressive social views"; and George Meredith's *The Case of General Ople and Lady Camper* is "against the English bourgeoisie" (K-lvi474).

Progressive novels (in Walter Rideout's understanding) that did get translated after Stalinism include such as *A Lantern for Jeremy* by V.J. Jerome, *Call it Sleep* by Henry Roth, and Mailer's *The Naked and the Dead*, and it could be argued that angry young men such as John Braine and Alan Sillitoe were translated at least partly because they were – or were perceived to be – critical of the social system in post-war Britain.[2] Similarly, Robert Penn Warren's *The Governor* may have been helped along by its criticism of American politics.

As regards censorship of translations, there is, after 1956, little point in treating "radical" or "progressive" novels as an entirely separate category. For one thing they are now far fewer and for another, the ones chosen for translation are now less overtly communist. With progressive novelists represented by writers such as Mary McCarthy (*The Group*) and Henry Roth (*Call it Sleep*) the censor has less work to do weeding out unflattering references to Stalin or the Molotov-Ribbentrop pact. Also, the censorship in general is less harsh. On the Polish literature front, 1956 saw the end, until at least 1980, of interference in the aesthetic side of literature (Maciejewski 2009: 327). Piotr Nowak notes the disappearance from censors' reviews after 1956 of the "intellectual omnipotence mixed with censors' arrogance" (Nowak 2012: 156). In a 1964 speech to the Writer's Union, First Secretary Gomułka said the Party would not interfere in the technical side of writing and would agree to "sensible experiments" (qtd. in Głowiński 1996: 127). Gomułka had made a similar declaration in 1959: the Party would grant artistic freedom without "administrative interference in matters of artistic technique" but would "fight for accessible art, understandable and close to working people and expressing their socialist aspirations". However,

Gomułka did also say that art should be realistic in form. There were limits to how hands-off the state would be (Gomułka 1959: 77).

The censors were ill-disposed towards naturalism, mysticism, pessimism, nihilism and detachment from social issues: nearly everything the socialist realist novel was not. The pessimistic ending of John Steinbeck's *Pearl* was noted by the censors in 1956, who decided, however, that it was forgivable, or at least could be read as a portrayal of the failure of "impulsive, blind, individualist opposition" (G-424, 31/36: 118). The authorities were keen on showing that organised, collective struggle was the way forward. It was still only 1956 and this looks like an attempt to "rescue" Steinbeck by reading socialist realist values into the book. As the years pass, there are fewer complaints from the censors about pessimism, although there was opposition in the press to "defeatist" drama from the West (Napiontkowa 1990: 225). Complaints of pessimism that I have found are usually about Polish or Eastern European writers, held to higher standards of optimism than westerners. A sentence was ordered struck from Stanisław Lem's introduction to his own *Summa technologiae* (published 1964) for being too pessimistic (G-771, 132/106). Vaclav Havel's play *The Memorandum* was deemed "pessimistic and very debatable" in 1967. In the same year, the censors levelled charges of "mysticism" against Polish writer Tadeusz Miciński (who died in 1918) (G-846, 86/1: 11, 85).

This is not to say that foreign writers could now get away with anything they liked. Also, although Polish writers may have learned to avoid certain subjects, western writers, naturally, did not – or at least they did not avoid the same subjects. In 1958, the censors recommended changes to the translation that was to appear in 1960 of Arnold Bennett's *The Grand Babylon Hotel* because it glorified the English too much (G-596, 68/3: 8-9). In 1970, the censor recommended that one story be removed entirely from the translation of William Carlos Williams's *The Farmer's Daughter*. The reason was that a character in the story, Fred, is a declared democrat and communist but also a drunken idler. "At the same time his behaviour, attitude to life and the views he expresses prove how far he diverges from a communist in our understanding". Since mere tinkering with the story would not change its meaning it should be removed. In the event, the story was not cut but changes demanded of another story were made. The censor wanted the word "sovietism"[3] cut because it was juxtaposed with "fascism" (G-861, 101/1: 26).

Polish writers had a harder time of it after the thaw. Where a Marek Nowakowski runs into trouble because his stories are "too realistic, even naturalist" in 1961 (G-704, 68/86: 635), western writers who avoided saying bad things about communism had little to fear. Censors seem to have accepted that once a translation had been slated for publication that meant it had been officially approved by the higher-ups: their reviews are shorter, fewer and show less ideological zeal after 1956.

John Braine's *Room at the Top* suffered cuts from the Polish censors in 1960. The narrator's idea of putting paid to communism by having "a hundred girls like Susan ride on 'buses the length and breadth of Great Britain" (Braine 1957: 144) is left untouched (Susan is "a justification of the capitalist system" (Braine 1957: 138), also uncensored in Polish). The lines quoted below made it into Polish, despite the questionable sentiments expressed:

> 'We're just fighting the war over again, sir,' Reggie said. He winked at us. 'We decided that we should have let the Russians polish off the Germans and then gone in and polished off the Russians with the atom bomb.' He winked at us again.
> 'Just what I've always said.' The Librarian fizzed with enthusiasm. 'The Allies have paid dearly for their mistake' (Braine 1957: 121-22).

However, the lines coming immediately afterwards, spoken by the librarian, were cut: "'When I was in Germany I saw what the Russians were really like. I don't mind admitting that I was a bit of a Communist before the war, but I soon changed my tune'" (Braine 1957: 122; Braine 1960: 143). This change was imposed by the censor (G-429, 34/15: 151). There is also a small cut to the line, "there were Commissar-harsh lines ruled from his nostrils to the corner of his mouth" (Braine 1957: 156), from which the commissar is absent in the Polish (Braine 1960: 183), though this is not mentioned in the censor's review.

Alan Sillitoe's collection of short stories, *Men, Women and Children*, was translated into Polish nearly 20 years after *Room at the Top*, and it is virtually impossible to find traces of political censorship. The first story, "Mimic", contains the words: "I had never any intention of working, but what society demands of you is in fact what life itself wants. So you must imitate it – instead of allowing your soul to be destroyed by believing in it" (Sillitoe 1973: 26). Such a rejection of collectivism might have been treated as heresy in 1950s Poland but in 1979 it was permitted, although it is altered, reading, in back translation, "But society demands of a person the same thing that life demands. And so you must pretend you are doing something instead of permitting your pride [duma] to be crushed by the belief that that is the way it must be" (Sillitoe 1979: 28). Additionally, where Sillitoe has, in the same passage, "Your soul is in danger" (Sillitoe 1973: 26), the translator has "osobowość" ("personality, character") instead of "soul" (Sillitoe 1979: 28). Although it is hard to discern the institutional censor's hand here, this readiness on the part of the translator to interpret for the reader shows a paternalism like that of the censor's – one that always knows better than either reader or author. It is always dangerous in translation studies to talk of one-to-one equivalents but the Polish for "soul" is not "duma" (which means "pride"); nor is it "osobowość", except by a long stretch of the imagination. The Polish word is "dusza". The correspondence between "dusza" and "soul", as might be expected given that Christian traditions underlie both the Polish and English speaking cultures, is close.

Other choices of words by the translator could be questioned. In "Pit Strike" some striking miners are described as "militants" in the original (Sillitoe 1973: 41) but as "zabijaków" (*sic*) ("brawlers") in the translation (Sillitoe 1979: 50). Although this may be simply a mistake (the translator also misunderstands "knackers" in the same story) it is not the only example of denigration of working class solidarity to be found in Polish translations (Looby 2013: 165) and could, at a stretch, be interpreted as an attempt to undermine or sneer at the dictatorship of the proletariat.

The Polish translation of Mary McCarthy's *The Group* came out in 1985 and, like *Portnoy's Complaint*, translated a year later, is remarkably frank in terms of ideology, sex, and religion. Lines such as "'the Soviet Union, where the services of doctors and scientists, no matter what their "bourgeois" background, are at a premium'" and "'The communists are completely unscrupulous. One day they're your bedfellow and the next day they're calling you a fascist'" are translated faithfully, as are the words "'the Stalinists and their dupes'" (McCarthy 1964: 88, 149, 281; McCarthy 1985: 107, 187, 352). So too are Mr. Schneider's accusations that Russian commissars are sabotaging the Spanish Revolution and a passage about how a profit-sharing co-op is being run by communists behind the scenes (McCarthy 1964: 281, 225-226). On the other side of the political coin in Poland, the words "[black is] the colour of reaction, of clerical parties and fascists" (McCarthy 1964: 131) are given in full too (McCarthy 1985: 163).

The translator, Cecylia Wojewoda, also seems to trust the reader more than many other translators. This can be seen in her translation of racist and anti-Semitic terms used occasionally by characters in the novel. One passage of free indirect discourse contains the words "to a darned lot of kikes' children" (McCarthy 1964: 114) and this is translated "as is". That is, the pejorative word is there and no inverted commas are used to "help" the reader understand that these are not the words of the author: "zgraję zatraconych gudłajskich bachorów" (McCarthy 1985: 139). Wojewoda also appears to trust readers not to turn into racists if they read an accurate translation of the words "the way Negroes could call each other 'nigger'" (McCarthy 1964: 370; McCarthy 1985: 471).

Any explicit suggestion that communism and fascism were alike remained a risky business but even here one can at times see some leniency. The 1981 translation of Philip K. Dick's alternative history *The Man in the High Castle* is notable for including such lines as "'They [the Nazis] saved the world from Communism. We'd be living under Red rule now, if it wasn't for Germany. We'd be worse off'" (Dick 2001: 87) and "'If Germany and Japan had lost the war, the Jews would be running the world today. Through Moscow and Wall Street'" (Dick 2001: 114). In 1981, censorship was particularly weak as the Solidarity movement reached a peak of activity and this may be why the book was permitted to be so forthright and yet equivocal on matters of politics – as well as race. However, the words "'Only, Communists sneaked in Pan-Slavic Peter the Great empire ambitions along with it, made social reform means for imperial ambitions'" are missing from the translation, as is a character's thought that in this the communists were exactly like Mussolini (Dick 2001: 158). Even in 1981, drawing parallels between communism and fascism was still dangerous.

Doris Lessing's "The Other Woman" (from *Five Short Novels*) contains the following exchange: "'Hitler's got to be stopped, hasn't he?' 'Hitler,' she said scornfully. 'Hitler and Churchill and Stalin and Roosevelt – they all make me sick...'" (Lessing 1960: 77). This passed the censor despite the suggestion of equivalence and what might in other times have been denounced as the speaker's failure to be *engagée* (Lessing 1956: 102). This may be because the translation was published in 1956, during the thaw.

Waugh's *Brideshead Revisited* at times sails a little close to the wind. The speeches of Rex Mottram, an MP, "seemed to incline to revolutionary policies, flirting, with Communists and Fascists" (Waugh 1962: 224). This subtle suggestion of equivalence is allowed to remain in the Polish, as is the idea that fascism might be revolutionary (Waugh 1970: 215). A rather ridiculous character's statement that there is no "'fundamental diversity'" between communists and anarchists (Waugh 1962: 234) is also allowed into the Polish, though it is unlikely it would have been tolerated 15 years earlier (Waugh 1970: 226).

Eric Linklater was not so lucky with his *Ripeness is All*, translated in 1962.[4] On the other hand, it must be admitted that his equation of Communism and Fascism was a lot more forthright than the passing suggestions in Lessing and Waugh. The episode where two teenagers, Rupert and Dennis, argue respectively for Communism and Fascism is described by one censor, rather delicately, as "somewhat debatable", a comment which applies to pages 179-185, 255, 256, and 258 – i.e. not a small incident in the book. An indication of the amount of informal censorship and decision-making that went on is the fact that the censor calls for publication "with changes", the final decision is "without changes" and the actual book does have changes made to the pages indicated by the first censor (G-736, 68/125: 205, 206). "'Think what they [Communists] did in Russia: murdering hundreds of thousands of people, and stopping others from going to Church, and plotting against everybody, and putting people in timber-camps, and I don't know what else'" (Linklater 1936: 169-170) is cut for obvious reasons, though young Rupert is permitted to say "'...Communism is inevitable. It's an historical necessity'" and to talk about the "'Class Struggle [...] Tyrants, and the Feudal System, and Aristocracies, and the Bourgeoisie [...] the People [and] Dictatorship of the Proletariat'" (Linklater 1936: 170). The Polish does not use capital letters as the English does to mock Rupert's views but the satirical intent is still there (Linklater 1962: 180). Missing, however, are his aunt's counterarguments about the hardship of establishing a utopia and the inevitable re-emergence of capitalists and an aristocracy (Linklater 1936: 170-171; Linklater 1962: 181). One censor wrote in 1961 of a book called *Gather no Moss* by Sean O'Hanlon that mentions of the USSR – even one slightly satirical one – were acceptable since the book was a satire (G-704, 68/86: 685-686). *Ripeness is All* benefited from this kind of leniency but direct criticism of Russian Communism – voiced by an adult, not an adolescent – was cut.

There are other changes to *Ripeness is All* that were not referred to by the censor. For example, the suggestion that Rupert (the communist) and Dennis (the fascist) be sent to Russia and Italy, respectively, is removed (Linklater 1936: 270; Linklater 1962: 290). The censor may have mentioned this informally or the editor may have realised, given the other cuts, that it would be safer to remove the lines.

The censor was also troubled by Thomas Wolfe's *You Can't Go Home Again*. The book's main strength, the censor wrote, was its progressiveness and anti-fascism as it showed the hero moving from dispassionate observer to a progressive. However, Wolfe's position on the question of Hitler is immature, while the liberal intelligentsia in the book are pessimistic and fail to appreciate the USSR's contributions to change. The censor demanded unspecified changes on certain pages (G-596, 63/3: 397-398). The pages in question show some evidence of interference: "the hordes of India [hate] the English" (Wolfe 1940: 497) is changed to "the peoples of India [hate] the English" (Wolfe 1959: 492). The line "Everywhere the Communists (so they say) hate their cousin Fascists, and the Fascists hate the Jews" (Wolfe 1940: 497) is translated without the mention of kinship between communists and fascists (Wolfe 1959: 492). Changed, too, was the line "there is no such thing as English chemistry or American physics or (Stalin to the contrary notwithstanding) Russian biology" (Wolfe 1940: 554), which was translated without mentioning Stalin (Wolfe 1959: 546).

A dozen or so years later, Kurt Vonnegut's science fiction novel *Cat's Cradle* also gave the censors pause for thought because of its politics. They objected to the passage listing the names of the people used in cardboard cutouts for target practice (G-919, 121/9: 203). Among them are Stalin, Fidel Castro, Hitler, Mussolini, "'some old Jap'" and Mao; that is, "'practically every enemy that freedom ever had'" (Vonnegut 1963: 187). In the translation, Mao and Castro are not on the list, while "some old Jap" has been replaced by "some decent old samurai" and Stalin has been replaced by "stary poczciwy generalissimus" ("a decent old generalissimo") (Vonnegut 1971: 164). This last alteration is an interesting attempt by the translator to get around censorship. The exalted title should bring Stalin to Polish readers' minds but the name itself has been avoided, satisfying the demands of the censors. If questioned, the translator or editor (or even the censor) could try to claim the title refers to, say, Franco.[5]

The censors were also exercised by the nationality of Zinka, "a Ukrainian midget, a dancer with the Borzoi Dance Company" (Vonnegut 1963: 26) and in the published translation her nationality is glossed over. The point here seems to be that she defects to the United States. Since her request for asylum is included in the Polish translation it is fairly obvious she is from the eastern bloc. Still the censors try to obscure the matter. In the original, tired of US materialism and wanting to go back home, she goes to the Russian embassy (Vonnegut 1963: 26); in the translation she goes to "her" embassy (Vonnegut 1971: 19). When she is first mentioned in Polish she is from "the Multi-coloured Ballet", not the Borzoi, and her Ukrainian nationality is not mentioned (Vonnegut 1971: 19). On another four or five occasions Zinka's nationality is given in the English but not in the Polish. However, there is one exception: on page 55 of the Polish version she is described as a "Russian Lilliputian" (Vonnegut 1971: 55). In the list of pages that required intervention, the censor included page 55, presumably with Zinka in mind, but his or her superior ignored page 55 in the "final" list of pages that needed attention. This could have been carelessness (the superior lists pages on which Zinka's nationality is revealed) but it could also have been a deliberate mistake. Zinka's nationality is revealed in the Polish (Vonnegut sometimes calls her Russian, sometimes Ukrainian), though it is not hammered home as in the English. Among the examples of "granfalloons", or spurious communities, Vonnegut gives the Communist Party (Vonnegut 1963: 82). The translation adroitly sidesteps the politically objectionable implications by stating merely that political parties are examples of granfalloons (Vonnegut 1971: 69).

Joyce Cary's *To Be A Pilgrim* was reviewed by the censors in 1959 and they objected to a passage that in the original runs, "'Concessions were the fatal weakness which opened the way to the French Revolution;' and the Communists, the Socialists answered, 'Nothing from the enemy but their blood'" (Cary 1958: 51). The translation of the last part was to have read, "A komuniści, socjaliści odpowiadali: Chcemy jedynie krwi wroga" ("And the Communists and Socialists answered, 'All we want is the enemy's blood'") (G-428, 34/12: 314). In the translation as it was eventually published the communists and socialists want "the destruction of the enemy" ("zniszczenie wroga") (Cary 1959: 92). The change is so small it seems pointless. The removal of a rhyme, unremarked by the censor, also seems to be the result of over-sensitivity. It runs, "Tyrants hate Truth, death takes them by surprise, / Hail Democrats, who love the larger lies". This is a particularly clumsy cut because the following sentence is "When I suggested to Ann just now that this would make a good heading for her war chapter..." (Cary 1958: 233). It is translated faithfully into Polish, despite having no antecedent (Cary 1959: 403). A panicky censor may have thought the first line was too open a reference to Stalin but generally speaking such vague references pass the censor. An example of this would be Ray Bradbury's *Fahrenheit 451*. The novel is all about censorship, something the Cold War generations would associate with the eastern bloc rather than the western, and yet it is translated fully and accurately into Polish. Captain Beatty's long speech about censorship is about the USA but obviously applicable to Poland too. He recommends filling people's heads with dry facts, for example about Iowa's corn yield (Bradbury 1980: 65), and this is reproduced in Polish (Bradbury 1960: 70) even though the communist propaganda technique of providing economic information in precisely such a way, without context, was widely known and mocked. The Soviet reviewers were far more wary of the book, suggesting cuts and the addition of footnotes before any publication (Sherry 2012: 112). In earlier years, Polish censors had been alert to analogies and parallels. In 1949, the censor recommended the addition of a foreword to a Polish novel about Robin Hood in case the young readers should draw an analogy between the Merry Men hiding out in the forests and anti-Communist partisans in Poland (Nowak 2012: 141). By 1960, when *Fahrenheit 451* was translated and published, censors were less jumpy.

In the translation of Sinclair Lewis's *Babbitt* meetings "for the denunciation of unions" (Lewis 1961a: 167) is translated "na celu wytykanie błędów w pracy różnych związków" ("for the purpose of pointing out the mistakes in the work of various unions") (Lewis 1961b: 263). The censor (translator, editor) seems to have been scared of coming out against trade union activity and adjusted the text accordingly, making it sound like the meetings are for offering constructive criticism rather than preserving the capitalist status quo. When some of the townspeople refer to others as "'skunks and reds like [the radical lawyer] Doane'" (Lewis 1961a: 265) this is translated as "shady characters like Doane" (Lewis 1961b: 421). These two changes are slightly absurd as a great deal of anti-socialist sentiment still issues from Babbitt and his ilk. From the point of view of Polish propaganda, Babbitt *should* come across as rabidly anti-socialist but caution and superficiality at times trumped both the needs of propaganda and the integrity of the source text.

The reasoning behind other changes is easier to detect.

'It was like suddenly realizing that the Americans might wipe out Russia, and then one
would have no more worries about war. That would be immoral, and tragic, but it would
be safe. Have you ever thought that? That they might one night just wipe the whole lot
out, and we would live in our lifetimes' (Drabble 1984: 196)

is cut entirely from the Polish version of *A Summer Bird Cage* (Drabble
1976: 229). "'For goodness' sake get rid of them before tonight.
Yugoslavia's a Communist country, and they won't hesitate to imprison
someone under age'" in Graham Greene's *Travels With My Aunt* is
attenuated in Polish. In back translation it reads: "Get rid of them before
Yugoslavia; they might not stop to think if a minor can be arrested there".
The sentence that follows it, "'I was always taught that Yugoslavs were *good*
Communists'" (Greene 1971: 101), is also altered so that the reference is to
Yugoslavians being good people, avoiding the implication that there are bad
communists (Greene 1970a: 95).

An entire story, "I am Dying, Egypt, Dying", was cut from the Polish
translation of John Updike's *Museums and Women*. The story takes place
during a cruise on the river Nile and there are two passengers presumed by
the others to be Russian. It contains the following passage, which must have
rung a warning bell for censors: "'Now what does the poor devil [the average
Egyptian] have? A war he can't fight and Soviet slogans.' 'They *hate* the
Russians, of course. The average Egyptian, he loves a show of style, and the
Russians don't have any. Not a crumb.' 'The poor dears'" (Updike 1973:
131). However, this is a small episode in the story and the two Russians do
not play an important role either. Even the dialogue quoted above is
commented on ironically:

And they passed on to ponder the inability, mysterious but proven a thousand times
over, of Asiatics and Africans – excepting, of course, the Israelis and the Japanese – to
govern themselves or, for that matter, to conduct the simplest business operation
efficiently (Updike 1973: 131).

This is all sensitive material but could have been dealt with by pruning rather
than banning the entire story. It may have fallen victim to sensitivities
concerning Middle Eastern conflict (the story dates from 1969).

By contrast, in Updike's "The Day of the Dying Rabbit", the censor
took a liberal view of the lines "he had made a million dollars in some deal
involving Stalin and surplus wheat. He had liked Stalin, and Stalin had liked
him. 'The thing we must realize about your Communist is that he's just
another kind of businessman'" (Updike 1973: 37-38; 1978: 37). They survive
intact in Polish. A slighting reference in *Travels With My Aunt* to communist

(Yugoslavian) agriculture is allowed to stay too: "In the fields horses moved slowly along, dragging harrows. We were back in the pre-industrial age" (Greene 1971: 115). By contrast, in 1950 a censor took an author to task for portraying harvest time in Poland with the use of items such as sickles and scythes rather than tractors and harvesters (Nowak 2012: 137). Much had changed since Stalinism.

Not for nothing was Poland known in Russia as a window on the world. The censorship regime was more relaxed and it is often said that Russians would learn Polish in order to be able to keep up with western literature (Walicki 2013: 80). Samantha Sherry gives several examples of ideologically motivated cuts in the 1959 Russian translation of Graham Greene's *Our Man in Havana*. Comparison with the Polish version shows that greater freedom was allowed in Poland. The second sentence was cut from the Russian version of the following exchange: "'He finds it necessary to return to Switzerland on a matter to do with his precision-instruments.' 'With a passage booked on to Moscow?'" (Greene 1970b: 232). The implication is that the person in question is mixed up in spying (Sherry 2012: 190-191). The sentence is kept in the Polish version, which also translates Captain Segura's nickname, "The Red Vulture", as "Czerwony Sęp" (i.e. "Red Vulture"), while the Russian is simply "Vulture" (Sherry 2012: 230). The Russian translation, but not the Polish (Greene 1975: 35), leaves Khrushchev out of the following passage:

> That evening hour was real, but not Hawthorne, mysterious and absurd, not the cruelties of police-stations and governments, the scientists who tested the new H-bomb on Christmas Island, Kruscev who wrote notes: these seemed less real to him than the inefficient tortures of a school-dormitory (Greene 1970b: 30; Sherry 2012: 200-201).

The Polish translation does leave communism out of the following passage, spoken by the Red Vulture himself: "'One reason why the West hates the great Communist states is that they don't recognise class-distinctions. Sometimes they torture the wrong people. So too of course did Hitler and shocked the world'" (Greene 1970b: 165; Greene 1975: 154). This was also cut from the Russian (Sherry 2012: 193). Poland's censorship may have been less severe than the USSR's – for example, censors' reviews were not passed on to the secret police (Nowak 2013: 42) – but the USSR was its model.

---

[1] Caldwell suffered something of a critical backlash after 1956. In 1958, one reviewer wrote that he was popular in Poland mainly because of the eroticism of his books, an eroticism which is wild and, for civilised people, unbelievable, with characters reduced to stimuli and reactions (Zengel 1958: 10).

[2] Sillitoe was on a list of authors considered suitable for publication because of their progressiveness in the German Democratic Republic in 1963 (Westdickenberg 2004: 196-197).
[3] The review is handwritten and hard to read but the Polish word appears to be "sowietyzm". The censor also objects to the term itself.
[4] Nazi Germany permitted publication (albeit in English) of the book in 1936.
[5] The censors also demanded, in 1962, that Stalin's name be removed from a list including Hitler and Mussolini in *Point of no Return* by John Marquand (G-745, 68/135: 216).

Chapter 4
Morals

Church-state relations in People's Poland have been widely studied (Pawlicka 2004: 9). Suffice it to say, the authorities did not succeed in any mission they may have had to turn Poland atheist, whatever about Marx's opinion of religion as the opiate of the people. The fortunes of the Catholic Church in post-war Poland, as set out by Katarzyna Pawlicka, run in tandem with the oppressiveness of book censorship. That is, from 1944 to roughly 1947, when the state was still quite weak, there was relative tolerance for the church. In these early years, Cardinal Hlond, the primate of the country, showed a willingness to work with the new order and high state dignitaries attended his installation in 1946 (Agnosiewicz 2010: 140). From 1948 to 1955 the church suffered the worst period of repression, under Stalinism. An anti-clerical campaign started in the press and the workplace. The bishop of Kielce, Czesław Kaczmarek, was charged in a show trial with spying for the US and the Vatican and in 1951 there were around 900 priests in jail (Pawlicka 2004: 20-24). Cardinal Stefan Wyszyński was arrested in 1953.

1956 brought "normalisation" of relations (Cardinal Wyszyński was released within days of Władysław Gomułka becoming First Secretary) but – as with censorship – things soon returned to their old course, though without the level of terrorising that characterised Stalinism. In 1957, the Atheist Intelligentsia Society was set up under the auspices of the Party, to be followed by the Nationwide Polish Association of Atheists and Free Thinkers and the Society for Secular Schools, while religion in school was first cut and then, in 1960, removed altogether (Pawlicka 2004: 28, 29-30), though not all will read these moves as "repression" of the church or of religion. In 1960, the Party's Central Committee ruled that radio and television should make more of an effort to tackle the issues of laicisation and anti-clericalism (Friszke 2003: 127). Flashpoints in the 1960s included the letter from Polish bishops to German bishops inviting them to participate in celebrations of the millennium of Christianity in Poland and extending their forgiveness and asking for forgiveness from the Germans. The government held this up as evidence that Polish bishops might support German territorial claims in newly Polish lands in the west of the country (Pawlicka 2004: 31). This was also accompanied by harassment that ranged from confiscations of copies of the icon of Mary from Częstochowa on tour around Poland to the breaking up of a Corpus Christi procession in 1966 (Roszkowski 1991: 280).

When Edward Gierek became First Secretary of the party in 1970, there were hopes for an easing of relations with the church as well as with writers and artists. Pawlicka admits that the number of permits for church building increased (Pawlicka 2004: 92-93, 157), while Agnosiewicz points out that from 1975 to 1990 1,500 churches were built and in the 1980s permission was granted for 1,500 new churches and chapels (Agnosiewicz 2010: 163; see also Brzoza and Sowa 2003, vol. 5: 715). By the end of People's Poland the Catholic Church had built a strong position for itself: among the pre-war intelligentsia, according to Czesław Miłosz, "Catholic" was nearly synonymous with "obscurantist". This was not the case in Poland in the 1980s (Agnosiewicz 2010: 164). In 1979, 31.5% of Poles with a higher education were atheists; by 1988 this percentage had fallen to 11% (Brzoza and Sowa 2003, vol. 5: 715).

The church worked with the democratic opposition in the 1980s, allowing members to use ecclesiastical buildings, while Cardinal Glemp called for a peaceful resolution of tensions. General Jaruzelski, who had become first secretary in October 1981, was able to assure Moscow that the church was an essential ally of the Party (Brzoza and Sowa 2003, vol. 5: 708). This may have been a lie designed to persuade the comrades (who were surprised to hear it) that the situation in Poland was stable and no intervention was necessary but the fact it could even be risked is suggestive: it is safe to assume the Soviet Union had its own sources of information about the situation in Poland. Jaruzelski might have been stretching the truth but he would have been caught in an outright lie. Permission was granted in the 1980s for many new Catholic publications (Roszkowski 1991: 386). In October 1984, prominent Solidarity supporter Father Jerzy Popiełuszko was abducted and murdered by security service officers. Whether this was part of an officially sanctioned policy to terrorise the church is still debated in Poland. The perpetrators were sentenced to sentences of between 14 and 25 years within four months of the crime.

The state had to reckon with the church. As Sabina Bober writes, with reference to the first twenty years of People's Poland, it was difficult to mount an all-out attack on the Catholic Church since the authorities wanted to win over the masses and the church was firmly embedded in society (Bober 2011: 51). The archives show, for example, that the authorities sounded out the hierarchy on the decision to raise food prices in 1976 (Pawlicka 2005: 97-98). Even in earlier, harsher years, the state tried to work with the church, a task not made easier by Pope Pius XII's threat to excommunicate Catholics belonging to Communist parties in 1949. An agreement was signed between the state and Cardinal Wyszyński in 1950, which, among other things, gave the episcopate the right to teach religion in schools. This should not be taken to mean the state would not use physical force against the church but by the 1970s, afraid of open conflict, the authorities usually tried to avoid confrontation. The existence of the PAX publishing house, among other things, is evidence of the authorities' desire to at least placate Polish Catholics, although its function has been seen as to divide any potential Catholic opposition (Bober 2011: 52).

PAX was a pro-communist Catholic organisation founded by Bolesław Piasecki, who had been associated with the far right before the war. Piasecki was given permission to publish a weekly paper, *Dziś i Jutro*, which was launched in November 1945, and by 1947 there existed a PAX publishing house. This subsequently became the PAX Publishing Institute, whose first three books were, as it happens, all translations: the New Testament, *Sous le Soleil de Satan* by George Bernanos and *All Glorious Within* by Bruce Marshall (*Stowarzyszenie* 1985: 94-95). Piotr Nowak has found that in the early post-war years the censors were much harsher on private religious publishers than on state publishers, with a peak of hostility reached in 1949/1950. The severity of the censorship immediately after the war was directly related to the state's hostility to the church (Nowak 2012: 66, 161). The intent seems to have been not so much to destroy Catholic writing as to destroy private publishers and channel Catholic writers into a tame, government publisher.

In 1948, PAX was not slavishly pro-government. Its organ, *Słowo Powszechne*, contains no pro-government declarations and its court reporting is neutral in tone (Friszke 2013: 4). However, Adam Michnik wrote in 1976 that from the very beginning it was "agenturalny" – a pejorative adjective formed from the root of "agent", as in secret agent (Michnik 1998: 168) – while Roszkowski writes that in their zealousness members of PAX often outdid communists. They followed the party line so closely that for some time they were threatened with excommunication (Roszkowski 1991: 160, 227). At key moments PAX sided with the hard liners in the Party establishment, for example in 1949, when the government clamped down on the church, and again in 1956, when PAX opposed the reforming wing of the party that eventually got the upper hand, returning Władysław Gomułka to politics amid promises of democratisation. When the Catholic newspaper *Tygodnik Powszechny* was shut down in 1953 for not publishing an obituary of Stalin it was PAX that took it over.

Much later, in 1982, a writer associated with PAX, Jan Dobraczyński, chaired the first meeting of the Provisional Council of the Patriotic Movement for National Revival, whose aim was to drum up support for martial law, which had been declared the previous year. It should also be noted that the only member of the Council of State that voted against the imposition of martial law was Ryszard Reiff, the chairman of PAX. Also, Poland's first post-1989 prime minister, Tadeusz Mazowiecki, came from PAX, although he broke with the organisation in 1955.

Whatever about PAX's reputation (of "servility" according to Michnik (1991: 224)) they did publish worthwhile books, and were indulged somewhat by the authorities (Jarosiński 1999: 18). They published Graham Greene's *Heart of the Matter* in 1950 and G.K. Chesterton's *The Adventures of Father Brown* in 1951, when it was difficult to get anything western published.

The state's initial softly-softly approach to the church is reflected in the publishing world. In 1947, when there was still some pluralism in the country at large and more tolerance for religion, the Łódź censors passed for publication an issue of the Marxist magazine *Kuźnica* containing pictures and texts that were insulting to "religious feelings". The issue was confiscated by the censors' Head Office and the censor responsible was sacked (Ciećwierz 1989: 275). Two years later, though, Polish writers Zofia Kossak and Antoni Gołubiew ran into trouble with censors for the religious tendencies in their fiction (Bates 2002: 86-87). At a censors' meeting devoted to theatrical performances in February 1949 the situations in which the censor should intervene in matters religious were set out: mystical or religious perspectives on Poland; plays proclaiming the supremacy of faith in life; suggestions that the Polish state was fighting religion; suggestions that the state was fighting religion in schools; attacks on civil marriages; suggestions that being a "good Pole" meant being a Catholic; and when the text was concerned with politics, rather than religious ritual. It was also recommended that workers not be permitted to stage nativity plays. The director of the Censorship Office, Antoni Bida (who was also the head of the Office for Religious Affairs, which was set up in 1950), returned to the subject later that year. Although he said censors should join battle with the "clerical offensive" there would be no religious persecution. There would also be no attacks on the pope (Nałęcz 1994: 23, 24).

In 1959, the censors were still concerned about needlessly antagonising Catholics. An internal report takes censors to task for permitting the publication in *Fakty i myśli* ("Facts and Thoughts", the organ of the Association of Atheists and Free Thinkers) of a satire: "Its contents had nothing to do with disseminating atheist thought. Leaving aside its political effects, the primitively ridiculed figure of God insults the religious feelings of believers. It is unacceptable from the point of view of the state's interests" (G-656 159/1: 164). This report was used for instructional purposes, so that other censors could learn from the mistakes of their colleagues. The censors appear to have realised that crude anti-clericalism would backfire. And yet, one finds in the archives a censor's review of a guide to Katowice which objects to the emphasis in the guide on churches that are not necessarily of any architectural interest. The censor ordered the removal from the book of a photograph in which a cross dominates the panorama of the town (G-756, 68/147).

The church itself was not averse to censorship. Grzegorz Boguta, in a discussion panel on censorship, remarked that in 1980 the creators of *samizdat* books had three sources of censorship to deal with, the state, Solidarity and the church (Boguta 1999: 133), while Andrzej Urbański claims that after 1956 the church continuously requested of the authorities that objectionable material be removed from the theatre (Urbański 1992, vol. 2: 264). Marta Fik writes that erotic films were sometimes blocked by the censor because of viewers' perceived religious feelings, giving the example of Ken Russell's *The Devils* and Pasolini's *Decameron* (Fik 1996: 138).[1]

In the early, less repressive post-war years, Anthony Cronin's books were frequent guests on private publishers' lists. With the monopolisation of publishing by the state, the number of re-issues fell and for a number of years the general climate did not favour his work. In 1949, the censors were divided about his 1932 novel *Three Loves*. Two reports on its re-edition note its lack of social significance, while admitting that it has literary value. One censor favours its re-edition because of its interesting psychological conflict, while the other writes that its Catholic "overtones" militate against its re-edition (G-173, 32/44: 84, 85). A third report from a few months later also points out the near-complete lack of social-educational content. The final verdict on publication, as is often the case, is left blank (G-173, 32/44: 122). In the event this particular book was not re-issued until 1957, although other novels by Cronin started reappearing under the PAX imprint in 1954. In the same year that the censors turned down Cronin's *Three Loves*, the Ministry for Culture and Art also rejected a work by Daniel Lord called *Czyste serce* ("Pure Heart") because of its Catholic character (M-705, Departament Twórczości Artystycznej; Wydział Wydawniczy). Daniel Lord, a Catholic priest, had been instrumental in drafting the Production Code for Hollywood in the 1930s.

If PAX tried to marry Catholicism and socialism, it is clear why Cronin would be ideal for their list. His novel *The Citadel* is an attack on the iniquities of the medical profession in Britain and is sometimes credited with inspiring the creation of the National Health Service, while *The Keys of the Kingdom* is about a humble priest whose loyalties are with the common folk. Both these books, as well as *The Stars Look Down*, were published by PAX in 1954, all three accompanied with instructive forewords. The overall intention of the three forewords seems to have been to damn Cronin with faint praise. Zygmunt Lichniak (*The Citadel*) writes bracingly, "Let us make one thing clear: Cronin has fallen behind. Even more clearly: he was never in the forefront" (Lichniak 1954: 5). Worse is to come: Cronin is no social revolutionary or artistic genius. He is not even profoundly Catholic. On the plus side, he is a decent man, not blind to the injustice of capitalism, and always ready to line up with the exploited and against religious hypocrites (Lichniak 1954: 6). The three books are distinguished by

> that clarity of ideologically correct content and that passion of a writer's engagement in a work which allows us to ascribe it [the passion] the useful function of a literary ally in the struggle for the great transformation, for the healing of the world of social injustice (Lichniak 1954: 7).

In the foreword to *The Stars Look Down* the same writer, this time using the name Mateusz Żurawiec, admits Cronin is not up there with Conrad, Chesterton, Greene or Van der Meersch. He is shallow and facile but he is also direct and lively, and he protests against egotism and social exploitation (Żurawiec 1954: v-vi). In *The Stars Look Down*, Cronin defends the working class exploited by capitalism but we – Żurawiec says – see what Cronin does not: the revolutionary power of the masses. In Cronin the workers look to make small adjustments to the system and have faith in the "good capitalist", which means that the book is incomplete (Żurawiec 1954: vii; see also Bates 2011: 68). The reader will be struck by the similarity between these public sentiments and those expressed privately by censors in relation to novels by progressive western writers.

Marian Michalski, in the foreword to *The Keys of the Kingdom*, is kinder, devoting himself mostly to the action of the book. Its hero, Father Francis Chisholm, achieves little in his 36 years of unspectacular work but in sum, the church, while it needs high-achievers, is based on the Chisholms of the world (Michalski 1954: vii; see also Bates 2011: 68). The particularly acute reader might see in the claim that the Catholic Church is based on mediocrities like Father Chisholm a masked attack but in fact Father Chisholm is humble and saintly, not mediocre. The small number of people he converts on his mission contrasts favourably with the impressive number of converts left him by his predecessor – but only on paper.

G.K. Chesterton's fiction, thanks mostly to PAX, was published in People's Poland. Even under Stalinism an edition of Father Brown detective stories appeared, in 1951, to be re-issued another four times over the next twenty years. *The Napoleon of Notting Hill* was published during the thaw, in 1957, and *The Man Who was Thursday* went through three editions (the first in 1958) more or less unscathed by censorship: even the line about how the police "'go to artistic tea parties to detect pessimists'" (Chesterton 1937: 45) is preserved in Polish, though it could easily be taken as a satire on socialist realism's emphasis on optimism and faith in a better, communist future. Zdzisław Łapiński was not so lucky as Chesterton. His review of the book was cut from the Catholic newspaper *Tygodnik Powszechny* in December 1958. In it Łapiński quoted the book's reference to police work being carried out on the basis of textual exegesis and added, "Sounds familiar, doesn't it? Chesterton sympathises with his policemen; we would be inclined to be more careful. What is for Chesterton a paradox is for us a truism" (G-656, 159/1: 158). Chesterton did not have things all his own way. *The Ball and the Cross* was blocked in 1968 because, the censor wrote, although it satirises the nineteenth century English bourgeoisie, it suggests that the Catholic Church is humanity's only "ostoja" ("sanctuary, mainstay, rock"). Also, the Catholic character in the book keeps winning the debates with the atheist (G-834, 77/6: 38). A 1968 Censorship Office report which is in the Party's Central Committee files mentions the case as well. Books from PAX are to be given some leeway, it says, but undermining communism and ridiculing communists is not permitted (K-lvi859). Hence, in 1968, two books were confiscated. One was a *Don Camillo* book by Giovannino Guareschi, confiscated for striving too hard to show that Catholicism is a natural part of life and that therefore other ideas – such as Communism – are foreign to human nature and insignificant in the face of eternal truths vouchsafed by faith. The other was *The Ball and the Cross* for its "attack on materialist philosophy and its simultaneous glorification of idealistic concepts, in particular Catholicism" (K-lvi859).

The fortunes of Graham Greene's *The Power and the Glory* in Poland have been described by John Bates. It was translated and published in Paris in 1956 but refused publication in 1957 in Poland, not appearing until 1967 (Bates 2011: 69-70). The 1956 and 1967 versions are very close, suggesting that once permitted into Poland the censors paid little attention to the text itself. The 1967 PAX translation contains a slight shift in stress from the original, where we read, "They had a word for his kind – a whisky priest" (Greene 1991: 60). In translation this is "Nazywano go przecież księdzem-pijaczyną" ("They called him a drunkard-priest") (Greene 1985: 56), leaving open the possibility that the priest at the centre of the novel is unique among priests in his alcoholism. This is not so in the original, which implies that numerous priests drank too much. The Greene threat was taken seriously. Whether it was more "harmful" to publish Dobraczyński or Graham Greene was discussed in the Clerical Affairs Group of the Administrative Division of the Party's Central Committee in the mid 1960s (*Tajne dokumenty* 1996: 122).

Once religious writers like Chesterton, Greene and Cronin had overcome the censors' objections to their being in print and in Polish they had to deal with the attentions of other, religiously motivated censors. Cronin's *The Keys of the Kingdom* is, in Polish, still an unmistakably Catholic novel. There is no sign of any anti-clerical tampering from the state censorship. But tampering there is. The book tells the life story of Father Frances Chisholm, a priest who is "unorthodox" in that he spurns materialism and devotes his life to pastoral and missionary work, especially among the poor. He is contrasted with his contemporary, Father Anselm Mealey, who makes a successful but worldly career in the Catholic Church. Chisholm has the occasional crisis of faith, one of them brought about by a dubious miracle that takes place at a dry spring in his parish: a young woman called Charlotte Neily (diagnosed by Chisholm's free-thinking friend as a manic depressive sure to be canonised if she stays out of the asylum) has a vision of Mary at the spring, from which water starts flowing. A passage describing Father Chisholm's inner struggle prompted by this miracle is significantly altered:

> If only he could believe like Anselm who, without a struggle, blandly, smilingly, accepted everything from Adam's rib to the less probable details of Jonah's sojourn in the whale! He did believe, he did, he did… but not in the shallows, only in the depths … only by an effort of love, by keeping his nose to the grindstone in the slums, when shaking the fleas from his clothing into the empty bath … never, never easily … except when he sat with the sick, the crippled, those of stricken, ashen countenance. The cruelty of this present test, its unfairness, was wrecking his nerves, withering in him the joy of prayer (Cronin 1956: 95-96; ellipsis in the original).

The first sentence is missing entirely from the Polish and it is the poverty he witnesses that unnerves Father Chisholm and takes away the joy of prayer.[2] While the nine-day-wonder of the holy well is continuing to its eventual conclusion (it is revealed as a sham) another, less showy miracle occurs, when a poor boy's injured leg heals, saving his life. This is all present and correct in the Polish, meaning that the general import of the episode is kept but the contrast with gaudy, crowd-pleasing miracles is lessened. Nor, it seems, is this a slip of the pen, although it is true the translation is not the best, with a few misunderstandings of the source text ("a patch beside", "Holy Rollers" and "bothy" threw the translator, and his translation of Mealey's telegram refusing aid to Father Chisholm is wrong). When Cronin returns to the subject of the miracle our "tacit censor" again makes his or her presence felt, cutting "The waters of Jordan, Lourdes, or Marywell – they mattered not a jot. Any muddy pool would answer, if it were the mirror of God's face" (Cronin 1956: 106), which hardly seems accidental. Such distortions might be written off as mere mistakes if they did not so often have the effect of increasing the text's orthodoxy. The last eight words of "'And quite the nicest thing about you, my dear boy, is this – you haven't got that bumptious security which springs from dogma rather than from faith'" (Cronin 1956: 109) go missing – accidentally? – from the Polish translation even though they are spoken by no less a personage than a bishop (Cronin 1974: 149).

Other changes are subtler than the frank censorship shown above but they also tend towards orthodoxy, if not subservience. At the start of the book Father Chisholm remembers "the vexation of the Bishop's letter, proposing, or rather announcing, this visit of his secretary" (Cronin 1956: 2). In Polish the ironic words "proposing, or rather" are missing (Cronin 1974: 8). Father Chisholm is still upset but the hint of peremptoriness in bishops' communications is missing: it is simply a letter announcing the visit. The town in which Father Chisholm grows up is described as "Sabbath-stricken" (Cronin 1956: 8) but in back translation it is "sunk in Sunday lethargy" (Cronin 1974: 17). Daniel Glennie goes through town with "*Love thy Neighbour as thyself*" printed on his horse's rump (Cronin 1956: 20). In Polish the part of the animal's anatomy is modestly left out (Cronin 1974: 33).

But – it might be argued – Father Chisholm's heresies are translated faithfully. True, but his heresies are not really all that heretical. Mother Maria-Veronica takes him to task for a number of such failings:

> 'For instance, some remarks you made when Dr. Tulloch was dying... and afterwards, when he was dead.'
> 'Please go on.'
> 'He was an atheist, and yet you virtually promised he would have his eternal reward... he who didn't believe...'
> He said quickly: 'God judges us not only by what we believe... but by what we do.'
> 'He was not a Catholic... not even a Christian!'
> 'How do you define a Christian? One who goes to church one day of the seven and lies, slanders, cheats his fellow men the other six?' He smiled faintly. 'Dr. Tulloch didn't live like that. And he died – helping others... like Christ himself.'
> She repeated stubbornly: 'He was a free-thinker.'
> 'My child, our Lord's contemporaries thought him a dreadful free-thinker... that's why they killed him.'
> She was pale now, quite distraught. 'It is inexcusable to make such a comparison – outrageous!'
> 'I wonder! ... Christ was a very tolerant man – and humble' (Cronin 1956: 162; ellipsis in the original).

This is translated in full, with the exception of the word "virtually", thus painting Father Chisholm very slightly "blacker". It is also interesting to note that the Catholic belief that God judges us by what we do is translated without any ambiguity, unlike the translation of the Presbyterian article of faith that you cannot earn or deserve God's grace, which, as will be seen, caused some translators problems.

Not all heresies in Catholic novels were treated with kid gloves: the later translation (1970) of *Brideshead Revisited* is an altogether more robust affair when it comes to the religious matters that loom large in the book.

There is no evidence of the translator or anyone else intervening to make the religious elements more orthodox. Thus, comments pertaining to Catholicism of the type "'feelings of guilt from the nonsense you were taught in the nursery. You do know at heart that it's all bosh, don't you?'", "'it's all superstition and trickery'" and "'It's such a lot of witchcraft and hypocrisy'" (Waugh 1962: 276, 309, 310) are translated in full (Waugh 1970: 265-266, 296, 297).

The general pattern is that when material that might be objectionable to Catholic sensibilities is central to a book it is translated faithfully. No special effort is made to spare Polish readers' "religious feelings" (as the matter is framed in present-day Polish legislation). This is true also of short passages whose anti-clericalism or hostility to religion is very pointed. Sometimes the harshness or, especially, vulgarity of the original is toned down but the central message is preserved. However, when the source text injures "religious feelings" only in passing, the target text often censors quite sweepingly, removing entirely sentiments that that might upset Catholics or question dogma or even cherished but erroneous beliefs about Catholicism. The two approaches are often found in the work of the same translator and in the same book.

An example of the latter kind of interference is the question of heaven, hell (in particular) and judgement. There is a tendency in translations to absolve God of the blame for judging people and sending them to hell. In passing references to God's cruelty the devil is sometimes substituted or agency is elided. Both Sean O'Casey (Looby 2008: 57) and Edna O'Brien (Looby 2013: 164) wrote passages in which God is depicted as being responsible for people suffering in hell (which as judge he is). Polish translators intervened to make it look like the devil sends people to hell. This may not simply be a case of translators trying to shield readers from some unpalatable truths about Christianity. The PWN-OUP English-Polish dictionary gives for "goddamn" the words "przeklęty" (adj.), "cholernie" (adv.) and "szlag by to trafił", none of which refer to agency in the explicit way that the English expression does. "Przeklęty" means cursed; "cholernie" comes from the disease, cholera; and "szlag by to trafił" means literally, "may it be struck". English, too, uses phrases such as "the devil take it" as if the devil took souls to hell when it is God that sends them. In other words, what may strike some readers as censorship may strike others as mere cultural adaptation, especially since expressions like "the best goddamn..." are fossilised and do not really express any desire that God damn anything. However, there are times when closer attention should be paid to the literal meaning of expressions like "damn". For example, in *The Keys of the Kingdom* Doctor Tulloch exclaims, "'Damn it to hell!'" at one point (Cronin 1956: 29). This is translated without any reference to damnation: "'Niech to cholera porwie!'" ("cholera take it") (Cronin 1974: 44). Arguably, this is "what a Pole would say" in the circumstances – a translation technique which can hardly be equated with censorship. However, there is an extra dimension to the issue here because Doctor Tulloch is an infamous free-thinking atheist in a community where religious tensions run high. The full quotation is "'Damn it to hell!' he cried. 'We use our children to build our battleships. We sweat them in our coal mines and our cotton-mills. We're a Christian country. Well! I'm proud to be a pagan!'" (Cronin 1956: 29). Doctor Tulloch also lets fly with a religion-based imprecation outside the house of Charlotte Neily: "'Damn it to hell!'" (Cronin 1956: 98). In Polish this is "Niechże to diabli porwą!" ("devils take it") (Cronin 1974: 134). Sometimes, when it is particularly clear that the word "damn" has its original, strict meaning, the translator is more likely to preserve it in Polish, as when the priest in *The Power and the Glory* says: "'Oh God help her. Damn me, I deserve it, but let her live forever'" (Greene 1991: 208). This is translated "as is" in Polish ("...Niech ja będę potępiony...") (Greene 1985: 185).

Religion, though not Catholicism, is central to James Baldwin's *Go Tell it on the Mountain* and the translation (published by PAX) is faithful, if a little cautious. The complicated relationship of the central character, John, to his faith, his preacher-father and his church is all accurately reflected in Krystyna Tarnowska's translation. Criticism is directed at the Protestant church so one might argue that faithfully translating "'I guess it takes a holy man to make a girl a real whore'" (Baldwin 1991: 154) came more easily in Catholic Poland. This would be a little uncharitable: the fact is that it is translated accurately, as is "she hoped that one day God, with tortures inconceivable, would grind them utterly into humility" (Baldwin 1991: 201). The sentiment is at one remove from God. It is what a fallible human being desires but the reader (Polish or of the original) does not need to be especially penetrating to see that Christianity requires of its followers that they believe in a God of inconceivable, humiliating and eternal torture. However, the translator balks at "'You can tell that puking bastard [Jesus] to kiss my big black arse'" (Baldwin 1991: 189), which she translates as simply "'Mam to gdzieś'" ("I don't care"; literally: "I have it somewhere", a euphemism for "I have it in my ass") (Baldwin 1966: 206). This evasion may have been cause by religious sensibilities or a simple aversion to vulgarity or a combination of both.

In either case it is interesting to contrast it with the translation of *Portnoy's Complaint*, published exactly 20 years later by a "secular" press (Wydawnictwo Literackie). Here no punches are pulled in the translation of the description of Jesus as "The Pansy of Palestine" (Roth 1969: 168), which in Polish is "główny pedał Palestyny" ("the chief fag of Palestine") (Roth 1986: 165). *Portnoy's Complaint* does, however, have a foreword in which excuses are made for the vulgarity. The novel takes the form of a psychotherapy session, the translator, Anna Kołyszko, writes. She continues: "this situation [...] justifies the hero's thorough-going self-exhibitionism, the naturalist details of the images he conjures up and the obscene language" (Kołyszko 1986: 7). In 1966, when *Go Tell it on the Mountain* was published, the Catholic Church was celebrating the millennium of Christianity in Poland. This, and the publisher's open identification with Catholicism, may have conspired with general Polish conservatism to reign in the disrespect for Jesus shown in the source text.

The translation of Sean O'Casey's *I Knock at the Door* illustrates some of the same points as *Go Tell it on the Mountain*, i.e. explicit, unambiguous attacks on clericalism and religion are translated with only very slight watering down. O'Casey himself was noted for his anti-clericalism and ran afoul of the Catholic Church (he was born into a Protestant family) in his native country, Ireland. *I Knock at the Door* shows his jaundiced view of the church in Ireland. In those parts of the text where he tackles religion and priests head on, the translation does so too, though not without a few small deviations to protect religion. In O'Casey's reminiscence about his father, Protestantism's implied superiority to "popery" (O'Casey 1971: 16) is kept in the Polish, which translates "popery" more neutrally as "nauka papistów" ("the teaching of Catholics") (O'Casey 1963: 15). The narrator's mother's belief that Roman Catholicism is a "terrible religion" for its doctrine that an unbaptised child would go "to hell, or limbo, or whatever they called it" (O'Casey 1971: 15) is reproduced in full in the Polish version (O'Casey 1963: 13-14). The unsympathetic, though not vicious, description of a Protestant clergyman in the chapter entitled "His Father's Funeral" is also given in full in Polish. The target text even keeps "The curse o' God on every school..." (O'Casey 1971: 104; O'Casey 1963: 143).

"In her heart she was glad that he had been baptised, though the Roman Catholic idea of original sin was ridiculous and laughable" (O'Casey 1971: 15) is a full frontal assault on the religious sensibilities of most Poles but it is not ducked: it is translated in full. In the Polish version the second "was" is replaced by "seemed to her" ("wydawało się jej") (O'Casey 1963: 13) but one could certainly argue that this is a reasonable interpretation since in the original "was" expresses Mrs O'Casey's views on the matter, not necessarily those of the author. A little harder to defend is the change of "– What about the priest who threatened to turn into a goat anyone that dared to say a word in favour of Parnell?" (O'Casey 1971: 59). In Polish the priest's alleged threat is to "do for" ("wykończyć") anyone who spoke out for Parnell (O'Casey 1963: 77). This looks like an attempt to suppress criticism of – in this case Catholic – clergy. Criticism of priests and the power they wield over "ignorant superstitious country gulls who walk in daily dread of their parish priests" (O'Casey 1971: 59) remains in the Polish but the outer reaches of ridicule are missing.

Staying in Ireland we find a short story called "The Miser" by Frank O'Connor translated into Polish in 1971. O'Connor, too, had many scrapes with the Catholic-inspired censorship in his home country and the story in question shows a priest, Father Ring, in a very poor light. This is also the case in the translation. A more substantial example from Ireland can be found in Brendan Behan's *Borstal Boy*, where the narrator's periodic outbursts against the church are just as strong in the 1982 Polish version. If we take a passage like the following one, two forces abroad in Poland come into play:

> Then I had difficulties, when I was thirteen or so, with myself and sex, and with the Church because they always seemed to be against the [Irish] Republicans. [...] I had been for the Republicans in Spain; and it seemed the Church was always for the rich against the poor (Behan 1990: 52).

Behan's problems with the church are largely political. His support for the Spanish Republicans would have endeared him to the censors, the ministerial reviewers and – we may surmise – Polish publishers seeking to get into the good books of the authorities and still publish worthwhile books. In Poland of 1982, however, the pope was Polish and the church stood squarely on the side of a mass movement opposed to the Party. Given the circumstances, a contemporary translator might have been tempted to tone down lines such as "'to hell with Rome, up the Republic'" (Behan 1990: 66). The translator, Krystyna Korwin-Mikke, did not tone down these or other lines.

It may even be that that the book was selected for publication because of such open, political, anti-clerical passages and that the translator would have been even more conscious than usual of the censor breathing down her neck. However, Korwin-Mikke cannot be accused of being a propaganda tool: she does not make lines like "It [religion] was all ballocks" (Behan 1990: 96) any more acceptable to Catholic Poland but nor does she go further than Behan in knocking the church. The translation, whatever its faults, is simply forthright without trying to protect the reader, the church or God from Brendan Behan. Other translators were quicker to protect God's reputation from the depravity of western writers.

Another example of forthright translation is supplied by *Manhattan Transfer*. When Marco, Congo and Emile discuss killing God (Dos Passos 1986: 44) this is kept in the Polish (Dos Passos 1958: 51). Sinclair Lewis's *Elmer Gantry* is explicitly critical of religion and to eliminate the criticism would defeat the purpose of translating the book in the first place. In the novel, Lewis takes aim at the evangelical movement in the United States and attacks on the clergy are front and centre throughout the book. It was translated in 1959 and the satire is reproduced in full – almost – in the Polish translation. A cynic might say the Polish version served two masters well: an anti-clerical Polish political establishment and an expansive but *Catholic* church. The former would be heartened by the faithful translation of lines in chapter two about how God (not the devil) burns unbaptised babies in hell (Lewis 1935: 40-41); the latter by the polite removal of the last ten words of "swallowed the Discipline with such friendly ease as a Catholic priest uses towards the latest bleeding Madonna" (Lewis 1935: 368) and their replacement with, in back translation, "with exceptional ease" (Łuszczewska 2012: 48). This is an unmistakeable attempt to preserve the dignity of the Catholic Church.[3]

Willingness to ruffle Catholic feathers is even more noticeable when the source text deals with the social teachings of the church rather than God and priests directly. This may be contrasted with the situation in democratic Ireland, where Frank O'Connor's novel *Dutch Interior* was banned presumably for alluding to abortion, affairs and prostitution (since it has no "overt sexual descriptions") (O'Drisceoil 2011: 34). The sex scene in chapter two of Mary McCarthy's *The Group* and the detailed descriptions of contraception are all present and correct in the Polish translation from 1985. Another example of uncompromising translation is Zofia Uhrynowska's 1972 version of Muriel Spark's *The Prime of Miss Jean Brodie*. At several points the book has direct references to Catholic social teaching: these cause no evasions in the target text, which faithfully translates, for example, the reference to birth control being "'the only answer to the problem of the working class'". The same is true of the claim that Roman Catholicism is a superstitious religion for people who do not "want to think for themselves" (Spark 1965: 43, 85) and that Catholics have to have lots of children. Various references to abortion in Mario Puzo's *The Godfather* are also kept in translation.

A large part of Margaret Drabble's *A Summer Birdcage* concerns the question of abortion, anathema to Catholics. The translator could hardly avoid the issue – at least, not without leaving huge gaps in the book, likely to be noticed by critics and readers. So the references to abortion are kept, including one character's statement, "'I know it isn't murder'". However, there is some slight prevarication, as when the speaker continues, "'I couldn't care less about abortions'" (Drabble 1984: 107) while in the target text she says she has never up until now cared about miscarriages (Drabble 1976: 128). Elsewhere, "'I felt it [the foetus] was a leech sucking my blood. Is that abnormal? I suppose it's not, really'" (Drabble 1984: 41) is changed to "wprost czułam, jak we mnie rośnie pijawka, która wysysa ze mnie krew. Czy to normalne? Chyba nie" ("I felt a leech growing in me and sucking my blood. Is that normal? I don't think so") (Drabble 1976: 47). In Catholic Poland, it would seem, it is *not* normal to think of one's unborn baby in this way, no matter what fictitious characters in a British novel might say about the matter. Some interventions give the impression of being accidental, based on misreadings of the source text. One might hypothesise that translators, steeped in a culture of respect for certain values, are inclined to see what they *expect* to see rather than what is actually there.

A value judgement about the propriety of monogamy might lie behind the change of the title of chapter eleven of Drabble's novel, in which Louise is caught cheating on her husband, from "The Collision" to "Disaster" ("Katastrofa"). Alternatively, the translator may have decided that this was a personal catastrophe, regardless of any Roman Catholic teachings about the sanctity of marriage, and re-named the chapter accordingly and – if one accepts this interpretation – well within the limits of poetic licence. Like the Sherwood Anderson example given in chapter one, one's opinion of whether it is censorship or not depends heavily on one's own understanding of the book.

William Faulkner's *The Wild Palms* revolves around an abortion, even if this is not immediately apparent. It would be pointless to translate the book without mentioning the abortion and the theme is present in the Polish but there is one concession to Catholic feelings that strikes a jarring note in the translation. Where Harry says, "'I will set up as a professional abortionist'" (Faulkner 1954: 103) the Polish has "będę zarabiał na życie jako zawodowy fabrykant aniołków" ("I will make a living as a professional manufacturer of little angels") (Faulkner 1987: 178).

In the above examples one can see small evasions and some timidity but in general sensitive issues are translated with only small attempts to soften the blow, as it were, for Catholic readers. When it comes to passing references to religion translators (or censors or editors) are quicker to intervene. Naturally there are exceptions, as when Mario Puzo writes, "'he's tricky as a priest'" (Puzo 1969: 202) and his translator, Bronisław Zieliński, follows suit with "podstępny jak ksiądz" (Puzo 1979: 266) but an accurate translation is usually unremarkable. Some of the numerous examples of intervention from Albert Maltz's *The Underground Stream* have already been seen, although other Stalinist-era translations of progressive American novels were tougher. For example, Caldwell's uncompromising "'[God will] send a man to hell and the devil for persisting in doing that'" (Caldwell 1947: 9) is translated as "Za bluźnierstwa Pan Bóg posyła człowieka do piekła" ("God will send a man to hell for blasphemy") (Caldwell 1949: 17). Likewise, "'I hope God sends you straight to hell'" (Caldwell 1947: 160) is translated "as is" (Caldwell 1949: 152). Various complaints made by the main character, Jeeter Lester, about God's presumed hatred of the poor (since they suffer so much) are also left intact. In Saxton's *The Great Midland*, Pledger's lines "'I'll pray, God strike dead every one of those white men. God strike them dead for what they done to us!'" (Saxton 1997: 82) are translated with no evasion, no attempt to suggest that maybe the devil should take white men (Saxton 1951: 111). Sally, in *Winged Seeds*, says, "'May God damn and blast your rotten soul – if you've got one – for ever and ever, amen'" (Prichard 1984: 334) and this is translated in full (Prichard 1951: 346).

Similarly, "'I spent all my money at the drugstore trying to get rid of that kid, but none of the damn stuff worked'" (Saxton 1997: 191) is present in the Polish and if anything even more explicit (Saxton 1951: 257). Also, in Howard Fast's story "Dumb Swede" the words "she became pregnant and got some medicine from the druggist to purge herself with" (Fast 1949: 165) are even plainer in the Polish translation (Fast 1950: 118). This might be down to the more zealously anti-clerical atmosphere of the early 1950s. The translation of Myra Page's *With Sun in Our Blood*, as seen, tries to put religion in the background but even here a few small alterations suggest there was some concern for Christian values in the translation process. Mention that the narrator's father was seldom ever in church (Page 1950a: 96) is cut from the Polish (Page 1950b: 88).

From a later period, Sherwood Anderson's "The Philosopher" from *Winesburg, Ohio*, shows the tendency to place respect for God, religion and associated taboos above respect for the source text. Doctor Parcival's possibly heretical belief that "everyone in the world is Christ" (Anderson 1946: 28) is present in the Polish, presumably since removing it would destroy the story. Kept, too, is Parcival's "'I was a regular ass about saying prayers. You should have heard me'" (Anderson 1946: 25) but his description of how he blessed his father's dead body is changed. He says, in the original, "'It was very amusing. I spread out my hands and said, "Let peace brood over this carcass." That's what I said'" (Anderson 1946: 26). In Polish he does not say it was amusing. Instead it reads, "Wzniosłem ręce i powiedziałem: – *Pokój temu ciału.* – Otóż to właśnie" ("I raised my hands and said '*Peace be upon this body.*' That's what I said") (Anderson 1977: 49). The story has created no expectation of a "normal" blessing; the signs are all there that Parcival's blessing will be unconventional: the first story in the collection is called "The Book of the Grotesque" and thus it seems unlikely that this was a translator's slip. Rather, it was a deliberate decision (not necessarily the translator's) to preserve a taboo: do not speak ill of the dead. In the translation of Cronin's *The Keys of the Kingdom* a similar respect for this taboo can be found, when the sentence "There was talk of a public funeral – with the confraternity band – for the mangled remains" (Cronin 1956: 61) is translated without mentioning the "mangled remains" (Cronin 1974: 86).

Respect for the dead is not unique to Christians but the next example, from Charles Portis's *True Grit*, goes to the heart of Christianity. The tale is narrated by Mattie Ross, a Presbyterian girl, and while it is by no means a religious tract, she does make her views known. "They love candles and beads" (Portis 2011: 121), she says of Catholics from Eastern Europe, and the translation's only fault – if it is a fault – is that is more literary than the characteristic deadpan delivery of the narrator: "Lubują się w świecach i paciorkach" ("They do so love candles and beads". "Lubować się" is used instead of the more usual "lubić") (Portis 1973: 136). But not all the translation is as forthright. She says of the Cumberland Presbyterian Church at one point, "That is all right but they are not sound on Election" (Portis 2011: 109). This is significant because the Polish version (which has many explanatory footnotes) explains what "election" is (Portis 1973: 122). Here, however, we see a slight evasion. The note avoids saying that Calvinists believe you cannot earn salvation, saying only that some are elected despite having done no good deeds. This leaves open the possibility that Calvinists believe doing good in this world can open the gates to heaven in the next. A more outrageous abuse of the source text occurs in the translation of "There is nothing free except the Grace of God. You cannot earn that or deserve it" (Portis 2011: 37), which is rendered "Nie ma nic darmo, poza łaską boską. Tego nie opłacisz pieniędzmi, możesz sobie tylko na nią zasłużyć" (Portis 1973: 38) ("There is nothing for free except the grace of God. That you cannot buy with money; you can only deserve it"). Did the translator (Zofia Uhrynowska, who had no difficulties with *The Prime of Miss Jean Brodie*) deliberately misrepresent Protestantism or was it an oversight – a case of seeing what one expects to see (i.e. that doing good leads to eternal reward)? The reader may decide but one thing seems certain: this change was not imposed by the Censorship Office. No socialist or communist ideological purpose was served.

Anna Chilewska has shown how translators of *Anne of Green Gables* tended to pass over the religious denomination of the family that adopts the book's heroine. Of the seven translations she studied (six made since 1989), the only translator to make explicit the denomination of the inhabitants of Avonlea is Agnieszka Kuc, whose translation appeared in 2003 (Chilewska 2009: 170).

> Inconsistency and lack of important cultural and religious details allow Bernsteinowa (1912) and Ważbińska (2002) to assimilate the Presbyterian faith to the religious denomination of most Polish people – Roman Catholicism – where normally a single priest performs all functions during a mass (Chilewska 2009: 171-172).

Rozalia Bernsteinowa's translation pre-dates People's Poland but this does not mean it was exempt from censorship (until the law changed in 1981) and it was her version that was used in Poland after the Second World War, though institutional censorship is less important here. It seems certain Polish cultural norms and expectations exerted themselves in religious questions before, during and after People's Poland.

As seen above, Sherwood Anderson was permitted to compare people to Christ but when such comparisons are not central to the story they are often removed in Polish translations. In John Braine's *Room at the Top*, for example, the words "'You've lovely eyes, like Christ's – '" (Braine 1957: 171) are translated as "'you have such lovely eyes'" (Braine 1960: 200). God comparisons were problematic during Stalinism too. In the Howard Fast story "Where Are Your Guns?" the sentence "He was an English gentleman and he was God too" (Fast 1949: 85) is not let stand in Polish, which has "uważał się za równego Panu Bogu" ("he thought himself the equal of God") (Fast 1950: 69). In Page's *With Sun in Our Blood* a doctor "standing in the doorway, lamplight on his white hair [...] was like God" (Page 1950a: 226). There is no comparison with God in the Polish (Page 1950b: 198) though the decision to leave out the comparison may have been caused by a communist-inspired desire to separate science and rationalism from religion. In the translation of Edna O'Brien's *Girl With Green Eyes* the words "I thought of [...] how I used to think he was God" (O'Brien 1964: 94) are translated as "Myślałam [...] o tym, jak go ubóstwiałam" ("I thought [...] of how I used to idolize him") (O'Brien 1978b: 88), which seems less potentially blasphemous.

Simple disrespect for Jesus is sliced out of Philip K. Dick's *The Man in the High Castle*, where the exclamation "Christ on the crapper, he thought" (Dick 2001: 17) is replaced by "Rany boskie, myślał" ("God's wounds, he thought") (Dick 1981: 13). In the same novel "Pray to what?" (Dick 2001: 232) is changed in Polish to "Pray to whom?" (Dick 1981: 221). Someone must have intervened to spare the blushes of Catholics in the translation of *A Summer Birdcage* when Gill says, "'but you can't believe in it all the time yourself either, like the Catholics or whoever it is and God. You just pretend you don't have any lapses of faith'" (Drabble 1984: 108). The central message is preserved in Polish but Catholics are left out, as if it were unthinkable that they might have moments of doubt. In back translation the Polish reads, "but you can't believe in all of that all the time yourself either. You just pretend you don't have any crises of faith" (Drabble 1976: 130). In the translation of "We talked about religious people who had perversions" in Kurt Vonnegut's *Cat's Cradle* (Vonnegut 1963: 29), "religious people" is rendered as "bigoci" (Vonnegut 1971: 21). The Polish word "bigot" means one who is excessively religious, one who flaunts his or her religiousness, a hypocrite. It is at first glance a reasonable interpretation but it narrows the field of potential perverts considerably: there are fewer holy joes than there are religious people.

Another small change in *Cat's Cradle* is the message on a Christmas decoration. In the original it is "Peace on earth!" (Vonnegut 1963: 40); in translation it is "Chwała Bogu na wysokości!" ("Praise be to God in the

Highest") (Vonnegut 1971: 32). This is arguably nothing more than domestication, returning us to the questions posed in chapter one: where does one draw the line between censorship and legitimate interpretation? The same might be said of such translations as "wykrzykujący przekleństwa" ("screaming curses") (Hammett 1988: 45) for the original's "screaming blasphemies" (Hammett 2005: 170); "'Chwała Bogu, nie ma'" ("no one, praise be to God") (Waugh 1957: 13) for "'No one, I am thankful to say'" (Waugh 1951: 7); "'do licha, nie możemy stanąć po żadnej stronie'" ("the devil take it, we can't take sides") (De Boissiere 1953: 323) for "'Gad dammit, we kean't take sides'" (De Boissiere 1956: 278); "'Niechaj diabli wezmą Sylwię. I niech diabli wezmą Bena Somerville'a'" ("devils take Sylvia. And devils take Ben Somerville") (Macdonald 1978: 145) for "'Damn Sylvia to hell. And damn Ben Somerville'" (Macdonald 1973: 129); "Niech diabli wezmą Gobi" ("devils take the Gobi") (Dickson 1972: 14) for "Damn the Gobi" (Dickson 1951: 11); and "Niech ich piekło pochłonie!" ("May hell consume them!") (Roth 1975: 23) for "'May the fire of God consume them!'" (Roth 1991: 22). This last example is a clear attempt to avoid saying that God is responsible for people burning in hell and one might seize on this as evidence of censorship. Yet the same translator (who also translated "Damn Sylvia" as "devils take Sylvia") rendered "'Shit on de pope, I says'" (Roth 1991: 411) faithfully – or at any rate equally disrespectfully – as "Sram na papieża, mówię" ("I shit on the pope, I say") (Roth 1975: 470), for which in modern day Poland he could end up in court.

This suggests that alterations of the type "cholera" for "God damn" are cultural adjustments, perhaps made unconsciously by translators, who, instead of writing what the English speaker *did* say, wrote what a Pole *would* say. And even an anti-clerical Pole, capable of saying, "shit on de pope" would likely say, "do licha" rather than "God damn". Thus, for example, in O'Casey's *I Knock at the Door* "–it was a God-damned shame" (O'Casey 1971: 103) is "To wstyd i hańba" ("It's a shame and a disgrace") – a common Polish collocation that sounds more natural than a literal translation (O'Casey 1963: 142). It will be recalled that this translator was not afraid to convey the agent behind the original's "'The curse o' God on every school'".

References to sex and sensationalism are more often to be found in the archives than references to religious issues. In some respects, the concerns of the authorities were close to those of the church and it is difficult to say who influenced whom. Were censors and translators mindful of the church's teachings on sex and morals or did their own views coincide with those of the church? Marta Fik writes: "in fighting against 'wantonness' Polish People's Republic censors quite often become self-appointed spokespeople for Catholic society" (Fik 1996: 138). Communist youth organisations were known for their puritanism and a poster reproduced in Kuroń and Żakowski's

PRL dla początkujących shows a stern looking member of the Polish Youth Association wearing a red tie and pointing at a numbered list of things a member should not do: laugh, dance, have fun, love and joke (Kuroń and Żakowski 1996: 63). Socialist realism passed over in silence anything rude or crude and demanded that "affairs of the heart be presented in an unbearably idyllic manner" (Jarosiński 1999: 81).

Kamila Budrowska reports surprisingly few references to eroticism and morals in the archives from 1948 to 1958 and puts forward three possible explanations for this: (a) the censors thought it unimportant, (b) "daring" texts rarely made it as far as the Censorship Office, (c) out of delicacy, censors avoided mentioning sex, preferring to accuse erotic books of other faults (Budrowska 2012: 230). Piotr Nowak, also, found only one reference to eroticism in his study of the Poznań censorship archives and concludes that such books probably never made it as far as the censors (Nowak 2012: 63). The period, Budrowska writes, was marked by prudishness compared to earlier years: the censors refused Leopold Buczkowski's *Wertepy* publication in 1953 on the grounds of being pornographic, although it had been published in 1947, at which time the censors made no such accusations (Budrowska 2012: 236). It appeared after the thaw, in 1957 and again in 1973. The prudishness Budrowska mentions can be seen as well in the translations of Albert Maltz, above. Wacław Sadkowski also draws attention to the softening of erotic scenes and vocabulary in translations published in People's Poland (Sadkowski 2002: 114).

In the 1980s, Poland saw a general loosening of strictures relating to sex and morals in novels. This is sometimes assumed to have been an attempt by the authorities to provide a safety valve and distract attention from the political situation in the country (Świstak 2010: 116). Among such distractions were Polish novel *Raz w roku w Skirołowkach* ("Once a Year in Skirołowki") by Zbigniew Nienacki, von Sacher-Masoch's *Venus in Furs* and Jerzy Kosiński's *The Painted Bird* (Świstak 2010: 117), as well as first-hand accounts of drug addiction like Christiane F.'s *Wir, Kinder vom Bahnhof ZOO* and Polish author Barbara Rosiek's *Pamiętnik narkomanki* ("Diary of a Female Drug Addict") (Świstak 2010: 119-120).

Unsurprisingly, the archives do not tell us if the censors were acting under the influence of the Catholic Church. It seems to have been taken as read that certain topics were taboo. There are few indications of the motivation behind the cutting of rude language and so forth. It was not explained why "sensationalism" was bad: rather, if words were cut or books withheld from publication the charge of "sensationalism" was sufficient explanation in itself. People's Poland is often remembered as a grey and buttoned-down place, where even entertainment could not be light. This impression is borne out by the archives.

Tadeusz Zaborowski, a censor who worked at the regional level in the 1980s, claimed that when it came to taboo subjects, censors were guided less by rules and regulations than by the taste of the general public. The censors took action against attacks on religious feelings and tried to prevent the flow of detailed information about crimes for fear that criminals might learn too much or that people might learn how to use drugs (Zaborowski 2003: 65). When it came to erotica, the written word was granted more freedom than the image. Zaborowski attributes the liberalisation of the 1980s to the public's demand for greater freedom. The authorities could hardly allow freedom in some areas and not others (Zaborowski 2003: 67).

Bates remarks that during "High Stalinism" Jack Lindsay was one of the only contemporary English writers published in Poland (Bates 2011: 65-66). His left wing credentials did not give him carte blanche and one censor recommended cutting some of the sex from his *Lost Birthright* in 1950, deeming the book good politically but not artistically. In fact, the censor contradicts him or herself, noting that in the novel the exploitation of the workers takes a backseat to the erotic adventures of the people who exploit them. This would mean it was politically weak and yet it passed. The same censor felt the amount of space devoted to the seduction of a chambermaid was, at 46 pages, excessive (G-145, 31/26: 877). A chambermaid is seduced at the start of the novel but – in the Polish version at least – it takes much less than 46 pages. In the same year, Curwood's *Gold Hunters* gave censors a headache because of its sensationalism: it had too many murders, too much gold and too much getting-rich-quick. The three editions that had so far appeared were enough, the censor wrote, recommending that paper not be allocated for publication (G-166, 32/24: 47).[4] Censors also worried about readers imitating or learning from sensationalist books. In 1957, the censor criticised the translation of *Knock on any Door*, Willard Motley's 1947 novel about juvenile delinquents, because it was "an excellent instruction manual for young hooligans and a justification for crime as being allegedly only the result of social conditions" (G-426, 34/4: 81-82). In addition, the book was accused of glorifying crime, which was "*against the ethical norms* obtaining in *any* society" – socialist or capitalist (G-426, 34/4: 81; emphasis in original). The censor recommended a small print run and that the book be published not by Iskry (for children and the young) but by Czytelnik (G-426, 34/4: 81-82).[5]

The censor's review of a collection of Samuel Beckett's stories is worth quoting for the insight it provides into the mentality of the censors/authorities of the times (1958):

Of little value. The object of the author's interest is an a-social individual – a beggar. Melancholic ruminations characterised by resignation and sneering at the surrounding world. It is hard to find any positivism in these short stories. In some places the descriptions are disgusting – pornographic. Seeing as the item is of little value – and translated from French to boot – I think (regardless of interventions) it would be better not to print it (a waste of time and effort).

There follows a list of the pages requiring censorship and the review finishes with the word "Pornography" (G-427, 34/5: 214).[6] The question of whether or not to publish the stories was discussed by the Party's Central Committee in March of 1958 where it was acknowledged that the censor's reservations were justified. However, since policy had now changed in favour of giving readers access (two words are illegible in the file here) the ultimate decision was to allow publication with a small print run (G-596, 68/2: 337). The translation appeared in 1958 with a print run of just 3,250 but as it is from the French its translation will not be considered here.

With the thaw, some of the horror of sensationalist, escapist books started to wear off but it did not disappear entirely. Agatha Christie was complimented by one censor in 1956 precisely for *not* being a cheap sensationalist (G-424, 31/36: 23-24). A batch of reviews of novels for serialisation in newspapers attests to increased tolerance for sensationalism mixed with continuing distaste. One, from 1959, is a review of Earl Derr Biggers's Charlie Chan novel, *Fifty Candles*. It is judged not too sensationalist and given the go-ahead. Another review of the same book also approves, though a hand-written note suggests that one crime story after another in the newspaper in question is perhaps too much. However, the censor leaves the decision to the newspaper editor (G-588, 55/1: 10). In the same batch there is a very positive review of one Arthur Conan Doyle story and a negative review of another. In neither case is any comment made on escapism or sensationalism (G-588, 55/1: 114, 136).

Caldwell's books are frankly sensationalist and it was almost certainly his criticism of the USA that allowed him to get away with as much as he did. The vulgar language of Caldwell's characters in *Tragic Ground* also gave censors pause for thought, as seen in chapter two. So too did "numerous interludes expressing the author's erotico-sexual obsessions" (G-710, 68/93: 240). Jan Kott's review of this book claims it is not even pornography, just vulgarity and sentimentalism (Kott 1961: 5).

Polish writers also copied the tricks of the sensational thriller trade and this drew some criticism from the censors. A 1967 report presents a number of books that were "questioned in their entirety" – i.e. banned. One of the books, which was to have been serialised in a Łódź newspaper, was *Szlafrok barona Boysta* ("Baron Boyst's Dressing Gown") by the prolific Samuel Zeydler-Zborowski. The novel's hero is a Polish policeman "gifted by the author with all the stereotypical features of the hero of a third rate crime novel" wrote one censor (G-833: 102). Another censor describes it as typical James Bond style writing with all its negatives, such as cosmopolitan spies and cheap eroticism (G-833: 104).

The impression one gets from surveying the archives is that sex, sensationalism and morals were a bigger issue for censors in film and theatre than in fiction. For example, one 1967 report states that the theatre periodicals *Dialog* and *Teatr*, as well as *Ruch Muzyczny*, cause a lot of problems and require very close control. *Dialog* published play scripts – when it was permitted to: Bonarski's *Panienki* ("Young Women") was banned. The excerpt quoted in the censors' files features teenage girls talking about boys and sex (G-846, 86/1: 61-62). In the mid 1960s, Roman Polański's film *Repulsion* was only permitted a limited release, to film clubs, because of its "graphic" scenes (G-846, 86/1: 77), although another reason (perhaps the real one) may have been that the director was living in the West.

In the 1970s, censors were still fighting to keep western sex at bay, blocking the distribution of the film *McCabe and Mrs Miller* for moral reasons: the film is set in a brothel and the characters use vulgar language (G-888, 105/3: 10). In 1977, extracts from Henry Miller's *Tropic of Cancer* were pulled from the periodical *Nowy Wyraz* because of their sexually explicit character (G-1277, 214/21: 105). In film, at least, the 1980s saw a significant easing of such restrictions, with the earlier puritanism giving way to nudity and sex (Kornatowska, qtd. in Kalinowska 2009: 66). It was in the 1980s, too, that D.H. Lawrence's *Lady Chatterley's Lover* re-appeared in Polish. A heavily cut version had been published in 1928; this new translation was based on the first English edition, which itself had been censored (Jabłońska 2007: 199).

Turning to other books, we find that the London of Margaret Drabble's *A Summer Birdcage* was too swinging for Polish tastes. The line "'It's bound to be an utterly sick-making drunken orgy, with foreign girls and models...'" (Drabble 1984: 77) is, in back translation, "There will be terrible drunkenness and it will be full of foreign girls and models" (Drabble 1976: 92). Even though the speaker is obviously disapproving, mention of an "orgy" was still cut by someone – translator, editor or censor. In *Manhattan Transfer* "'they [Arab dancing girls] got slippery belly buttons'" (Dos Passos 1986: 105) is translated simply as "One są słodkie" ("They are sweet") (Dos Passos 1958: 137). The translator of Caldwell's *Trouble in July* cut the following words altogether: "'Where her legs came together at her belly it looked exactly like somebody had poked his finger in one of those toy balloons, and the place had stayed there'" (Caldwell 1979: 50; 1949: 234).[7] Some of the book's violence is toned down, but not by much. Shep Barlow punches his daughter in both the Polish and the English version but the words "Oscar had often boasted that he had killed so many Negroes that he had lost count" (Caldwell 1979: 44) are missing from the Polish (Caldwell 1949:

228), though this may have been simply an oversight. This only very slight attenuation of violence in Caldwell may be contrasted with the treatment of Irish writer Edna O'Brien, who in Polish translation is less shocking than in the original. The violence aimed at women, in particular, is cut (Looby 2013: 166). It may have been thought that Caldwell had a serious message about the dark side of capitalist America but O'Brien's books (*Girl With Green Eyes, The Country Girls, A Sinful Woman*) were "only" for women, who needed to be protected from such ugly scenes. Despite the propaganda posters showing women driving tractors and despite even occasional disapproval in the censors' archives of the traditional stereotyping of women (Nowak 2012: 147) People's Poland was a patriarchal society.[8] Some fairly innocuous ribald humour even goes missing from the translation of O'Brien's *The Country Girls*, as when a boy in the street says, "'Thirty-two degrees is freezing point, what's squeezing point?'" (O'Brien 1963: 136), which becomes "–Proszę pani, która godzina? Niech pani sprawdzi na termometrze!" ("'Excuse me, Miss, what time is it? Check it on the thermometer'") (O'Brien 1978a: 126).

The Polish translation of Nathanael West's *Day of the Locust* appeared in one volume with his *Miss Lonelyhearts* in 1963. Although West, like Caldwell, may have been considered a "serious" writer since he exposes the rotten underbelly of Hollywood and by extension capitalism, the violence is toned down considerably in the Polish version, which attempts to shield the reader from some of the unpleasantness of the original's portrayal of decadence and decay. This paternalism is especially noticeable in the treatment of the narrator's rape fantasies: "Nothing less violent than rape would do" (West 1975: 53) is, in back translation, "Nothing other than brutal violence would do to take her" (West 1963: 95); "hit her with a bottle and rape her" (West 1975: 127) is "knock her out with a blow from a bottle and take her by force" (West 1963: 217); and "Tod tried to start the rape going" (West 1975: 128) is "Tod tried to continue the interrupted attack" (West 1963: 218). What is actually going through the narrator's mind remains fairly obvious but the little evasions are there to be seen when one compares source and target texts.

A tendency to be more delicate in matters of sex and physiology can also be seen in the translation of Alan Sillitoe's *Men, Women and Children*. "'Milk out of a virgin's tit'" (Sillitoe 1973: 57) becomes "milk from a virgin" (Sillitoe 1979: 77); and "sweet evening fuck on the grass" (Sillitoe 1973: 151) becomes "sweet caresses on the grass" ("słodkie karesy na trawie") (Sillitoe 1979: 208). The use of a foreign word ("karesy") hints to the reader that the original was more direct in an example of what Matthew Reynolds calls "semi-censorship" (Reynolds 2007).

Room at the Top also provides examples of Poland's coyness. Sex is not always portrayed in a romantic light in the original and the Polish version is in places less blunt. Joe Lampton's face is described as "unused by sex" (Braine 1957: 8), whereas in Polish it is "unused by adventures in love/erotic dalliances" ("nie zużytej miłosnymi przygodami") (Braine 1960: 6). The narrator writes, "she behaved as if she wouldn't welcome sex from me in any shape or form; and I took her at her face value. Which is the last thing that any woman wants" (Braine 1957: 70-71). The second sentence is dropped, leaving, in back translation, "she always gave me to understand that she would not permit even an attempt at courtship and I took that at face value" (Braine 1960: 83). Whereas in the original the narrator could "get sex at any pub or dancehall" (Braine 1957: 84), in translation he can satisfy his "erotic needs" (Braine 1960: 99).

Despite the foregoing, there is still some sex and violence in Polish translations of English language books. For example, Edna O'Brien's translator (Maria Zborowska) made no attempt to censor the violence directed at women in Naipaul's *Miguel Street*. Other notable examples would include descriptions in *Borstal Boy* of the warders beating the author and the reference to the song "Fanny by Gaslight" – not only present in the Polish translation but explained in a footnote (Behan 1982: 398n). References to beating women in Braine's *Room at the Top* also survive. Charlotte, in Faulkner's *Wild Palms*, cries, "'Bust the hell out of me!'" and "'You bastard! You damned bastard! So you can rape little girls in parks on Saturday afternoons!'" (Faulkner 1954: 108, 111). These are contained in the Polish, although "bastard" is rendered as "kretyn" ("cretin") and "idiota" ("idiot") (Faulkner 1987: 188). The villain in Raymond Chandler's *Big Sleep* is a man who blackmails Carmen Sternwood by drugging her and taking nude photographs. This sleazy atmosphere is preserved in translation, while the references to "queens" and "fags" are usually less insulting but scarcely any less homophobic. The sex scenes in the later, and far more explicit, *Godfather* are reproduced in full in Polish.

Apart from a progressive loosening of strictures after 1956, it is difficult to discern a pattern in the translations studied here. That is, translations done by men and women of men and women's books and in different decades are all as likely to be more coy than the original. The suggestion that the translations of Edna O'Brien are more delicate because the books were perceived as being for women must remain just that: a suggestion.

Overall, Polish translations have less sex and violence than their English source texts but there are exceptions and some target texts are as frank as their sources. The same is true of swearing but there are fewer exceptions to the rule of using milder language in Polish than in the original. In 1946, George Orwell wrote that Britain was usually a few years behind the US in the unexpurgated use of swear words (Orwell 1998, vol. 18: 511).

Poland was further behind again. In a 1976 review of *Catch-22*, Zbigniew Lewicki castigated the translator for his work and also noted that the swearing in the Polish version was weaker (Lewicki 1976: 346). Writing some 28 years after the end of institutional censorship in Poland, Joanna Jabłońska claimed that contemporary Polish literature was only now breaking linguistic taboos that writers such as Norman Mailer, Charles Bukowski and Saul Bellow had tackled in the middle of the twentieth century (Jabłońska 2007: 191). To this day, the translations of English-language films, especially if shown on terrestrial television, tend to use euphemisms in place of the swearing in the original.

There are not too many references to strong language in the archives, which may suggest that reluctance to use swear words – like racist terms – was a Polish literary norm that did not have to be forced on translators by the state. That is, the manuscripts the censors saw had already been cleaned up. In 1952, the censor objected to the use of the word "skurwysyn" ("son of a whore") in Howard Fast's *Freedom Road*, suggesting that ellipsis be used (G-386, 31/123: 266). In the event the word was printed in full. In 1970, the censor hesitated over Hemingway's *Death in the Afternoon*, recommending the book be published but only after making changes on page 141. The censor's superior's decision, however, was to "publish without changes" (G-879, 101/19: 156). On page 141 of the published translation an artillery officer swears repeatedly. This is shown in the text with ellipses after the first letter or letters of the swear words (Hemingway 1971: 141), much the same as in English editions (Hemingway 2000: 125-126).

Graham Greene's *Travels With My Aunt* was first published in 1969 and translated into Polish only a year later. It contains the line "'Peter can talk about nothing but cricket. [...] Nothing but the fucking Ashes'" (Greene 1971: 23). The translation uses the standard Polish euphemism, "pieprzone" (literally: "peppered") (Greene 1970a: 20) and this is the choice of word to be seen over and again. In *The Godfather*, "'I don't give a fuck'" (Puzo 1969: 115) is translated "Ja pieprzę to" (literally: "I pepper it") (Puzo 1979: 150) and "'You fucking bastard'" (Puzo 1969: 68) is translated "Ty pieprzony draniu!" ("You peppered blackguard") (Puzo 1979: 86). The translation may sound absurd to English readers but it is simply a case of substitution based on sound properties, as when English speakers say "crikey" instead of "Christ". "Pieprzony" is so often used that it may now have been "besmirched" by association (i.e. it is now a "dirty" word itself) but there is no doubt that it is less offensive than what it stands for, "pierdolony", a word which does not appear at all in the Polish translation of *The Godfather*. There is a faint possibility the translator wanted to use this word to translate "fug" in Vonnegut's *Cat's Cradle*. The published version uses "cholerny" (the adjective of cholera) and "pieprzony" on the page castigated by the censor for its overuse of indecent language (G-919, 121/9: 203). The unreliability of the censors' records means that we cannot now tell for certain whether the presence of "cholerny" and "pieprzony" on the page in question (24) is an effect of the censor's complaint or a cause of it.

Since many of the English source texts also use euphemisms like "fug" and "frig" anyway (Maltz, Mailer, Behan etc.) the attenuation of the word "fuck" is less noticeable than the toning down of "bastard", a word which presents problems for Polish translators. There is a direct equivalent, "bękart", but it is seldom used as an insult. It occurs in the translation of Kingsley Amis's *Lucky Jim* – "'I'll wring that little bastard's neck one of these days'" (Amis 1954: 57; Amis 1958: 75) – and Zofia Kierszys used it with absolute consistency – including instances of closely-spaced repetition – in her much criticised[9] 1957 translation of Faulkner's *Sanctuary*. By 1967, however, when Kalina Wojciechowska translated *Wild Palms* by the same author, "bękart" had fallen out of favour: for example we have "'decent is such a bastard word'" (Faulkner 1954: 35) while in Polish it is an "idiotic" word (Faulkner 1987: 52). Also used as substitutes in the Polish version are "łobuz" ("rascal"), "osioł" ("donkey"), "kretyn" ("cretin") and "dureń" ("idiot") (Faulkner 1987: 163, 163, 25, 25). In general, translators use words such as these and "łajdak" ("rogue") and "drań" ("blackguard"), all of which are milder than the coarse English insult they replace. They are insulting but not obscene. In *Day of the Locust*, "bastard" is translated as, variously, "łobuz", "łajdak" and "drań" (West 1963: 8, 77, 131), while in *The Catcher in the Rye*, the narrator's comment on his own behaviour "What a *rude bastard*, but I couldn't help it!" (Salinger 1953: 171) is rephrased in translation as: "Co za chamstwo" ("What rudeness") (Salinger 1967: 175).

Some Irish writers have a fondness for "whore" as a form of address. This is not usually translated as "kurwa", the direct Polish correspondent and probably the most frequently used swear word in the language. Sean O'Casey's "'Yeh whore's get'" (O'Casey 1971: 82) is translated "Ty, ścierwo" (literally "You carcass") (O'Casey 1963: 111) and Frank O'Connor's melancholic "'we poor whores'" (O'Connor 1963: 95) is in Polish "my nieszczęśliwcy'" ("we poor unfortunates") (O'Connor 1971: 47). O'Connor, too, gives us "plank their ass" (O'Connor 1963: 214), which in Polish is "wygrzewać d..." ("warm their a...") (O'Connor 1971: 214). Although in other respects the Polish *Brideshead Revisited* is quite a daring translation, preserving the racist terms and most of the hints of homosexuality (though the translator may have missed a few clues), ellipsis is also used for the word "arse". Where the original has "'Green arse, Samgrass – Samgrass green arse'" (Waugh 1962: 124), the translation has "pocałuj mnie w d... w sam raz" ("kiss my a... that's right") (Waugh 1970: 120).

Expressions using the word "shit" ("gówno") cause translators fewer headaches. Portis's "'shitpoke lawyers'" (Portis 2011: 63) is translated with the use of the word "zasrani" ("shitty") (Portis 1973: 71). Brendan Behan's "'You fughing shit-house'" (Behan 1990: 67) is translated "ty pieprzone gówno" ("you peppered shit") (Behan 1982: 93). "Gówniany" ("shitty") is sometimes used to translate "fugging" (for example in Mailer's *Naked and the Dead*), and in *The Maltese Falcon*, translated in 1963, "gówniarz" (derived from "gówno") is consistently used to translate the original's "punk". The word "cunts" is used by John Updike in the story "Sublimating" in *Museums and Women* (Updike 1973: 276). It is neither translated nor replaced but simply removed from the Polish version (Updike 1978: 216).

Against the background of translations that are more decorous than their source texts, two books in particular stand out. The first of these is *Ulysses*, translated by Maciej Słomczyński and published in 1969. Słomczyński translates obscene English into equally obscene Polish, including even Private Carr's "God fuck old Bennett!" (Joyce 1994: 583). Credit for this forthrightness must go to the translator but it is likely that the prestige and notoriety of the novel ensured the censor let the obscenities pass. Limited print runs were a way of ensuring that material that had passed the censor did not then go very far but even here *Ulysses* is exceptional. The initial print run was a respectable 40,290 and there were successive editions, in 1975 and 1981, of just over 20,000 copies each.

However, *Ulysses* did not, in fact, escape unscathed. A June 1969 Censorship Office report entitled "Notes on certain negative phenomena in the artistic programme of television and in the repertoire of cinemas and theatres" states that "serious interventions" were made in the stage version of the novel (G-848, 86/3: 160). The report does not say what it was the censors changed but it comes immediately after a passage in which the writer bemoans the invasion of "so-called 'black literature' from the West" and the tendency of theatres to choose plays for production that allude to "our reality" (G-848, 86/3: 159, 160). This suggests the production may have been censored for political reasons but Marta Fik claims it was sex that was at issue (Fik 1996: 138). Also, Kamila Budrowska is of the opinion that censors' references to western influences and naturalism was sometimes code for sex (Budrowska 2012: 233).

The second exception is the translation of *Portnoy's Complaint*, which is also very frank. The translator, Anna Kołyszko, uses the Polish word "pierdolony" and translates the chapter title "Cunt crazy" (Roth 1969: 78) as "Ocipiały" (Roth 1986: 83), a word the dictionary defines as "bonkers" but which is formed from the word "cipa" ("cunt"). It is, nevertheless, a little less offensive than the original. Elsewhere the Polish word "pizda", also very offensive, is used (Roth 1986: 264). However, the sheer volume of swear words is not reproduced in the translation. For example, "And doesn't speak in those fucking *syllables!*" (Roth 1969: 74) is translated without any swear word (Roth 1986: 78), and "Mrs. Nimkin, you shit, I remember you [...] YOUR FUCKING SELFISHNESS AND STUPIDITY" (Roth 1969: 98) becomes "Pani Nimkin, ty ścierwo, pamiętam panią [...] PANI CHOLERNY EGOIZM I GŁUPOTA!" (roughly: "Mrs Nimkin, you carcass, I remember you... your bloody egotism and stupidity") (Roth 1986: 100). "Hideous Catholic bullshit" (Roth 1969: 98) is a milder, though still insulting, "obrzydliwe katolickie banialuki" ("hideous Catholic nonsense") (Roth 1986: 101).

There is inconsistency in the treatment of swear words but the *Maltese Falcon* ("punk"/"gówniarz") is the only example I have come across where the target text is ruder than the source text. That is to say, translations are either as obscene as the originals or less obscene so the overall effect is that Polish translations are less vulgar than their source texts.

Samantha Sherry gives numerous examples of cuts and evasions concerning sex in translations that appeared in the Soviet periodical *Inostrannaia Literatura*.[10] When these are compared with Polish translations, it can be seen that while they were guided by similar considerations of decency, Polish translators were more daring – or allowed to get away with more – than their Russian counterparts. In the Russian translation of *Lucky Jim* "sexual encounters" is translated as "dates"; "sexual feelings" as "sensual attractions"; and "start any kind of sexual relationship with her" as "to come together with her" (Sherry 2012: 133). The Polish translation (from the same year as the Russian) reads, respectively, "love dates" ("randki miłosne"), "sexual desires", and "get involved in any kind of sexual dealings with her" (Amis 1958: 76, 96, 318). As can be seen, the Polish is quicker to use the word "sexual" than the Russian but still tends to substitute love for sex, as is also shown by the following example: "even the mildest sexual entanglement" (Amis 1954: 58) is rendered "w żadną historię miłosną bodaj najbardziej umiarkowaną" ("in any love story, even the most temperate") (Amis 1958: 76).

Sherry also considers the Russian translation of *The Grapes of Wrath*, in which some of the details in a description of childbirth are euphemised (Sherry 2012: 136-137). The Polish translation of the passage ("For on the night when Noah was born..." (Steinbeck 1939: 69)) leaves nothing out (Steinbeck 1959: 121). However, the references to sex which Sherry finds are euphemised or otherwise censored in the Russian translation (Sherry 2012: 154) are censored in the Polish, as, for example, when Casy asks himself, "'What's gnawin' you? Is it the screwin?'" (Steinbeck 1939: 19). In Polish he asks himself if it is his groping of a girl that is troubling him (Steinbeck 1959: 37).

Also more robust in Polish than in Russian is the translation of *The Quiet American*. Pyle says he has never had a girl – "'not properly. Not what you'd call a real experience'" (Greene 1977: 102). By translating "experience" as "romance", Sherry points out, the Russian translator turns this from sex into a relationship (Sherry 2012: 134). Not so the Polish version, which reads, in back translation, "It was never an experience in the full sense of the word" (Greene 1966: 121). A little later Pyle asks the narrator, "'If somebody asked you what your deepest sexual experience had been, what would you say?'" (Greene 1977: 103). "Sexual experience" is rendered "physical pleasure" in Russian (Sherry 2012: 151) but in Polish it remains "sexual experience" ("'przeżycie seksualne'") (Greene 1966: 122). The word "sexual" in the following short passage is translated as "indecent" in Russian (Sherry 2012: 152) but left as "sexual" in Polish: "'*Sans vaseline*,' Vigot said, throwing a four-two-one. He pushed the last match towards me. The sexual jargon of the game was common to all the Sureté" (Greene 1977: 137; Greene 1966: 161).

However, some concessions were made in the Polish *Quiet American* that are close to those of the Russian. In "I had experience to match his virginity, age was as good a card to play in the sexual game as youth..." (Greene 1977: 67) "sexual game" is translated more modestly as "gra miłosna" ("the game of love") (Greene 1966: 81). In addition, "'You [English people] all talk like poufs'" (Greene 1977: 184) is translated as "'Wszyscy gadacie, jakby wam śmierdziało pod nosem'" ("You all talk as if something stank right under your nose") (Greene 1966: 215). In the former example, the Russian translation also used "love" rather than sex, while in the latter the Russian translator used an idiom meaning "mumble". Sherry points out that this may have been because the translator was not familiar with the slang word "pouf", which applies to the Polish translator as well (Sherry 2012: 134, 139-140).

In both the Russian and the Polish translations of *The Catcher in the Rye* the graffiti that haunts Holden Caulfied in the last chapter but one – "Fuck you" – is toned down significantly. The Russian translator (in 1960) used a descriptive translation: Caulfield sees "an obscenity" on the wall (Sherry 2012: 154). The Polish goes a little further, supplying the first two words and using ellipsis for the rest: "Pies cię..." ("May a dog...you") (Salinger 1967: 184). Sherry notes that on one occasion the Russian avoids translating "flit" as homosexual, even though it is used to describe a man who has just made a pass at Caulfield, an episode which is given in full (Sherry 2012: 139). As seen in the Polish context too, it seems sometimes that words themselves rather than the meanings attached to them are what exercise censorious minds, although as it happens in this case the Polish does not shy away from translating "flit" as, variously, "pedzio" and "pedał", derogatory terms for homosexuals, for example at the start of chapter 19.

Samantha Sherry cites Russian translator Viktor Golyshev's argument that softening the "erotic content and non-normative language" of western books was an artistically motivated choice, not a censorious decision. Westerners "have already become used to this, and when you repeat it, you destroy the proportions, so it comes out stronger than it does there" (qtd. in Sherry 2012: 71). This is an argument that could be made in Poland: Sadkowski describes the level of obscenity in *Ulysses* as unprecedented in Polish writing (Sadkowski 2002: 136). However, it raises a chicken-and-egg question: are Polish translations less vulgar because Polish literature is less vulgar or is Polish literature less vulgar because Polish translations are less vulgar?

The historical record suggests that the timidity in matters of religion, sex and sensation described above was not forced on translators or writers by the new political regime. Morality-based censorship, Kamila Budrowska writes, had a long history in Poland before the Second World War (Budrowska 2012: 230). Pre-war Poland, despite an encouraging start and the guarantee of free speech in the 1921 constitution, was also censorious, with blank white columns in newspapers indicating the parts that had been cut. Particular targets of the censorship were left wing poets (and later all political opposition), morals, pornography, blasphemy and insulting religious feelings. The poet Anatol Stern spent several months in jail for blasphemy and works by luminaries such as Słonimski, Jasieński, Iwaszkiewicz and Tuwim were censored (Gazda 2008: 35-36). One of the most often cited cases of censorship involved Emil Zegadłowicz's novels *Motory* (*Motors*) and *Zmory* (*Ghosts*) with their sexual explicitness and mockery of the Catholic Church. The entire print run of the former was confiscated in 1938. In 1920, Iwaszkiewicz's *Zenobia Palmura* was confiscated for outraging "the sense of shame and the sense of beauty" and the editor who had published it spent three weeks in jail (Zawada 1995: 202). Zawada points out that some politicians were even harsher: one called for books like *Gargantua and Pantagruel* and *Tristan and Isolde* to be banned on the grounds that they were pornographic (Zawada 1995: 203). In 1936, Julian Tuwim shelved his poem *Bal w Operze* ("Ball at the Opera"), evidently thinking Poland would not accept lines like the following: "Prancing across the coin-flooded floor,/ Enters a dazzling Fucking Whore!" (Tuwim 1985: 22; lines 670-671). Tellingly, the widely available, canonical, Polish version is not as explicit as this English translation, using ellipsis for the last two words ("K... Mać") (Tuwim 1986: 242-243; lines 659-660). Writers did attempt to push the boundaries (Tuwim published less outrageous parts of the poem in journals (Barańczak 1984: 234)) but the boundaries pushed back. In 1935, critic

Ignacy Fik railed against authors whose development had been arrested at puberty, who were hypochondriacs, homosexuals, drug addicts, exhibitionists, psychopaths and degenerates (Fik 1979: 126).

Cinema too was forced into timidity before the war, with films that had already passed the Hays code in the United States being further cut in Poland, with the result that some made no sense in their Polish incarnations (Madej 1994: 84). The censorship was vaguely defined, leading Słonimski to complain that the officials cut anything they thought was not "nice" or "tasteful" (Madej 1994: 83). However, among a set of guidelines was a ban on scenes showing the exhumation of bodies (Madej 1994: 80). As seen above, respect for the dead was probably behind a change made many years later to Sherwood Anderson's "The Philosopher" and Cronin's *Keys of the Kingdom*.

Polish literature was influenced by translations. Writing in 1971, Leszek Elektorowicz claimed that verbosity in Polish letters had been reigned in under the influence of American literature and noted Hemingway's influence on Polish writer Marek Hłasko. William Faulkner and – Elektorowicz acknowledges – his translators made themselves felt in the 1960s in Poland (Elektorowicz 1971: 24-25). However, the coarse language of writers like Henry Miller, John Updike, William Faulkner, Ernest Hemingway and also Graham Greene did not make its presence felt in Poland to anything like the same extent. Polish prose may have become more snappy and hard-boiled but if it became more obscene it was not so much because of western literary examples. Much of the swearing had been filtered out – and continues to be filtered out. The English Bridget Jones resolves not to fall for "emotional fuckwits" (Fielding 1997: 2) but in Polish this undesirable type of person is rendered "popaprańcy" ("mess-ups") (Fielding 2001: 7).

---

[1] Aleksander Pawlicki suggests the film, which was released with drastic cuts, was permitted (in film clubs only) in order to show the church what the West was like and how good they had it in Poland ('Zabijanie' 2004: 23).

[2] "On miał swą wiarę, miał ją, lecz źródła jej tkwiły w miłości dla biednych, nędznych, w dziele miłosierdzia dokonywanym w cieszących się najgorszą sławą dzielnicach miasta, skąd przynosił pchły, które potem wytrząsał codziennie do nie używanej wanny. Wiara ta nigdy nie przychodziła mu spokojnie i łatwo, z wyjątkiem tylko tych momentów, gdy siedział przy chorych, ułomnych i konających, którym śmierć powlekała bielmem oczy. Ale bezmiar nędzy, na którą patrzył, i rozmiary panoszącej się krzywdy rozstrajały mu nerwy i zabijały w nim radość modlitwy" (Cronin 1974: 131). It will be noticed, also, that the bath which was "empty" in English is "unused" in Polish.

[3] The film of the book was ordered banned in Poland because although it showed that religious sects were all about money it also showed "the enormous influence of a religious cult on society" and "scenes of collective religious ecstasy". This and the final scene, when a man regains his hearing, contravene the "secular character of cinema" (G-848, 86/3: 227-228).

---

[4] This review is also quoted by Nowak, who found it in the Poznań branch office archives (Nowak 2012: 138).

[5] In 1969, the censors axed the television series *The Avengers* because it contained helpful hints for criminals – including karate (G-848, 86/3: 71).

[6] Kamila Budrowska also quotes this review (Budrowska 2012: 241-242).

[7] This was also cut from the 1940 Russian translation which, unlike the Polish, cut the following paragraph describing the sex act (Sherry 2012: 125-126).

[8] See, for example, Trawińska (2010). Katarzyna Bereta notes that even in socialist realist books for children the heroes were still men, with women mostly seen in the kitchen (Bereta 2013: 77).

[9] See, for example, Sadkowski (2002: 126).

[10] See also Marianna Tax-Choldin's comparison of Studs Terkel's *Working* with its Russian translation (1986: 345).

Chapter 5
Racists

At a meeting of censors in 1949, one speaker presented a list of situations in which the censor should intervene. Among other things, the speaker said: "it is correct to cross out characters of Jewish usurers or [Jewish] publicans leading the countryside to alcoholism...it is correct to cross out the characters of Jews presented in a negative light that ridicules them" (Nałęcz 1994: 23). Another early indicator of the direction state control would take was the list of books for withdrawal from circulation drawn up in 1951 (*Cenzura PRL...* 2002). Among the titles were *Mein Kampf* and *How to Free Oneself of Jews* (*Jak uwolnić się od Żydów*). Also on the blacklist were the yearbooks of *Seas and Colonies* (*Morze i Kolonie*) and all works by H. Rider Haggard. Distaste for eurocentric colonial adventuring and any accompanying racism was to be a feature of the censorship, with writers like Evelyn Waugh, Somerset Maugham and Graham Greene occasionally running afoul of it. In literature translated from English, it generally remained the practice to excise racist and anti-Semitic epithets.[1] In this respect, at least, the official, though not widely publicised, policy of censorship is borne out by practice. Cormac Ó Cuilleanáin writes of "liberal censorship", which may "be located largely inside the translator's head" and seeks to spread "desirable and usually libertarian values and objectives" (Ó Cuilleanáin 2009: 184). Polish translators may not have needed any prompting from the authorities to encourage racial tolerance and respect for one's fellow human beings.

Although the communist mission was to make a new, progressive person, who would turn her back on the irrational racist prejudices (and dreams of empire) of the past, there is evidence that even without institutionalised censorship or more or less overt prompting from the Party the practice in translation was to avoid racist epithets. For example, the 1898 Polish version of *Huckleberry Finn* (which would have been subject to Tsarist censorship) generally avoids using "czarnuch" for "nigger", instead preferring "murzyn" ("black person") even when the speaker is obviously an unsympathetic character. In chapter six, Huck's father refers to "niggers" several times in the course of a diatribe about (among other things) the government and the law. This is translated as "murzyn" throughout (Twain 1898: 51-52).[2]

The force and offensiveness of such words changes over time and in different contexts but the word used in Polish translations is nearly always "Murzyn". "Murzyn" may be coming under fire now (Cieśla 2011) (as have "Negro" and "coloured") and the diminutive ("Murzynek") can cause offence but there is no question that the word is much less offensive – and intended to be less offensive – than "nigger", the usual term of abuse used without any great invention by racist characters in the books studied here. The nearest equivalent to it in Polish would be "czarnuch". Widely recognised as unmistakeably offensive, it would be the obvious choice of translation for "nigger" in the absence of other constraints.

Even in the "colonial/imperialist" books that offended the authorities, racist epithets were toned down or erased before the war. Rudyard Kipling's *Kim* ("all editions") was withdrawn from circulation in 1951 (*Cenzura PRL...*2002). In the 1926 edition "nigger" is translated "murzyn" on the few occasions that it occurs. This causes a distortion of the meaning: the drummer boy "styled all natives 'niggers;' yet servants and sweepers called him abominable names to his face, and, misled by their deferential attitude, he never understood" (Kipling s.d.: 135). In Polish, he calls all natives "murzyni" (Kipling 1926: 132) and it is therefore a little more difficult to understand why they dislike him so. In the pre-war translation of *The Man Who Would Be King*, "niggers" is also translated as "murzyni". A translation of Waugh's *Black Mischief* appeared before the war, with racist epithets removed or neutralised. It was not renewed in People's Poland. The pre-war translation of Conrad's *Heart of Darkness* also avoids translating the original's "nigger" as "czarnuch" (Kujawska-Lis 2008: 169).

Another pre-war example comes from Upton Sinclair's *They Call Me Carpenter*: "'I bring 'em to you; I bring de Japs and de Chinks and de niggers – de vooly-headed savages vot vould eat your missionaries if you sent 'em. I offer you de whole vorld, Mr. Carpenter; and you vould be de boss!'" (Sinclair 1971: 102). The 1928 Polish translation uses neutral words for all the nationalities and races and gets rid of the speaker's accent (Sinclair 1928: 74). One last example comes from the translations of Graham Greene's *The Power and the Glory* (see also Bates 2011). The Polish translation was first published in Paris, in 1956, away from the eyes of the Polish censor. Both the Paris version and the later, People's Republic version avoid the word "dago", spoken by Captain Fellows (Greene 1991: 33), using instead "native" ("tubylec") (Greene 1956: 39; 1985: 31).

After the war, the censor supported the tendency to remove racist and anti-Semitic abuse from translated English and American literature. Only sometimes, on the basis of archival evidence, is it possible to state categorically that the change from a derogatory word to a neutral one was forced by the censor. Evidence of the censors' ongoing sensitivity to racism can be found in the minutes of official meetings of the type mentioned above and also in the book reviews in the archives. For example, in a 1971 review of Isaac Asimov's *Whiff of Death* (*Powiew śmierci*), the censor seems to be trying to "rescue" the book from potential accusations that it is anti-Semitic:

> That the murder victim is probably a Jew (vide p. 95) is not a shocking element because he has been given negative character traits and besides, he falls victim to a scientific maniac. At play here are conflicts related purely to ambition, with no political basis (G-863, 101/3: 250).

The individual censor was not all-powerful and had to protect himself from his superiors. What we have here may well be a junior censor trying to head off any future criticism for failing to spot "anti-Semitic" elements in the book. Whatever the individual censor's exact motives were, it can be seen that anti-Semitism was thought better avoided.

A 1973 second quarter report into "the main tendencies observed in questioned material" tells how suggestions of universal anti-Semitism in Poland were censored and shows how the censors contributed to an idealised self-portrait of Poles: "...accusations of anti-Semitism during the war, inadequate help for the Ghetto Rising and cruelty to German prisoners were removed from journalism and war diaries" (G-1117, 176/22: 47). The censors delayed Poland's coming to terms with anti-Semitism. For example, a short story by Wincenty Burek, "Ścigany" ("Pursued"), was prevented from appearing in 1969. The story tells of a Jew hiding from the Nazis in Poland during the war. At one point, he says to the man sheltering him that he has to pay for shelter from other Catholics and although he is now penniless, they all think he – being a Jew – has gold and dollars. This story had appeared in 1956 but it is not in the 1969 edition of the same book. The Party infamously used anti-Semitism as a weapon in 1968 but I have found little or no evidence of a policy, however fleeting, of promoting anti-Semitic English or American authors. In any case, foreign literature was rarely the burning issue that, for example, Polish-Russian relations or World War Two was for the authorities.

Another example from the archives of this sensitivity concerns Virginia Woolf's *The Years* and has been described by John Bates (Bates 2011: 69). Briefly, the censors demanded the cutting down of repeated references to a certain character's Jewishness. Unmentioned in the files is another change in the published translation: from "'Burnt as brown as a nigger!'" (Woolf 1948: 259) to "Tanned like a Black" ("Opalona jestem na Murzyna!") (Woolf 1958: 389). This change did not merit a comment from the censor, which may mean that the translator made it without prompting. The situation is similar in the case of H.G. Wells's *Kipps*. The censor noted with approval changes made by the publisher to parts of one character's speech concerning socialism and society in general. The same character,

Masterman, in the same scene, says, "'There isn't a woman in the swim of society [...] who wouldn't lick the boots of a Jew or marry a nigger, rather than live decently on a hundred a year!'" (Wells 1941: 243). The Polish has, in back translation, "'... who wouldn't lick the boots of a lout [cham]...'" (Wells 1950: 291). This change was not remarked by the censor, again suggesting it was made by the translator before the censor saw it (G-145, 31/25: 168-175). Similarly, a reference in the translation of Howard Fast's *Freedom Road* to a Jew being "pyszny" ("haughty" – the original is "uppity" (Fast 1979: 52)) attracted the censor's ire (G-386, 31/124: 131). "Pyszny" does, in fact, appear in the published version – but not "nigger", the word used by the speaker about the black Jewish man in question. This is translated as "Murzyn" (Fast 1952: 68) with no record of any prompting from the censor.

Another archival example of the authorities' sensitivity to racism concerns a film called *The Dutchman* (directed by Anthony Harvey). It was withheld from circulation in 1967 because, among other things, it promoted "the view that the races are biologically and insurmountably foreign and cannot coexist" (G-846, 86/1: 326).

A revulsion against anything that might smack of the "white man's burden" can be seen in the censors' archives. Polish classic Henryk Sienkiewicz came under fire in 1948 for his approval of missionary activity in Africa in his *Listy z Afryki* (*Letters from Africa*). The censor wrote that the author failed to notice that "'the missions, showing that working for whites was the path to heaven, only changed one form of slavery for another: the substance remained the same. The author sees the people's poverty but he does not notice the causes'" (qtd. in Nowak 2012: 143). The book was, in fact, published, as volume 43 of Sienkiewicz's collected works, in 1949, and the initial rejection may be an example of over-zealousness at the lower levels of the censoring bureaucracy. The book was published as a stand-alone volume in 1956. A ministry-level review of *The Cruise of the Snark* by Jack London approves of the book's socialism and claims London is generally very sympathetic to native peoples, though not those of the Solomon Islands. Also, London does not highlight colonial exploitation strongly enough. However, the final verdict is to pass the book for translation (M-705, Departament Twórczości Artystycznej; Wydział Wydawniczy). In 1959, the censor ordered the cutting of Somerset Maugham's preface to *The Casuarina Tree* because it spoke "of the life-giving and civilising mission of the English in Malaysia" (G-591, 60/3: 57). Graham Greene's *Heart of the Matter* nearly ran into trouble for similar reasons in 1950. A review of the book (produced by the Publishing Division of the Ministry for Culture and Art) reads, "there is no racism here but one can feel the belief in the civilising mission of the 'higher' culture of whites". For this reason, among others, the ministry official recommends it not be published. The decision was overridden: "Due to the political situation and the publisher [PAX] posit [ive]" is entered in the report (M-709, Departament Twórczości Artystycznej; Wydział Wydawniczy: 41). The book did indeed appear in 1950. The translation is faithful except in one respect. All references to "niggers" (made mostly in chapter one by the disaffected and slightly ridiculous Harris, never by the narrator) are translated "Murzyni", giving slightly absurd results when "'I hate the bloody niggers. Mustn't call 'em that'" (Greene 1948: 3) is translated without the word "nigger" (Greene 1950: 11). It may be because the translator, Jacek Woźniakowski, used "Murzyn" throughout that the ministry report did acknowledge there is no racism in the book (assuming, as seems likely, the reviewer read the translation rather than the original). Furthermore, Woźniakowski may have deliberately chosen the safe word "Murzyn" to "rescue" the book from censorship.

The issue of racist language is approached without any great subtlety. Derogatory words for Irish, black people, Jews and so on are simply replaced with neutral words or removed entirely, with no regard for the intricacies of characterisation. Few, if any, of the novels discussed below are racist but they occasionally feature racist characters, often with the intent of satirising them. If and when the characters are polite enough to use non-racist vocabulary, their prejudice is captured in translation. For example, there is faint hint of anti-Semitism in a character in Faulkner's *Pylon*: "'Sales can ground it [an aeroplane], though,' Jiggs said. 'Yair.' The reporter was already turning, moving. 'But Sales aint nothing but a Federal officer; Feinman is a Jew and on the sewage board'" (Faulkner 1951: 132-3). The reporter is peddling the stereotype that it is the Jews who run the show (Feinman can overturn the inspector's decision because he is a Jew – not because he is on the sewage board). But because he calls Feinman a Jew (and not, for example, a "kike") the passage is rendered faithfully in Polish, prejudice intact (Faulkner 1967: 205).

Zofia Kierszys's translation of Faulkner's *Sanctuary* is in some respects quite daring. Nonetheless, "nigger" is usually translated as "Murzyn", with "czarnuch" and "Negr" (also pejorative) used on only a few occasions. At one point, Snopes launches into a quite vicious attack on Jews. Apart from expressions like "jew lawyer" (Faulkner 1997: 320) instead of "Jewish lawyer", however, no derogatory words are used for Jews and so this passage went uncut, although a neutral equivalent for "Jew" (as an adjective) was used (Faulkner 1957: 268-269). This translation dates from the thaw in Poland, 1957, when for a time censorship was in disarray. This may account for the leniency with which Snopes's anti-Semitic peroration was treated, not to mention the very fact that a book about murder, alcoholism, prostitution, rape, sex slavery and masturbation was permitted at all.

Edna O'Brien's *Girl With Green Eyes* was translated much later, when censorship had firmly re-established itself. However, the anti-Semitic prejudice of some characters is left untouched in translation, seemingly because no one comes out directly with derogatory words. Also, the passages in question are much shorter and less vicious than Snopes's speech in *Sanctuary*. Caithleen's Austrian landlady's dislike of Jews for their alleged meanness (O'Brien 1964: 35) is left in place, as is Andy's remark "'Look at the nose of him – you know what he is? They'll be running this bloody country soon'" (O'Brien 1964: 131). Andy, however, is an unequivocally unsympathetic character and his remarks do not indicate any authorial anti-Semitism and perhaps this, along with the absence of an explicit racial or ethnic slur, meant the passage was let stand.

But satirical intent is often lost or weakened in translation with the cutting of an offending epithet. Polish readers are more often than not presented with racist characters who refer in respectful or at any rate neutral terms to the minority groups they so dislike. An example from Sinclair Lewis's *Elmer Gantry* will serve to illustrate the point. In a 1959 censors' report we learn that "żydlak", a derogatory word for Jew, was changed by the censor to "Żyd", the neutral Polish word, on page 366 of the 1959 Polish translation (G-428, 34/9: 344). "Żyd" is indeed the word that appears in the published translation (Lewis 1987: 284) of Gantry's words: "'darned if I don't think the Yid'll win'" (Lewis 1935: 339). The point is, though, that Elmer Gantry (the fictitious character, not the novel) is – at least casually – anti-Semitic and "Yid" is precisely the word this morally dubious character would use. Similarly, his companion in the evangelisation business, Art Nichols, speaks of "'using some of these nigger songs'" (Lewis 1935: 183) but in the Polish version Nichols is much less cynical and dismissive, saying "Negro songs" ("murzyńskie piosenki") (Lewis 1987: 155).

In *Elmer Gantry*, we can also observe an apparent lack of consistency that is a feature of many other translated novels. A direct quote from Gantry in the original runs, "'he looks like a page of Yid himself'" (Lewis 1935: 141) but this time the Polish maintains the pejorative tone of the original, using the word "Żydzisko" (Lewis 1987: 119). This may have been an oversight (this and the following examples from the novel are not noted in the archives) or the censor may have decided it was a question of degree: in "'It says here in Deuteronomy that God chased these Yids...'" (Lewis 1935: 37) "Yids" is translated neutrally as "Żydzi" ("Jews") (Lewis 1987: 32). Perhaps it was thought there was a threshold for the number of racist epithets; that at some point the censor must step in and say, "enough is enough". Possibly, also, the censor was protecting himself. If accused by his boss of allowing anti-Semitism ("Żydzisko") he could always point to other "neutralising" decisions ("Żydzi") as evidence of – if nothing else –

sensitivity to the issue. In addition, he could use the "enough is enough" argument in his own defence.

Whatever the precise reasons, the effect is to make Elmer Gantry and his circle appear less racist. The effect may be small but it is repeated over the pages and through the years so that the Polish reader's image of English language literature is altered. Another example from *Elmer Gantry* is quite typical of the books examined here. Gantry refers at one point (in free indirect discourse) to "Italy and all those Wop countries" (Lewis 1935: 313). Elsewhere we find reference to a "'Bunch of Wops'" (Lewis 1935: 342). In both cases the pejorative tone is kept in translation ("makaroniarskie" and "makaroniarze") (Lewis 1987: 263, 287). It would seem as if Italians were considered fair game by Polish translators/censors/editors, while Jews and black people were not, though again Sinclair Lewis himself can hardly be accused of racism here. It may also be that "makaroniarz" (from "macaroni" and there appears to be no stronger term of abuse for Italians in common use) is simply not as offensive to Polish ears as, for example, "czarnuch" or "żydlak". A final example from *Elmer Gantry* is the following piece of dialogue: "'wops and hunkies and yids and atheists and papes'" (Lewis 1935: 461). In translation only the Italians are treated with a similar level of disrespect ("makaroniarze" (Lewis 1987: 387)). "Papes" is translated with "papiści", which means "papist" but is not marked as derogatory. "Yids" become "Żydzi" and "hunkies" is mistranslated as "wywrotowcy" ("subversives"). The speaker is not transformed into a beacon of tolerance but some of the rough edges are knocked off him.

It seems that black people and Jews in particular were treated with kid gloves. Italians and Chinese, when referred to pejoratively in the original, are more likely to be similarly slandered in the Polish translation. For example, in a passage of free indirect discourse from *East of Eden* we come across "Bacigalupi's garbage wagon went by, and Martin looked after it spitefully. *There* was a good business. Those wops were getting rich" (Steinbeck 1992: 537). "Wops" are "makaroniarze" in translation (Steinbeck 1963, vol. 2: 334). Dr Murphy, who has a "genuine admiration" for Lee, says, "'That Chink knows more about the pathology of cerebral hemorrhage than I do...'" (Steinbeck 1992: 589). In the Polish "Chink" becomes "Chiniec" (Steinbeck 1963, vol. 2: 401), a less derogatory word than Polish is capable of but still derogatory. When a visitor addresses Lee as "'Ching Chong'" (Steinbeck 1992: 205) this insult is translated more or less as is. Lee emerges from the book as a strongly positive character and no amount of racist abuse from any other characters in the novel has any chance of tarnishing his image. Accordingly, the translation reproduces the racism directed at him by incidental characters without fear of the Polish reader thinking any less of

Lee or Chinese people in general. With black people and Jews translators and censors are less willing to trust authors or readers.

Examples abound in *Babbitt* by Sinclair Lewis, an officially approved writer (the censor's 1957 review of *Main Street* notes that it shows the American drive to make money and dislike of anything undermining the holy law of property (G-424, 31/37: 339-340)). De Valera, a "'Mick agitator'" (Lewis 1961a: 20) in Babbitt's words, is simply an Irishman in translation. When Finkelstein says, "'if a fellow wants to be a Jew about it'" (Lewis 1961a: 48-49), in Polish we read, "if you like being a skinflint" ("Jeżeli ci się podoba być dusigroszem") (Lewis 1961b: 75). The racist stereotype is gone but so too is the irony of an American Jew (in all probability) slandering his own forebears in an effort to be accepted as one of the boys. "'Hun science'" (Lewis 1961a: 83) is rendered "German science" ("nauka niemiecka") (Lewis 1961b: 127); "'a coon's age'" (Lewis 1961a: 108) becomes "ages and ages" ("kopę lat") (Lewis 1961b: 166); "'Dagoes and Hunkies'" (Lewis 1961a: 121) is "Spanish and Portuguese" ("Hiszpanie, Portugalczycy") (Lewis 1961b: 187); "'But my folks ain't kikes'" (Lewis 1961a: 233) is "But my parents were not Jews" ("Ale moi rodzice nie byli Żydami") (Lewis 1961b: 369); and "plantation darkies" (Lewis 1961a: 259) is "Black people from a plantation" ("Murzyni z plantacji") (Lewis 1961b: 411). In Polish, the men of Babbitt's circle remain smugly xenophobic, parochial even, but in a strange way more "politely" so. Their narrow-minded opinions may even sound more carefully considered in translation since in Polish they are not so quick to resort to lazy stereotypical labels. But there is an edge of racism in the original that is missing in the translation. When Babbitt says "'no decent white man'" would want to live in New York, Philadelphia or Chicago (Lewis 1961a: 149), the Polish version has "no self respecting citizen" ("żaden szanujący się obywatel") (Lewis 1961b: 233). Babbitt remains a man of limited horizons but he is not the racist he is in the original.

In *Babbitt* there is little enough about racist brutality and exploitation but the scarcity of black (Irish, etc.) characters does not mean the characters portrayed are not racist. In Babbitt's conversation with his fellow train passengers the generally racist tone is preserved in translation. For example, the offending words in "'The old-fashioned coon ... these young dinges'" (Lewis 1961a: 120) are translated as "czarnuch" and "smoluch" (from "tar", highly offensive) (Lewis 1961b: 186) but the concentration of racist terms is diluted: in "'what's come over these niggers'" and "'glad when a nigger succeeds'" (Lewis 1961a: 120) the offending words are translated as "Murzyn" (Lewis 1961b: 186). No amount of pruning could excise the racism of the speakers in this passage and perhaps this is why the word "czarnuch" was permitted. It is so obviously the speakers who are being satirised that there is little risk of even the dullest reader thinking the point of the scene is to abuse black people. Racism is central to this episode in the book but the theme is often mentioned in passing in *Babbitt* and elsewhere. When passing indications of racism go missing in Polish translation the reader may be left with the impression that racism is a problem only in certain parts of the USA or at certain times.

For example, in *Grapes of Wrath* a number of references to black people as "niggers" by working class white people are missing from the Polish, in which they are called "Murzyni". Tom Joad hitches a lift with a trucker who recites a rhyme: "'An' there we spied a nigger, with a trigger that was bigger...'" (Steinbeck 1939: 8). The Polish version uses "Murzyn" (Steinbeck 1959: 19), as it does when Joad himself repeats the rhyme. Chapter 27 begins with snatches of speech (no inverted commas are used but it is plainly a mixture of voices), one of which reads, "They was a lady back home, won't mention no names – had a nigger kid all of a sudden. Nobody knowed before. Never did hunt out the nigger. Couldn' never hold up her head no more..." (Steinbeck 1939: 373). The translation is still racially hostile but less so, as it avoids the word "nigger". Without the racial abuse it is even possible – just – that the Polish reader will think the woman's shame comes purely from having had a child outside of marriage. It is precisely because black-white relations are not a big issue (at least not explicitly) in *Grapes of Wrath* that the Polish reader needs every possible clue to fully understand the situation – the unlikeliness of a working class revolution, for example, given the racial divisions among the working class. This should have been grist for the Polish propaganda mill but it was an opportunity lost due to the delicacy of the translation. One might expect the authorities to embrace literary evidence of US imperfections, the most glaring of which was racism. To a certain extent they did, as the example of Erskine Caldwell shows.[3] However, delicacy sometimes resulted in missed opportunities.

Another propaganda opportunity to criticise the West is lost in the translation of Irish writer Michael Farrell's *Thy Tears Might Cease*. A character's words "'Even the Nigger Minstrels sound nice up here, Martin'" (Farrell 1963: 173) are rendered without the word "Nigger". Instead it is "those Negro songs" ("te murzyńskie piosenki") (Farrell 1967, vol. 1: 221). Far from illustrating the racism of the decadent West (Ireland is the setting) with a faithful translation and, say, a footnote explaining minstrelsy, the publishers push the casual racism of early twentieth century Irish society out of sight.

Brendan Behan's racism – if it can be interpreted as such – is cut from *Borstal Boy*, a line of which reads, "the black boy from Tiger Bay [...]. Now Darky had his feelings, as good as anyone else" (Behan 1990: 309). "Darky" is translated "Ciemnoskóry" ("dark-skinned") (Behan 1982: 399), not generally perceived – at least not in the 1980s – as abusive. One could debate if Behan really is revealed as racist in the words quoted – possibly the person in question calls Behan "Mick" in a kind of prisoners' familiarity – but Polish readers cannot really have such a debate in the first place.

The censor found fault with some parts of Dos Passos's *Manhattan Transfer*. The review is handwritten and hard to read but the censor notes the anti-Semitism of the characters revealed on pages 128-129 of the new, 1958, Polish edition. It appears that the censor does not accuse Dos Passos of racism, that he understands the satirical intent, but he writes that "given the Polish reader" ("z względu na polskiego czytelnika") parts of the passage should be "przeredagowane" ("edited, redrafted" – a commonly used euphemism for censoring) (G-596, 68/3: 369). In the version published in 1958, we find a translation of the following passage (the speaker is Jimmy's uncle Jeff): "'City's overrun with kikes and low Irish ... I tell you the Catholics and the Jews are going to run us out of our own country...'" (Dos Passos 1986: 99). The Polish reads, in back translation: "'The city is overrun by lousy [parszywi] Jews and repulsive [wstrętni] Irish ... The Jews and Catholics are going to run us out of our own city before long'" (Dos Passos 1958: 128). A little further on there is "'the ignorance of these dirty kikes and shanty Irish'" (Dos Passos 1986: 100), whose back translation is "the ignorance of these Jews and raggedy [obdarci] Irish" (Dos Passos 1958: 129). As can be seen, the 1958 translation is attenuated but fairly close, despite the censor's concerns. In this respect it is similar to the 1931 version (by the same translator: the 1958 edition makes no mention of the existence of this earlier edition).

When it comes to black people, however, both pre-war and post-war translations of *Manhattan Transfer* temper the roughness of the American vernacular. One character, Congo, says, "'Hell I'm going out to Senegal and get to be a nigger'" (Dos Passos 1986: 44). In Polish he refers to himself as a "Murzyn" (Dos Passos 1958: 51) (the pre-war version also uses the word "Murzyn", with a small "m" throughout). The Polish reader is shielded not so much from American racism as from the ribaldry of conversation and the subtleties of relations between the characters. Later, Congo explains how he got his nickname, again using the word "nigger": "'When I very leetle I first go to sea dey call me Congo because I have curly hair an dark like a nigger'" (Dos Passos 1986: 207). In Polish "Murzyn" is used (Dos Passos 1958: 280). The 1931 version also uses "murzyn" (Dos Passos 1931: 276).

When Stan says, "'Ah guess youse one o dem dere foolish virgins'" his interlocutor replies ,"'Stan you're feeling your liquor, you're beginning to talk nigger-talk'" (Dos Passos 1986: 164). This is translated as "you're starting to talk nonsense" ("pleść trzy po trzy") (Dos Passos 1958: 219) in 1958 and "you're starting to blather Negro stories" ("pleść murzyńskie historje") (Dos Passos 1931: 217) in 1931. Elsewhere, the upper-crust James

Merivale, "abandoned [...] to reverie" (Dos Passos 1986: 344), pictures himself making a speech at some social or business gathering: "Reminds me gentlemen of the old darky" (Dos Passos 1986: 345). Again, this is translated using a more respectful or at least neutral "Murzyn" in both Polish versions (Dos Passos 1958: 477; 1931: 472). Both Merivale and Congo use racist terms (if only in "reverie" in the former's case) but they function quite differently. When the word is "Murzyn" in both cases, Merivale is transformed into a condescending but not necessarily racist man, while Congo becomes a curiously anachronistic figure, minding his p's and q's even when referring to himself in the company of fellow immigrants and friends.

A similar respect is shown to the Chinese: "He [Jimmy Herf] walks faster, the chinks are terrible kidnappers" (Dos Passos 1986: 83). The neutral word for Chinese people is used in Polish (Dos Passos 1958: 106), perhaps counterproductively as the words are now less obviously Jimmy's free indirect discourse (no inverted commas are used either in the English or Polish). They are therefore more likely to be attributed to the author: Dos Passos, rather than Jimmy (a child) thinks Chinese are kidnappers.

In *Manhattan Transfer*, derogatory words for black people and Chinese are neutralised, with side effects that go beyond merely decreasing the book's superficial offensiveness, and in fact distort Dos Passos's picture of US society. The censor took pains to highlight the "Jewish question" but perhaps only to "cover" himself. In any case the pejorative tone with reference to Jews (if not all the actual epithets) is kept in the translation. We might speculate that this is because in Jeff's tirade Jews are mixed in with Catholics: there is therefore less chance that the offending expressions might incite in Polish Catholics hatred for Jews. Even a hardened Polish, Catholic, anti-Semite could scarcely applaud Jeff's words since they express equal disdain for Catholics.

Failure to differentiate between a narrator who uses neutral language and characters who do not becomes a big problem in the Polish translation of Flannery O'Connor's short stories, where censorious intervention (from whatever precise source) plays havoc with O'Connor's carefully constructed linguistic system of differentiation between racists and non-racists. In short, with some exceptions, "Murzyn" or "Murzynka" (female), the neutral Polish term, is used to translate the following: "Negro", usually used by the third person omniscient narrator; "Negro", when used by characters within the stories; "nigger", when used by characters within the stories, either in quoted speech or free indirect discourse; "coloured man"; and "white nigger". "Murzyn" is used without regard to the interpersonal relations of the speakers, again with a few exceptions. The overall effect is one of "levelling". O'Connor and her characters – black and white – appear to have the same relationship to race matters and to belong to the same social class, even though class distinctions, often expressed through language, are often central to the stories.

In "A Stroke of Good Fortune", Ruby says, "It was a boil. A nigger woman up the road told me what to do and I did it and it went away" (O'Connor 1971: 104). As we have come to expect, "nigger woman" is neutralised as "Murzynka" (O'Connor 1975: 27). This unwarrantedly brings Ruby's speech a little closer to that of Flannery O'Connor as narrator. The use of language in general, and racist epithets in particular, to differentiate between various voices is especially marked in the story "Greenleaf". The social order to which the May family and the Greenleaf family belong is one which is greatly concerned by the class difference between Mays and Greenleafs and not at all concerned about the much deeper and more invidious division between black people and white.

Both Mrs May and her son Scofield are racists – at least judging by the language they use. Mrs May mutters to herself, "Some nigger's scrub bull" (O'Connor 1971: 311) at the start of the story. Scofield "would shout, 'Mamma don't like to hear me say it but I'm the best nigger-insurance salesman in this county!'" To which Mrs May would say, "'if you sold decent insurance, some *nice* girl would be willing to marry you. What nice girl wants to marry a nigger-insurance man?'" (O'Connor 1971: 315). In all three examples the translator avoids the word "czarnuch", favouring neutral words or avoiding translating the word "nigger" altogether. These avoidance tactics mean there is less distance between the characters and the author, since the author, Mrs May and Scofield all refer to black people as "Murzyni". But Flannery O'Connor is not the racist her characters are. The narrator, as in "A Stroke of Good Fortune", uses the word "Negro" – "He [Scofield] was what Negroes call a 'policy man'" (O'Connor 1971: 315) – very clearly setting herself apart from the characters she writes about. This distance is eliminated in the translation – to the narrator's cost in this case, since the characters do remain racists in the Polish version.

In "He [Scofield] said there was more money in nigger-insurance than any other kind, and before company, he was very loud about it" (O'Connor 1971: 315) the author temporarily abandons her own point of view (and inverted commas) and adopts that of Scofield, who is the kind of person who would call black people "niggers" even in company. Here too, however, the translator takes no chances. The Polish reads, "He claimed there was more money to be made in this kind of insurance than in others and he was quick to boast about it in company" ("Twierdził, że na tym rodzaju ubezpieczeń zarabia się więcej niż na innych, i chętnie się tym chwalił w towarzystwie") (O'Connor 1975: 111). Not only do Scofield and Southern "company" come out as less racist but the whole artistic device of free indirect discourse is missing since the words seem to come from the point of view of the narrator, unmarked in any way by Scofield's vocabulary. This might be described as "levelling upwards" in that the characters' language is raised up to that of civilised society, as represented by the narrator/O'Connor herself.

Mrs May does not use the word "nigger" indiscriminately. When she drives to the Greenleafs' farm she asks the children: "'Where's the colored man?'" (O'Connor 1971: 324). Yet this, too, is translated "Gdzie jest wasz Murzyn?" ("Where is your black man?") (O'Connor 1975: 123). Mrs May uses at least slightly more acceptable language in front of children. In translation, though, her consideration for youthful susceptibilities is missing: black people are always and everywhere "Murzyni". Mrs May speaks to the black man on the Greenleafs' farm using the familiar "Ty" form (you singular). While this is a sign from translator to reader of the relations that exist between white and black people, it might also be interpreted simply as the presumptuous, over-familiarity of a land owner speaking to a labourer.

O'Connor does not go into any great detail about the nature and extent of, for example, Scofield's racism. This means that his occasional use of the word "nigger" represents the fleeting chance the reader gets (if permitted by the translator) to form an opinion on this aspect of his character. The same is true in many of O'Connor's stories. The racism is so deeply engrained that it need only be revealed with an off-hand reference to "niggers". When this is missing from the translation the stories are not set against the proper background and when the word "czarnuch" *does* appear – for appear it does – it seems to be the exception, not the rule, of the Southern society portrayed by O'Connor. The translations in which "czarnuch" appears are "The Displaced Person" and "Judgement Day".

The word "nigger" or "niggers" appears over 30 times in "The Displaced Person", usually in the speech of characters and in a few instance in free indirect discourse, for example: "The next thing to go, she reminded herself, will be niggers" (O'Connor 1971: 205). The failure to shift the tense for reported speech is the clue here. If it were the narrator's voice we were hearing here it would be "The next thing to go, she reminded herself, would be..." This is translated with the word "Murzyn" (O'Connor 1975: 70). Polish does not shift tenses in reported speech so the lexical choice is the only indicator that the author is using free indirect discourse. That indicator is gone in the translation.

However, it seems the translator had recourse to the word "czarnuch" under the sheer weight of numbers. It is so insistently repeated throughout the story that it becomes impossible to ignore – though not impossible to tone down. "Czarnuch" appears just a handful of times. One passage will illustrate this. The words are spoken by Mrs McIntyre: "'The niggers don't leave – they stay and steal. A nigger thinks...'" (O'Connor 1971: 203). In Polish this becomes "The Negroes don't even wait to go. They stay here and steal. The nigger thinks…" ("Murzyni nawet nie czekają na odejście, siedzą tutaj i kradną. Czarnuch uważa…") (O'Connor 1975: 67). Of two occurrences of the word "nigger" the translator translates one faithfully. In "Judgement Day" the tally comes to over 30. In the translation "czarnuch" appears less than half as often.

This lack of consistency, or half-heartedness, often has detrimental effects on the translation. An illustration of this is the 1966 version of *Huckleberry Finn*. It is a little more adventurous than the 1898 version mentioned earlier (it is a fresh translation), using "czarniuch" (sic) a number of times in chapter six, when Huck's father is giving out (Twain 1966: 32). However, "Murzyn" is also used in the passage: the translator stops short of faithfully capturing the all-pervasiveness of racism. Elsewhere too, in the 1966 version, we find "Murzyn" for "nigger", e.g.: "he had an uncommon level head, for a nigger" (Twain 2001: 225). This time the speaker is Huck. It seems the translator or the censor did not like to admit the possibility that even sympathetic characters used racist language as a matter of course. As a result, the post-war Polish reader was deprived of an important dimension of the tale. Consistency would in this case have served the Polish reader better: even if "Murzyn" rather than "czarnuch" were used the reader would have a better appreciation of the blanket racism of the South that causes even Huck to speak of his companion in the same way that his father does.

Erskine Caldwell's *Georgia Boy* shows the same problem in translation, although it is less acute because the indictment of racism in this collection of humorous stories is less powerful. The narrator's parents occasionally refer to Handsome Brown and other black people as "darkies". His mother speaks of "'the best darkey we ever had'", "'that poor innocent darkey'" and "'a poor innocent colored boy'" (Caldwell 1950: 49, 122, 151). As terms of endearment go, this may not be very endearing but the tone is far from the vicious racism of Ned, who says at one point: "'I'll bash your head in with this rock! You hear me, nigger!'" (Caldwell 1950: 215). In all these examples, the Polish translation is "Murzyn", "Murzynek" or "czarny". "Murzynek" might be construed as insultingly condescending but that still leaves the problem of Ned addressing a black person in terms inappropriately close to those used by the family. To make matters worse, on one occasion when the mother uses the word "darkey" (Caldwell 1950: 49) the translation goes so far as to use "czarnuch" (Caldwell 1973: 27), presenting the reader with mixed messages. In addition, the narrator at one point says, "one of the *Negro* boys" (Caldwell 1950: 121; emphasis added). This is in marked distinction from his mother and father – but only in the English, as it is translated with the adjective "murzyński", which is just the word his parents mostly use in the translation. The distance between the views of the narrator and his parents is reduced in this way. The English reader sees that the narrator has outgrown the racism of his parents and of his background in general but it is a little less obvious to the Polish reader.

Charles Portis's first person narrated novel *True Grit* also illustrates the danger of inconsistency. In one episode, a train conductor says to a black man, Yarnell Poindexter, "'Get that trunk out of the aisle, nigger!'" (Portis 2011: 16). Somewhat unusually, the translator uses the word "czarnuch" (Portis 1973: 14). The story continues thus: "I replied to him in this way: 'We will the move the trunk but there is no reason for you to be so hateful about it.' He did not say anything to that but went on taking tickets. He saw that I had brought to all the darkies' attention how little he was" (Portis 2011: 16). The translator misses the racism of "darkies", translating it as "czarni" ("blacks") (Portis 1973: 15) although the narrator, Mattie Ross, is no abolitionist. This is only a small episode in the novel (Poindexter is a minor character), one of few mentions of race, and therefore of key importance to understanding the issue. The translator has given the impression that Mattie Ross is something she is not and there is no opportunity in the rest of the book for the reader to correct this judgement.

The 1958 translation of *Uncle Tom's Cabin*, like the post-war version of *Huckleberry Finn*, shows a little more willingness to tackle the racist language of nineteenth century white Americans but "Murzyn" is still often used in place of the original's "nigger". In the original we have, for instance, "'them high forrads al'ays shows calculatin' niggers [...] Now, a nigger of that ar heft and build...'" (Stowe 1909: 153), spoken by a trader, while the Polish not only uses "Murzyn" both times, but also does not attempt to differentiate the speaker's accent from that of the narrator ("takie czoło zawsze znamionuje przemyślnego Murzyna [...]. Wiadomo, że Murzyn tak zbudowany...") (Stowe 1958: 53). However, there is also the following back translation of the original's "'Some folks don't believe there is pious Niggers, Shelby'" (Stowe 1909: 10): "There are those who don't believe in these pious niggers [smoluchy]" (Stowe 1958: 20). As in the translation of *Huckleberry Finn*, it may be argued that this inconsistency means Polish readers see gradations of racism where none were intended in the original. In chapter one, entitled "A Man of Humanity", Haley contrasts himself with a former associate in the slave trading business, Tom Loker, "the very devil with niggers" (Stowe 1909: 14). Since Haley in translation calls them "Murzyni" some of the irony is lost. In the original, Haley's use of the word "nigger" puts him on the same level as Loker, though he does not know it. In the Polish translation Haley does – it is true – use racist terms but less often, damaging the overall effect.

Evasive tactics can be found in translations of O'Casey's *I Knock at the Door*, Vonnegut's *Cat's Cradle*, D.H. Lawrence's "Monkey Nuts" from

England, My England, Dreiser's *Sister Carrie*, Waugh's *Handful of Dust* and Maugham's *The Moon and Sixpence*. In *The Moon and Sixpence*, as in *Thy Tears Might Cease*, a mention of "nigger minstrels" (Maugham 1935: 45) is softened to "black singers" ("murzyńscy piosenkarze") (Maugham 1959: 43), a much vaguer term than the original's reference to the white-face music hall acts of nineteenth century America. The minstrels come up again in act one of O'Casey's play, *Red Roses for Me*. When he hears that a "Minsthrel Show" is being organised, Roory O'Balacaun replies "I'm one o' th' men meself, but I don't stand for a foreign Minsthrel Show bein' held, an' the Sword of Light gettin' lifted up in th' land. We want no coon or Kaffir industry in our country" (O'Casey 1956: 280). This time (1961), the translator makes some effort to capture the speaker's unpleasantness, translating "Kaffir" as "kefirskie", but she does not follow through with "coon" (O'Casey 1961: 58; act 1). (The translator also fails to translate the obscenity hidden in Roory's "Irish" surname: O'Balacaun.)

The narrator's flash of anger in *Cat's Cradle* ("I called Bokonon a jigaboo bastard" (Vonnegut 1963: 229)) is less mean-spirited in translation ("I said Bokonon was an old black son of a bitch" (Vonnegut 1971: 201)). O'Casey's stream-of-consciousness style indictment of British imperialism in *I Knock at the Door* is toned down. In the Polish version of "…far more important than Gladstones an' Gordons who are here today an' gone tomorrow where the good niggers go…" (O'Casey 1971: 76) the word for "niggers" is "Murzyni" (O'Casey 1963: 102). His pen portrait of a Jewish glazier repeatedly refers to the man as "the Jew" (O'Casey 1971: 135-137) where the Polish version – perhaps for stylistic rather than censorious reasons – uses various pronouns (and faithfully reproduces the anti-Semitism of the Irish characters that come into contact with the glazier (O'Casey 1963: 187-188)). The Irish-American Shaughnessy is abused (behind his back) as "'a slow, greedy "mick"!'" by Hurstwood in *Sister Carrie* (Dreiser 1959a: 277). In Polish translation, Shaughnessy is still abused but without reference to nationality (Dreiser 1959b: 356).[4] An example from Scott Fitzgerald's "The Diamond as Big as the Ritz" once again shows that Italians are more likely – in translation – to feel the force of the original's slur, although in this case the speaker is probably not a racist: "'Hey, I can speak Italian! My mother was a wop'", says one character (Fitzgerald 1986: 94). In Polish the word "makaroniarka" (feminine of "makaroniarz") is used (Fitzgerald 1973: 78). The translator of Doris Lessing's *Five Short Novels* (some of which are set in Africa) nearly always changes the numerous derogatory words for black Africans to neutral terms, except on one or two occasions. She also permits words like "'Gooks'" (Lessing 1960: 251) to be equally offensive in Polish (Lessing 1956: 345).

Ulysses in translation shies away from the word "nigger", which occurs eight times in the original, as in, for example, the phrase "where the bad niggers go" (Joyce 1994: 224). Here and elsewhere, "Murzyni" is used in translation (Joyce 1981: 229). "Czarnuch" does appear, in the translation of "Of all de darkies Massa Pat was verra best. […] Lay you two to one Jenatzy licks him ruddy well hollow. Jappies? High angle fire, inyah!" (Joyce 1994: 452). Also, "Jappies" is translated with the (at least mildly) pejorative "Japońcy" (Joyce 1981: 461). However the tendency is to attenuate.

A notable exception to the rule is the 1970 translation of *Brideshead Revisited*. When Rex Mottram fails to understand what a "mixed marriage" is he says, "'How d'you mean "mixed"? I'm not a nigger or anything'" (Waugh 1962: 184). The translation preserves the derogatory term (Waugh 1970: 177). Similarly, "dago", which occurs a few times in speech (Waugh 1962: 49, 259), is translated with the pejorative "mieszaniec" ("half-breed") (Waugh 1970: 47, 249).

John Updike's short story "The Witnesses" contains the innocent enough words "Negro men and Puerto Rican women" (Updike 1973: 71), faithfully and accurately rendered in Polish as "Murzyni i Portorykanki" (Updike 1978: 67). But there is a problem here. Despite the best efforts of the censors, Poles knew that everything was censored – certainly by 1978 when this translation was published. Poles, used to reading between the lines, used to decoding Aesopian language, outguessing the censors and most of all used to the indiscriminate use of the word "Murzyn", even in contexts where a racist word was more likely, may have thought that the original in fact used pejorative terms here. This could have been strengthened by the ambivalent attitude to the civil rights movement displayed in another story in the same collection, "Marching Through Boston", where Richard Maple repeatedly mocks the oratorical style of the speakers.

The picture that has emerged is one of caution on the part of censors and/or translators. This is especially noticeable in the case of derogatory terms for black people and Jews, which are very often neutralised with little or no account taken of context or the difference between the authorial voice and the voice of fictional characters. Other nationalities and ethnic groups are more likely to feel the full weight in Polish of the source text's racist epithet. In particular, "makaroniarz" seems to have been freely used for "wop", whose offensiveness was perhaps not fully appreciated by Polish translators. The translation of Faulkner's *Wild Palms* is a particularly good example of this bias. The frequent occurrences of "nigger" in the original are always translated as "Murzyn" but "wop" is usually translated as "makaroniarz". Nevertheless, as we have seen, "Micks" and "dagos" etc. are also sometimes neutralised. The picture is somewhat mixed. For example, the translation of Chandler's *Farewell My Lovely* (1969) preserves the accumulation of racist terms in the opening chapters, while the Polish versions of James Baldwin's *Go Tell it On the Mountain* (1966) and Mario Puzo's *The Godfather* (1976) both scrupulously render the racist epithets used by the characters in the original texts. In addition, the translation of Caldwell's *Tragic Ground* even uses a pejorative term where the original has the less insulting "colored". However, the context of the original does suggest the speaker was not favourably disposed to the person in question: "'that old fat colored woman'" (Caldwell 1979: 70). The speaker here is the main character, Spence, who has earlier used the word "nigger" (Caldwell 1979: 7), translated as "czarnuch" (Caldwell 1961: 8). A similar argument can be made for another substitution of "czarnuch" for a less insulting English word, this time in Waugh's *Brideshead Revisited*. In the original, the speaker, Boy Mulcaster, is, if not explicitly racist, then certainly coarse and narrow-minded. He has already had to be told that the black musicians at the party he is attending are "'not animals in a *zoo*, Mulcaster, to be *goggled at*'" (Waugh 1962: 195). Mulcaster speaks: "'Not a soul in the place I ever set eyes on before – all black fellows'" (Waugh 1962: 196). Somewhat unusually, the translator took the step of translating "black fellows" as "czarnuchy" (Waugh 1970: 189). The narrator uses the word "Negroes" (Waugh 1962: 197); the translator replies with "Murzyni" (Waugh 1970: 189).

Generally, however, the replacement of neutral terms in the source text by racist terms in the Polish is rare. I know of only two other cases in which the original is unambiguously neutral and the translation pejorative. The first is Jerzy Krzysztoń's translation of the words "a Jewish travelling salesman" in Sherwood Anderson's *Winesburg* (Anderson 1946: 138). He uses the pejorative "Żydek" (the diminutive of "Jew") (Anderson 1977: 224) to describe this incidental character, who is described in the original as looking "unwashed" but otherwise attracts no negative comments either from the narrator or any characters. The second is in Hammett's "The Farewell Murder", where the Continental Op's words "the black man" (Hammett 1984: 220) are translated using the word "czarnuch" (Hammett 1990: 159). This is an exception that proves the rule, however: the translation was published in 1990. Institutional censorship was lifted in April 1990, with the law taking effect from the 6th of June but it had ceased to function in 1989, even before it was removed from the statute books (*Kalendarium* 2007: 520).

Comparison of pre-war practices with those of the People's Poland strongly suggests that the authorities' injunctions against racist epithets coincided with the widely accepted convention in translation. The tendency was to treat readers like impressionable but not very clever children who would automatically think an author was a racist if a racist word appeared in his book, or worse still – that if racist language is allowed in books then racism is acceptable in real life too. The fear that readers might be so naïve can only have been amplified by the nature of People's Poland, where every novel that was published appeared under the aegis of the state. In the clash between forthright western authors who permit their characters to say unpleasant, even despicable things, and polite and proper Polish translators, the latter were doomed to victory as they had institutional censorship on their side. The side-effects frequently went against the official propaganda line about the reactionary, and racially and socially divided West. On the one hand, prominence was given to foreign books and authors who highlighted racial divisions and exploitation, especially in the United States. But, on the other hand, passing references to "Micks" or "niggers" are sometimes the only clue to the existence of racism. For some characters it is words like "black" or "Negro" that are marked. For a white character from the deep South in Flannery O'Connor's fiction to refer to a black man as a Negro or even as a person is to mark himself out as a bleeding heart liberal. In Polish translation the situation is often reversed: the user of the word "nigger"/ "czarnuch" is – as would be the case in polite, educated Polish society – marked. This misses the point. Scofield, in "Greenleaf", *is* polite society. By intervening in "defence" of black people and Jews – less often Italians, Chinese and other nationalities – translators and/or censors present Polish readers with less deeply entrenched racism. Half-measures do not work. Translating some but not all racist epithets often means that prejudice, rather than the norm – a state of affairs or of the mind that requires no comment other than a one-word epithet – becomes, in Polish, an exception.

1986 saw the translation of Philip Roth's *Portnoy's Complaint*, something of a breakthrough in terms of social mores in prudish, People's Poland. As well as the vulgarisms, Roth's translator unflinchingly translates the plentiful racist epithets into similarly offensive Polish with just a few exceptions. "Chink" (Roth 1969: 34) becomes the neutral "'Chińczyk'" (Roth 1986: 42) and "'Hebe eyes'" (Roth 1969: 210) becomes "Jewish eyes" (Roth 1986: 205) but elsewhere "kike" (Roth 1969: 180) becomes the very insulting "parch" (Roth 1986: 175) and "nigger" is generally translated "czarnuch", although "dago" (Roth 1969: 182) is mistranslated as "makaroniarskie" (Roth 1986: 177). Similarly, the 1987 translation of the Hammett short story "Dead Yellow Women" preserves many of the original's derogatory words for Chinese people (Hammett 1987).

In 1986, Jack London's *A Daughter of the Snows* reappeared in Polish translation after nearly 40 years, complete with its glorification of Teutons in the passage beginning "'We are a race of doers and fighters, of globe-encirclers and zone-conquerors'" and including such sentiments as "'The Negro has adaptability, but he is servile and must be led'" (London 1962: 67; 1986: 53). Also present and correct in the Polish translation are the words "'There must be a reason for the dead-status of the black, a reason for the

Teuton spreading over the earth as no other race has ever spread'" (London 1962: 114) – although in translation, the development of black people has merely stopped ("czarni zatrzymali się od tylu lat w swoim rozwoju") (London 1986: 93). It should be noted, however, that London does not use derogatory words for the non-Teutonic races, and the book also contains the line "'It's a common characteristic of all peoples,' he proceeded, 'to consider themselves superior races, – a naïve, natural egoism, very healthy and very good, but none the less manifestly untrue'" (London 1962: 66).

Earlier still, in 1981, a time when censorship was very weak, Philip K Dick's *The Man in the High Castle* had appeared in Polish. The novel presents an alternative reality in which Germany and Japan won World War Two. Racial tensions in the occupied USA are reflected in frequent use by characters of derogatory terms for Japanese, Italians, Jews and occasionally black people – often in passages of free indirect discourse. These are usually kept in translation. Within the alternative reality portrayed by Dick there is a book which portrays an alternative reality in which Germany and Japan *did* lose the war. Without going into all the complications of this fictional set up and the sympathies and motivations of the various characters in the novel, it is enough to say that the Polish translator, publishers and censors trusted readers to make their own judgments about the racism that is undoubtedly in the book, even if the book is not itself racist. However, certain taboos remained. Where the original has "backward people in Africa and Asia" (Dick 2001: 154) the translation refers to backward *regions* (Dick 1981: 143).

By 2003 the following line from Zadie Smith's *White Teeth* was translated with all the abuse intact (though the translator appears to have mistaken "wog" for "wop"): "Killed by the Hun, the Wogs, the Chinks, the Kaffirs, the Frogs, the Scots, the Spics, the Zulus, the Indians (South, East and Red)..." (Smith 2001: 89). The fear that Polish readers might understand this as official, high-culture approval of racism seemed to have faded (Smith 2003: 90).

---

[1] This was a feature of post-war Hungary too (Scholz 2011: 215).

[2] It was common practice before the 1930s to write the names of nationalities and races with a small letter in Polish. In quoting I follow the practice of the times from when the material under discussion comes.

[3] It should be noted, however, that writers such as Booker Washington, W.E.B. Du Bois, James Weldon Johnson, Countee Cullen and Ishmael Reed went untranslated in People's Poland, although a volume of Du Bois's autobiography had appeared in Polish in 1905.

[4] The translation was done before World War Two but it was still subject to post-war censorship.

154

Chapter 6
Children

In terms of sheer numbers, translations for children and the young dwarf translated literature for grown ups. In the period 1944 to 1963, London, Curwood, Cooper and Kipling each had combined print runs of over half a million books, with Hugh Lofting and A.A. Milne not far behind them (Bromberg 1966: 137-138). For example the tenth edition of Curwood's *Nomads of the North* had a print run of 50,250; the sixth edition of *The Voyages of Doctor Dolittle* had a run of 150,300; the eighth edition of *Treasure Island* had a run of 100,275 and so on. Compared to the one and only ever edition of *With Sun in our Blood* (10,350) these are impressive indeed. However, these numbers are in turn dwarfed by Polish writers for children: Wanda Chotomska wrote over *200* books for children and the young (Chotomska 2013: 11). From 1944/45 to 1980 seven million books by Chotomska appeared in print. For Janina Porazińska, another Polish children's writer, the figure is eight million and for Jan Brzechwa the figure is 18.2 million. In this period, Brzechwa was second only to Henryk Sienkiewicz (also popular with children), whose books had a combined print run of 18.7 million (Czarnik 1993: 229). Jack London's books had a combined print run of 4.8 million in the same period – the most of any translated author (no distinction is made here between books for children and books for adults). Twain, Curwood and Fenimore Cooper had from two to three million each, while A.A. Milne, Robert Louis Stevenson, Lucy Maud Montgomery and Rudyard Kipling each had between one and two million (Czarnik 1993: 249-250). From 1980 to 1989, the average print run for adult belles lettres was around the 40,000 mark; for children's it was closer to 100,000 (*Ruch Wydawniczy* 1990: 92).

In the immediate post-war years, translations made up from 12% to 17% of books for the young, rising to 42.6% in 1949. This proportion remained high during the first half of the fifties but by 1956 had declined to 26.4%. In the early 1960s, translations constituted roughly 16% to 20% of books for the young (Frycie 1978: 237, 254-255). A little over 20% of books for children and the young published in 1989 were translations (*Ruch Wydawniczy* 1990: 60). Although in theory, and in some of the rhetoric, children were highly prized targets of indoctrination, children's books were the Cinderella of literature. In 1978, Halina Skrobiszewska calculated that only 3% of criticism in periodicals was of children's literature (Skrobiszewska 1978: 15). From 1945 to 1970, at least, reviewers of children's literature in translation distinctly favoured classics and Frycie calculates that 82.5% of all children's literature was ignored by reviewers (Frycie 1982: 220). Maria Ostasz counts 1,320 articles (including reviews, sketches, potted biographies) on children's literature in the years 1945 to 1956 in Poland and concludes that literary criticism of books for children and the young was not a "marginal phenomenon", though the situation deteriorated in later years (Ostasz 1999: 30, 31). However, a glance at the *Polish Periodicals Bibliography* (*Bibliografia Zawartości Czasopism*) shows that the number of articles on literature for grown-ups was far higher than the corresponding figure for children's literature. In 1954, in one month alone, to take a representative example, there are roughly 217 entries for "nauka o literaturze" ("literary science") and four for "theory and criticism of literature for children and the young". In the same month there are around 280 entries for belles lettres and five for literature for children. The bibliography is biased (it excludes a leading periodical for children) but even still, the total number of articles on adult's literature in 1954 alone is around 2,500.

Books like *Robinson Crusoe, Uncle Tom's Cabin* and *White Fang* were not originally written for children and adaptations were often made. Maria Zaleska's adaptation of James Fenimore Cooper had been popular before the war and Stanisław Stampfl adapted *Robinson Crusoe* in 1958. However, even the unabridged versions of Cooper that appeared after the war came out under the imprint of Iskry, which specialised in children's books. *White Fang, Treasure Island* and Curwood's *Nomads of the North* were also Iskry books, as was Owen Wister's western *The Virginian*. The difficulty of distinguishing between adaptations and translations has been discussed by Adamczyk-Garbowska, who writes that because Irena Tuwim's translation of *Winnie the Pooh* is addressed only to children (and not to adults too, like the original) it is more strictly speaking an adaptation than a translation (Adamczyk-Garbowska 1988: 139-142). In turn, Kruszewska-Kudelska notes that philosophy, naturalism, physiology and politics were cut from Polish adaptations of *Robinson Crusoe* and *Gulliver's Travels*, leaving behind adventure and fantasy and turning the narrators from satirists into bourgeois writers (Kruszewska-Kudelska 1978: 111-112). This could be considered a form of censorship but is excluded from this book for two reasons. One is that though it may indeed be hard to draw the dividing line between adaptation and translation with great precision, children's versions of *Gulliver's Travels* are almost certainly and uncontroversially on the adaptation side of the line. The other, more important, reason is that unabridged, unadapted versions of these works existed in Poland and one may compare them with the source texts. Indeed, the censor wrote of Jan Kott's introduction to the 1953 translation of *Robinson Crusoe* that it showed how the bourgeoisie had presented a false, truncated version of the book or one "fabricated by other writers" (G-386, 31/124: 517).

A report written by the chief of the Regional Office for Information and Propaganda in Olsztyn in 1946 reads in part:

> 'I believe we should devote 99% of our energy to subjugating young people, to freeing them from the influence of Polish teaching and to raising them in such a spirit that it will be possible to build a better and happier homeland on the basis of their friendship and spirit' (qtd. in Kossewska 2005: 206).

This fervour is reflected in the surviving censors' reviews from the Stalinist period, which Michał Rogoż has studied. However, most of the books were translations from Russian (Rogoż 2013: 107). Excluding books that have "become" children's literature, the only mentions of children's literature translated from English that I have come across in the archives are of Rose Wuhl's *The Cap of Wisdom and Other Tales* and Oscar Wilde's fairy tales. Three reviews of the former, dating from 1950, are in the censors' files. Two are positive, recommending no changes. They commend the author for including social questions in the fairy tale and for making a connection between kings and capitalism (G-145, 31/25: 93-98). The third reviewer is cooler, though he or she still recommends publication, albeit with a small print run. This review describes the author as progressive by Western European standards and the book itself as "bourgeois-progressive, liberal-humanist; it leads children into a false, fairy-tale world". The review provides an insight into the ideology of the times: "In general the traditional fairy-tale form is an unfortunate choice – it would be better to avoid it in new, contemporary books!" (G-145, 31/25: 93).[1] Despite such misgivings, the censor only proposes one small intervention: changing the colour of a boat's sails from red. No reason is given but presumably the problem is that red is the colour of the Russian revolution and the author therefore ruffled some feathers.[2]

The Oscar Wilde reviews also date from 1950. One is straightforwardly positive, mentioning the strong element of fantasy in the tales (G-148, 31/69: 83), but the other censor is not too happy with "The Happy Prince". The handwriting is hard to decipher but it appears the question of God bothered the censor, who also wrote, "similarly, 'The Nightingale and the Rose' is too sickly-sweet for me". The proposed print run was only 10,000 – very low for a children's book but still higher than that of *The Cap of Wisdom*: 7,400. The final verdict is left blank (G-148, 31/69: 84) but the stories, under the title *The Remarkable Rocket*, appeared in 1950.

One finds few cuts in children's fiction translated from English (1945-1989, especially after 1956) that can be attributed to politics, narrowly understood. Numerous scholars have pointed to the freeness with which children's literature (and especially the inferior kind) is treated by translators and publishers (O'Sullivan 2005: 77, 98) but I have not seen any large-scale cutting and bowdlerisation in the books studied here. This was not necessarily the case in all of the eastern bloc. The Russian translator of the *Wizard of Oz* intervened quite drastically at one point, adding an episode in which the companions consider how to save the Scarecrow, who is clinging to a pole in a river (Inggs 2011: 87). In the Polish translation, as in the original English, they seem relatively unconcerned. Anna Chilewska has demonstrated that the rebelliousness of Pippi in Astrid Lindgren's *Pippi Långstrump* was toned down significantly in the 1961 Polish translation: the "passages where Pippi is at her most rebellious were not translated into Polish" (Chilewska 2009: 100). But Lindgren seems to have been too much for many adults, East and West, to take: a similar fate met *Madicken* in the US (where the book is known as *Mischievous Meg*), though English publishers/translators were less hasty to cut taboo subjects (Nikolowski-Bogomoloff 2009; see also O'Sullivan 2005: 83-85). Political the changes may be but they were not specifically socialist. However, as shown by the red sails in *The Cap of Wisdom*, there was always a chance that one might accidentally blot one's copybook. Wanda Chotomska relates how the word "patyk" ("twig, stick") in one of her children's television scripts was changed to "kijek" ("stick, club") because it happened that "Patyk" was also the surname of an official in the television company (Chotomska 2013: 14).

Although there may have been few cuts, censorship made itself felt in the selection of books for translation, especially in the years 1949 to 1955. The 1951 list of books to be withdrawn from circulation has a section devoted to children's literature (*Cenzura PRL...*2002). It includes Burnett's *A Little Princess* (all editions), Hughes's *Tom Brown's School Days*, and a number of Lucy Maud Montgomery's books. Even earlier, in 1946, a reaction against the magic wands and apoliticism of books for children had been visible on the pages of periodicals *Kuźnica* and *Odrodzenie* (Ostasz 1999: 38). Under Stalinism, socialist realism was promoted in children's literature too, with fantasy only permitted in fairy tales because at the time it was thought harmful to the development of children.[3] For a time there was hostility even to the Brothers Grimm (Skotnicka 2008: 441n), and an edition of Hans Christian Andersen stories was blocked by the censor in Poznań for being outmoded with its "'glorification of unearned wealth'" (qtd. in Nowak 2012: 143-144). For children, socialist realism meant a certain kind of subject matter and ideological zealousness. There were a lot of stories about peace because the class struggle and the party line were deemed too complicated

(Jarosiński 1999: 277-280). Common themes also included work (farming, mining), mechanisation, collectivisation and co-operation between farmers and industrial workers (Bereta 2013: 75-76).

A flavour of the times can be got from reading Grzegorz Lasota's speech to the Writers' Union in 1951 during a session devoted to literature for children and the young. He talks of children being the key to building socialism and later communism in Poland and praises books about the "romanticism of the revolutionary struggle" (Lasota 1951: 113, 119). He stresses the need for role models in children's literature, giving as an example Feliks Dzierżyński, the Pole who was the first head of the Cheka. "Our literature should show a positive hero in the process of development, in the process of the fight of the old with the new, in the process of the strengthening of his outlook in a warm, human collective". Children's literature should not shy away from bad and dirty things. Using the royal "we", Lasota claims Poles do not want saccharine literature or "sugar-coated heroes" ("lukrowani bohaterowie"). Out, too, are psychological naturalism and children of the inter-war intelligentsia filled with "internal contradictions" (Lasota 1951: 114). Lasota condemns "obscurantism and medieval clericalism" and among bad writers he includes Brand, Baxter (Brand and Baxter were actually the same writer), Karl May and Maine Reid, all of whom wrote westerns (Lasota 1951: 116).

Wanda Grodzieńska and Seweryn Pollak addressed the same meeting in terms similar to Lasota's, providing some explanation of the hostility to "mysticism" in children's books. In pre-war books children often receive unexpected inheritances and there are often "supernatural forces" at work. From here it is only a step away to religiosity (Grodzieńska and Pollak 1951: 132). These two are more forgiving of fantasy, reassuring listeners that it does not teach children to think unrealistically and pointing out that Gorky praised folklore, which, he claimed, knows no pessimism (Grodzieńska and Pollak 1951: 142-143). However, fantasy "must be based on logical thinking; it cannot be detached from reality". Kipling's talking animals are all right but the animals in Doctor Dolittle books are "perverted, devoid of their natural characteristics; Lofting's books merely pile improbability on improbability" (Grodzieńska and Pollak 1951: 144). In 1949, *Doctor Dolittle's Circus* had been passed, somewhat grudgingly, by the censors (Rogoż 2013: 106).

The implications for literature translated from English under Stalinism are clear: there would be a lot less of it since not many English language writers wrote books about Feliks Dzierżyński or other revolutionary heroes. In fact, there was a drop in the number of Polish-authored children's books as writers found it difficult to conform to the demands. The gap was filled with translations, mostly from Soviet countries, of books about the everyday environment of children, such as home and school (Rogoż 2013: 101;

Pacławski and Kątny 1996: 172-173). Fairy tales did not disappear entirely but "books for girls" did (Pytlos 2013: 113) and adventure books were frowned on by the censors, "though for want of better models many such books were tolerated, especially if they appeared to be ideologically neutral" (Rogoż 2013: 106). Marta Nadolna-Tłuczykont quotes a critic, Maria Gutry, from the mid 1940s on the subject of novels for girls: "'they teach coquetry and give the mirage of an easy life restricted to visits, parties, excursions and picnics'". Gutry explicitly ruled L.M. Montgomery out of this class of writing but, as seen, Montgomery did make the list of books for withdrawal from libraries (Nadolna-Tłuczykont 2013: 57). Monika Adamczyk-Garbowska notes that English translations were hit especially hard by Stalinism because so many English children's books were fairy tales and fantasy (Adamczyk-Garbowska 1988: 42).

Later (pre-1989) Polish scholars frequently mentioned the Stalinist period's dislike of escapist fairy tales, adventure stories and science fiction, though understandably they tend to refer to it in a roundabout way, or as if it were no more than a school of thought in pedagogy (Skrobiszewska 1971: 337-339; Białek 1978: 123). Czabanowska-Wróbel goes so far as to claim that books by Białek, Kuliczkowska and Frycie (especially his *Literatura dla dzieci i młodzieży w latach 1945-1970*) are obsolete. Quoting Heska-Kwaśniewicz, she describes them as "'ideologically entangled'" (Czabanowska-Wróbel 2013: 16). However, it is worth bearing in mind Skrobiszewska's observation that calls to abandon sickly-sweet stories about privileged children had been around long before Lasota. Progressive writers and educators, she wrote in 1971, had for decades been calling for the children of peasants and workers to appear in books in roles other than beneficiaries of rich children's charity.[4] But in 1901 there had already been a reaction against this condescending treatment of poor children and the portrayal of bourgeois ideals as desirable. Skrobiszewska also quotes Karpowicz from 1904 complaining about nature and history stories being written as if the whole world existed merely for the pleasure of aristocrats' children (Skrobiszewska 1971: 541-542). Moreover, Ursula Le Guin's 1974 article "Why Are Americans Afraid of Dragons?" tells of disapproval for escapist books in 1960s America (Hunt 2001: 174-175). Jarosiński points up the weaknesses of children's socialist realist verse (Jarosiński 1999: 277-297) but the legacy of Stalinism in children's literature was not all bad or at any rate some of the period's concerns were not so unreasonable. Skrobiszewska claims that standards in children's literature in Poland rose after the war (Skrobiszewska 1971: 337) and Pacławski and Kątny, writing after the end of censorship, agree (Pacławski and Kątny 1996: 167). Adamczyk-Garbowska concludes from her study of nine English children's books that the quality of their translations was not related to when they were translated but rather to the translator. However, she does note that downright bad translations were fewer after the war. The editing was better, corrections were made to re-editions and fewer "howlers" passed into print (Adamczyk-Garbowska 1988: 173-174).

The thaw affected children's literature too, filtering through to school reading lists in the academic year 1957-58 (Skotnicka 2008: 66). In late 1955, Wanda Grodzieńska wrote in *Nowa Kultura* that socialist realism in children's books had been misunderstood, leading to joyless books (Ostasz 1999: 73). *Anne of Green Gables* returned to circulation. Adventure stories like *Treasure Island*, fantasies like *The Wonderful Wizard of Oz*, and even the perverted animals of Doctor Dolittle found places on publishers' lists. Westerns came in from the cold, like, for example, Owen Wister's *The Virginian*, accompanied by a foreword dissociating the book from the image of the wild west propagated by Hollywood (Kieruzalska 1977: 8). Some difference in emphasis can be seen, however, even after the end of Stalinism. Krystyna Kuliczkowska mentions a 1964 article in *Kultura* about a series of children's books called "The Seven Adventures Club". The stories would have a basis in science and real-world knowledge. Another article, in *Nowe Książki* in 1970, claimed that adventure stories were no longer just about exotic and fantastic places and that 13 to 15 year olds now liked literary reportage and popular science. However, Kuliczkowska cites research showing that what 13 to 15 year olds really like most is, in fact, unsophisticated, escapist adventure stories (Kuliczkowska 1978: 102).

By the 1960s concern was growing over the casual sexism, racism and classism of children's books in the West. In particular, Enid Blyton (who was not published in Poland during the existence of the People's Republic) came under fire for the sexism of her Famous Five stories and the racism apparent in the Golliwog characters. In a 1975 British report entitled *Children's Reading Interests*, Richmal Crompton, W.E. Johns, and Anthony Buckeridge, none of whom enjoyed much of a career in post-war Poland, were marked as "non-quality" (Delaney 2013: 114n). Books that challenged the bourgeois values of older children's literature emerged. Lissa Paul illustrates the change using the example of Ursula Le Guin. The first three parts of her Earthsea trilogy, written from 1968 to 1972 are, in Le Guin's own words, written in a genre which is "'a male preserve: a sort of great game-park where Beowulf feasts with Teddy Roosevelt, and Robin Hood goes hunting with Mowgli, and the cowboy rides off into the sunset alone'". However, in the fourth part, *Tehanu*, published well over a decade later, there is no "traditional male hero" (Paul 1999: 116).

Michael Moorcock famously criticised Tolkien for writing "Epic Pooh" – that is, an infantile story (as in Winnie the Pooh) expanded to epic proportions. Tolkien, he complains, is conservative, and hankers after a safe, bucolic past of "petit bourgeoisie, the honest artisans and peasants, [...] the bulwark against Chaos" (Moorcock 1987: 123). Tolkien portrayed the evil goblins as mass-producers of utilitarian things of no beauty – an industrial proletariat, in other words (Grenby 2008: 155). One might expect socialism with its rhetoric of building a braver, better tomorrow to reject such writers as Tolkien, who pines nostalgically for "that Surrey of the mind, the Shire [from *Lord of the Rings*]" (Moorcock 1987: 125), and yet they were published. The three volumes of *Lord of the Rings* appeared in Polish from 1960 to 1963. It is true, however, that the Narnia stories by C.S. Lewis, whose conservatism Moorcock also found irksome, had to wait longer for publication. They were put out by PAX from the mid to late 1980s.

In the translation of the passage from *The Hobbit* mentioned by Grenby, describing the "goblin proletariat", one can in fact discern a few small evasions. Where the original has "They make no beautiful things, but they make many clever ones" (Tolkien 1997: 59) the translation omits cleverness, saying that they make no beautiful things but "they are good at other work" (Tolkien 1985: 52). The goblins especially hate "the orderly and the prosperous" (Tolkien 1997: 59) but in Polish back translation they hate those who "are happy and like order" (Tolkien 1985: 52). Thus, in Polish the thing to aspire to is happiness, not prosperity, though in both source and target text "order" is seen as desirable.

Some writers in the West, as in Poland, had been aware of the preponderance of middle class (orderly and prosperous?) heroes for some time. A German socialist book called *Fairy Tales for Working Children* was translated into English and published in 1925 in Chicago (Lathey 2010: 136) and Eve Garnett wrote *The Family from One End Street* in the 1930s about a working class family, while E.W. Hildick's *Jim Starling*, about a working class school, was written in the 1950s. Poland was not entirely unresponsive to the new winds blowing. Geoffrey Trease, a communist who has been credited with "drawing attention to the politically conservative bias of historical fiction" (Sarland 1999: 41), was translated into Polish in the 1950s (*Comrades for the Charter, Bows Against the Barons*) and 1960s (*A Thousand For Sicily*). Some of Hildick's books, including *Jim Starling*, were also translated. Other "progressive" writers fighting racism and sexism and challenging taboos in their books for children, such as Maurice Sendak, Judy Blume, Robert Leeson and Jan Needle, had less luck in Poland. None of these authors were translated. The reason may be simply that the new wave of socially aware books came a little too late to make an impact in the Polish People's Republic. Ursula Le Guin's *Tehanu*, for example, was only published in 1990. *A Wizard of Earthsea*, the first of the Earthsea books, was translated into Polish in 1983.

Leaving aside the more outlandish notions of Stalinism, Polish grown-ups, like grown-ups everywhere, generally want books for children to set good examples, teach children to share, be educational, character-building and so on (while children may just want an exciting adventure). If one takes the wide view then all literature is censored even before it gets to any official censoring institution, whether it be by commercial constraints, the writer's own prejudices or power relations in the publishing industry. However, the drive to censor is particularly strong with books for children. Society traditionally places greater restraints on writers of children's literature. Having said that, in the late 1960s the range of topics tackled in English language children's books opened up dramatically. Anne Scott MacLeod notes that in 1964 Roald Dahl ran into trouble for having an adult tell a child in *Harriet the Spy* that sometimes lying is necessary. By the mid 1970s, children's books dealing with topics such as rape, prostitution and drug abuse were accepted (MacLeod 2006: 127-129), although Alan Garner was still criticised for portraying "unsupervised sledging" in a 1977 book (Hunt 1999: 7).

A key difference between self-censorship of books for adults and books for children is that manipulation of children's texts is undertaken much more casually: authors of books for seven year olds deliberately and consciously leave out things they would include in books for adults or young adults and no one thinks any the worse of them. Few would even consider it censorship. Frank Baum writes in the introduction to his *The Wonderful Wizard of Oz*:

> the time has come for a series of newer 'wonder tales' in which the stereotyped genie, dwarf and fairy are eliminated, together with all the horrible and blood-curdling incident devised by their authors to point a fearsome moral to each tale. Modern education includes morality; therefore the modern child seeks only entertainment in its wonder-tales and gladly dispenses with all disagreeable incident.
>
> Having this thought in mind, the story of 'The Wonderful Wizard of Oz' was written solely to pleasure children of today. It aspires to being a modernized fairy tale, in which the wonderment and joy are retained and the heart-aches and nightmares are left out (Baum 1997: 3-4).

Polish translators worked with versions that may already have been censored in the source culture. For example, the Project Gutenberg edition of *The Voyages of Doctor Dolittle* contains the word "nigger" but not all printed versions do. In this respect we can see that the concerns of Polish adults do not always diverge so greatly from those of adults on the other side of the socialist-capitalist political divide. At times, the issue here is not so much the censorship of children's books by communists or socialists but by adults.

Adamczyk-Garbowska's account of the development of Polish children's literature shows that it freed itself from the requirement to be solemn and educational (and patriotic) later than its English counterpart (Adamczyk-Garbowska 1988: 148-149). She quotes an extraordinary passage from a 1927 book on children's literature in which Janina Porazińska is criticised for scaring children into neurasthenia and possibly even suicide by having all kinds of inanimate objects talk in one of her books. The pre-war translation of Carroll's books about Alice openly introduces the kind of moralising that Alice makes fun of in the original. However, changes were usually more subtle, consisting of attempts to make books more "child friendly" by referring to characters as "our hero" rather than by their names, or by using diminutives. For Adamczyk-Garbowska, this is nothing more than Polish conventions influencing translations of foreign literature, although it does deform the text (Adamczyk-Garbowska 1988: 150-152). Emer Delaney argues that using diminutives like this – albeit in English translations – changes "the perceived authorial attitude to childhood" and excludes the adult addressee (Delaney 2013: 115). Adamczyk-Garbowska deals with interference by publishers and censors in a separate section, entitled "the influence of non-literary factors on translations", dividing them into two types, pedagogic and politico-historical, which often are intertwined. An example of the former is the cutting of particularly sad or cruel scenes, which affects the 1958 translation of a Peter Pan book (Adamczyk-Garbowska 1988: 155-156). Karl May's books about Surehand and Winnetou were re-issued in 1956-57 with sadistic scenes (but also prolixity) cut (Skrobiszewska 1971: 301). Adamczyk-Garbowska does not give many examples of political censorship (she was writing in 1988 after all) but she does mention the disappearance of religion from certain parts of Thackeray's *The Rose and the Ring* and the avoidance of the issue of social class from one passage in an *Alice in Wonderland* translation in the early 1950s. She remarks that in those years books for children could not allude to the class nature of the book. The passage in question runs, "'I must be Mabel after all, and I shall have to go and live in that poky little house, and have next to no toys to play with, and oh! ever so many lessons to learn!'" The 1950s Polish version cut the reference to the scarcity of toys and the pokiness of the house (Adamczyk-Garbowska 1988: 157). However, both Maciej Słomczyński's 1972 translation and Robert Stiller's 1986 translation restore the reference to Mabel's relative poverty (Carroll 1972: 24; 1986: 20). Adamczyk-Garbowska's example dates from the Stalinist period but, as will be shown below, this kind of sensitivity to social class in translated children's books does not seem to have been the case in general. The major exception is the neglect of class markers in the speech of children.

When it comes to literature for the very young even Grodzieńska and Pollak are at something of a loss. It is all very well to say, for example, that books about schools should be about *socialist* schools (Grodzieńska and

Pollak 1951: 137) but their discussion of verses and tales for the youngest children is almost entirely limited to technical matters such as the desirability or otherwise of consonant clusters (Grodzieńska and Pollak 1951: 146). Adamczyk-Garbowska notes that by comparison with prose, little poetry for children was translated from English, attributing this to the nature of English poetry: it relies more heavily on word play and, stemming from the nursery rhyme tradition, uses mostly rhythmic, short words (one or two syllables), which are difficult to translate into Polish, with its typically long words (Adamczyk-Garbowska 1988: 43). Sure enough, the *Bibliography of Literature Translated into Polish Published Between 1945 and 1976 (Bibliografia literatury tłumaczonej na język polski wydanej w latach 1945-1976)* and its follow-ups for the years 1977 to 1980 do not list many authors of books for the very young (Oscar Wilde's fairy tales a notable exception), while in the 1980s publishers shied away from new titles, preferring re-editions and tried and tested translations (Pacławski and Kątny 1996: 185). The economic crisis of the 1980s meant hard times for the books industry in Poland: contemporary translations of children's literature were held up for many years and there was a lack of forward planning (Staniów 2013: 150).

In the narrow sense of not leaving anything out, the books for young adults that I have examined are faithful translations. Although, as mentioned above, Karl May's books were made less gory, the snapping, ripping, slashing and tearing, as well as the warm blood spurting from jugulars so characteristic of Jack London's *White Fang* and James Curwood's *Kazan, the Wolf-Dog*, are reproduced in all their bloodthirsty glory in Polish translations aimed at the young. In this respect, these books are not adaptations and they have not been brought into line with any Polish norms that may have existed of sparing young people graphic depictions of the horrors of life. "Now with her dulled and broken teeth at his throat she was lashing him with her sharp hind claws until the blood streamed from the old barbarian's sides and he bellowed like a choking bull" (Curwood 2003: n. pag.) from *Nomads of the North* is, if anything, even more vivid in translation: "She sank her rotting fangs into his throat and ploughed up his sides with her sharp claws until the old barbarian, streaming with blood, started bellowing like a slaughtered ox" ("Spróchniałe kły wpiła mu w gardło, orała boki ostrymi pazurami, aż stary barbarzyńca zlany krwią począł ryczeć jak zarzynany wół") (Curwood 1982: 21). The following line from *Nomads of the North*, but typical of London as well as Curwood, also closely follows the source text: "A little more and Maheegun's teeth would have snapped his shoulder, or slashed his throat to the jugular" (Curwood 2003: n. pag.). In back translation from the Polish this is "A little more and Mahigun's teeth would have crushed his shoulder, or torn open an artery" (Curwood 1982: 80). From *White Fang* we have "Major staggered to his feet, but the blood spouting from his throat reddened the snow in a widening path" (London s.d.: 210) which in Polish is just as bloody.[5] Similarly, *Treasure Island*, where the victims are human, is no less bloodthirsty in Polish than in English.

Death, though usually less gory, is a feature of books for younger children, like *The Wonderful Wizard of Oz* and C.S. Lewis's *Prince Caspian*. Here too, the Polish translators robustly communicate the unpleasantness to young Polish readers: the Wicked Witch of the East is squashed by Dorothy's house just as definitively in Polish as in English, with only her silver-shod feet protruding from under the house. The translator does not shrink from the Tin Woodman's massacre of the wolves sent to kill them or from the Scarecrow's twisting of King Crow's neck till he dies (Baum 1997: 143-145). In *Prince Caspian*, a dwarf says, "'But I always wondered if they didn't really drown 'em or cut their throats" (Lewis s.d.: 34). This is dutifully translated in the Polish version (Lewis 1985: 27), as is the decapitation of a witch in a fight (Lewis s.d.: 150; Lewis 1985: 121).

Nor are Polish children spared the seal clubbing and skinning in Kipling's *Jungle Book*: "...the men clubbed the seals on the head as fast as they could. Ten minutes later little Kotick did not recognise his friends any more, for their skins were ripped off from the nose to the hind flippers..." (Kipling 1939: 140) is translated "as is", no punches pulled.[6]

The modern day scholar, having read her Said, can point to the sordid exploitation implicit in much children's literature from England. Edward Said pointed out that *Robinson Crusoe* is about "'a European who creates a fiefdom for himself on a distant, non-European island'" (qtd. in Grenby 2008: 188).[7] Or, as Orwell put it, "We all live by robbing Asiatic coolies, and those of us who are 'enlightened' all maintain that those coolies ought to be set free; but our standard of living, and hence our 'enlightenment,' demands that the robbery shall continue" (Orwell 1998, vol. 13: 153). Polish scholarship was well aware of this. The 1955 afterword to the translation of *Roderick Random* (by an Englishman, George Bidwell, as it happens) has much to say about English colonisation, mentioning the fact that Roderick's father made his fortune "at the expense of the native inhabitants of South America" (Bidwell 1955, vol. 2: 276). Kipling, Burnett, Nesbit, Stevenson – did they all not write stories for and about the children of the exploiting class? The little princess in Burnett's story of the same name is the daughter of an Englishman exploiting a diamond mine in India so that his daughter may attend an expensive private school in Britain. Her mysterious neighbour lavishes his charity on her through the agency of an Indian servant, as if to make the exploitation theme all the clearer. *Treasure Island* is less nakedly colonial but the fact is that all that wealth on Spyglass Island was robbed from ships laden with the ill-gotten gains of colonial adventuring. Skrobiszewska resolutely defends Edith Nesbit, saying the children in *The*

Story of the Amulet are not from a wealthy family (Skrobiszewska 1971: 231) but we know better. They have a servant and their mother goes to Madeira to recuperate after giving birth. And yet perhaps Skrobiszewska was not so far off when she wrote elsewhere, in defence of Burnett, that the young care for the values of their heroes, not for their circumstances (Skrobiszewska 1973: 233). What do children understand of subalterns? Or, more to the point, what did the censors of the Polish People's Republic care of subalterns? They were not entirely insensitive to the subject – in 1950 they accused Jules Verne of glorifying colonialism and proposed changing parts of his *Deux ans de vacances* (Rogoż 2013: 108) – but it was not a very high priority, especially after 1956.

"One view of fiction", writes Charles Sarland,

> is that it constructs readers in specific ideological formations, and thus enculturates them into the dominant discourses of capitalism – class division, paternalism, racism. Such views are not totally fatalistic, but do require of readers a very conscious effort to read against texts, to deconstruct them in order to reveal their underlying ideology (Sarland 1999: 52).

When it comes to children's literature in translation, the Polish censors do not seem to have tried very hard to make that conscious effort.

Once the questionable books were allowed back into children's libraries after Stalinism, it seems little attention was paid to their colonial underbelly. No thoroughgoing attempts were made to re-write or "adapt" the books to make them more politically correct, although changes of individual words were made. The censors, as usual, were interested mainly in the surface level. Adamczyk-Garbowska gives the example of a racist play on words (Malaysians are "Malazy"-lazy) in Kipling's *Just So Stories* which was avoided in the post-war translation but not the pre-war version (Adamczyk-Garbowska 1988: 157). Despite such tinkering, it remains the case that in the Polish *Treasure Island*, for example, Long John Silver is just as ambiguous a character and also escapes in the end.[8] The power relations between the working classes and the ruling classes of Britain and the imperial designs that enable the child heroes to have such wizard adventures during their hols lie beyond the ken of the censors. If the word "nigger" should appear in the source text it will be excised from the translation but the underlying racism that sees Africa as "a wonderful country" for white people to bring back exotic stories from is still there.

And so, in *The Voyages of Doctor Dolittle*, the third, offensive sentence from the following passage is simply removed: "'He was the first man from that country to go abroad. He thought he was going to be eaten by white cannibals or something. You know what those niggers are – that ignorant!'" (Lofting 1923: 45). A few lines later, in the same story, related by Polynesia the parrot, there is the following offensive reference to Africans:

> 'Well, he brought back something which he *said* was The Sleeping Beauty. Myself, I think it was an albino niggeress. She had red hair and the biggest feet you ever saw. But Bumpo was no end pleased with her and finally married her amid great rejoicings' (Lofting 1923: 45-46).

The Polish avoids the slur "niggeress" but the general ribaldry at the expense of "Bumpo", the clownish African, is still there (Lofting 1985: 32-33). Doctor Dolittle himself remains, if not racist, then certainly paternalist towards the people he meets on his voyages. "'And then there are the babies: these native mothers are so frightfully ignorant'", he says at one point, explaining why he cannot take a holiday from his duties as their king (Lofting 1923: 305). This is reproduced in the Polish (Lofting 1985: 269).

Other writers were less insulting. Slighting references like "'confounded son of a Dutchman'" (Stevenson 1939: 56) and "'rank Irelander'" (Stevenson 1939: 168) are preserved in *Treasure Island* (in back translation they read, "Dutch herring" and "dyed in the wool Irishman" (Stevenson, 1974: 63, 169)). Censors seem to have had no serious ideological problem with the word "savage", at least in children's books. It occurs several times in *Treasure Island, Last of the Mohicans*, and *The Jungle Book* and is generally translated "as is". However, in *The Scarlet Letter*, the translator tries to avoid the word "savage" when it is applied to the native Americans. So, for example, "his savage companion" (Hawthorne 1994a: 52) is "czerwonoskóry towarzysz" ("red-skinned companion") (Hawthorne 1947: 28) and "savage priests" (Hawthorne 1994a: 108) is "z kapłanami indyjskimi" ("with Indian priests") (Hawthorne 1947: 76). Interestingly, the 1994 translation restores the word "savage" here and elsewhere (Hawthorne 1994b: 78, 163).

It might be expected that Kipling's *Jungle Book* would fall victim to the censor, as Kipling was a "jingo imperialist" (Orwell 1998, vol. 13: 151) and at least one Polish critic had cast aspersions on the imperialism of the tales (Jasienica 1950b: 7). In fact, no changes relating to imperialism or colonialism were made to the Polish text. In the last of the tales, "Her Majesty's Servants", the animals are talking about their life in the English army in India. The censor has little room to manoeuvre: either the whole story must be cut for glorifying (if it can be said to glorify) British imperialism or it must be entirely re-written, defeating the purpose of translating Kipling in the first place. Having been permitted in the first place, the book underwent few cuts from the censor: even the exclamation by one of the animals, whose pride has been injured at the suggestion that his master is black, is left untouched in the Polish: "'Of course he is [white],' said Vixen.

'Do you suppose I'm looked after by a black bullock-driver?'" (Kipling 1939: 269). The Polish conveys the very same message (Kipling 1963: 182). There is one sensitive point, though: "gipsies" (Kipling 1939: 8) is translated as "vagrants/tramps" ("włóczędzy") (Kipling 1963: 8). However, Stevenson's reference to "gypsies" in *Treasure Island* (Stevenson 1939: 151) was translated "Cyganie" ("Gypsies/Roma") (Stevenson, 1974: 153), while Edith Nesbit got away with the following: "'Gipsies are awfully fond of children,' Robert hopefully said. 'They're always stealing them'" (Nesbit 1959: 180), which in Polish is "–Cyganie przepadają za dziećmi – wtrącił Robert. – Nawet je kradną" ("'Gipsies love children,' Robert put in. 'They even steal them'") (Nesbit 1963: 176).

Frances Hodgson Burnett does not give the censor, concentrating on the surface level, much opportunity to intervene in *A Little Princess*. Sara Crewe's dreams and her fortune may be built on the exploitation of Indians but when a (plainly sympathetic) Indian character, Ram Dass, appears no derogatory words are used to describe him by the characters or the narrator. Sara does him the courtesy of speaking to him in what she remembers of Hindustani. This warmth and approval is present and correct in the 1959 Polish translation, as is Ram Dass's status as a servant.

An interesting omission from the Polish version of *The Story of the Amulet* is the lecture the children attend on "our soldiers in South Africa", which ends with the lecturer saying:

> 'And I hope every boy in this room has in his heart the seeds of courage and heroism and self-sacrifice, and I wish that every one of you may grow up to be noble and brave and unselfish, worthy citizens of this great Empire for whom our soldiers have freely given their lives.'

It is followed by Nesbit's authorial comment: "And, of course, this came true – which was a distinct score for Camden Town" (Nesbit 1959: 260). It may be the obscurity of this remark, which would probably not be understood by most Polish children, that caused the passage appearing to glorify empire to be excised. On the children's travels throughout time and space Cyril repeats that they come from a place where the sun never sets, i.e. the British Empire. The irony is more obvious here, since it is repeated over and over and Cyril says it "mechanically" on one occasion (Nesbit 1959: 103). It is translated into Polish each time it appears in the original, with "mechanically" becoming "odruchowo" ("involuntarily") (Nesbit 1963: 96). The general tendency in censorship is to assume the reader cannot be trusted to interpret the text "correctly" (i.e. as the censor believes it should be). One would think that in the case of children's literature the censor would be particularly paternalist, cutting anything that might be too much for the children to understand, and yet at least some ironic twists remain in the Polish translations of Nesbit.

In chapter eight there is an episode in which the workers of London are magically granted their fill of food and drink. In this context we read: "'I think it is chust a ver' bad tream,' said old Levinstein to his clerk; 'all along Bishopsgate I haf seen the gommon people have their hants full of food – *goot* food. Oh yes, without doubt a very bad tream!'" (Nesbit 1959: 151). The Jews here (Levinstein, Rosenbaum, Hirsh, Cohen) are members of the Stock Exchange, dismayed that the working classes have food. The whole episode is translated, but with some important changes. Firstly, the Jewish characters have no tell-tale accents. They speak standard Polish. Secondly, only Levinstein is given a surname in the translation (Lionel Cohen is translated as "Lionel"). Thirdly, the Queen of Babylon's words "'They'd be rather fine men, some of them, if they were dressed decently, especially the ones with the beautiful long, curved noses. I wish they were dressed like the Babylonians of my court'" (Nesbit 1959: 150) are translated without reference to curved noses (Nesbit 1963: 145). With all these clues removed it is likely that Polish children would not realise Nesbit is attacking Jewish financiers. Nesbit has been criticised for negative stereotyping of Jews and steps were taken to play this aspect down in the translation. The children buy their part of the amulet of the title from a man notable for his dirty finger, large diamond ring and little else. Later on we learn this man's name: Jacob Absalom (Nesbit 1959: 46). The name is left out of the Polish.

Notable, too, is the failure to intervene in very unsympathetic portrayal of the workers. On being given food and drink they immediately down tools:

> ...the cabman stopped.
> 'I ain't agoin' to drive you no further,' he said. 'Out you gets.'
> They got out rather unwillingly.
> 'I wants my tea,' he said; and they saw that on the box of the cab was a mound of cabbage, with pork chops and apple sauce, a duck, and a spotted currant pudding. Also a large can.
> 'You pay me my fare,' he said threateningly, and looked down at the mound, muttering again about his tea (Nesbit 1959: 149).

This unflattering picture of the working classes is translated faithfully into Polish (with the exception of their accents). This may have passed the censor because of the mixed messages of the piece. After this particular episode is all over, Nesbit writes ironically of "mad dreams including such dreadful things as hungry people getting dinners, and the destruction of the Stock Exchange" (Nesbit 1959: 153). This reverses the earlier message, that material goods are wasted on the poor.

Or maybe this passed the censor by because it is a only a children's book, mere make believe, in which the Jews who are slaughtered in this scene are magically returned to life and everything is as it was before. The lack of attention paid by literary critics to reviewing children's books may have been matched by censors' lack of attention to censoring them. This, however, is different to the fate of children's books in the West, where, Peter Hunt suggests, they are censored precisely because their low status makes them easy targets (Hunt 2001: 255). There is less outcry if "golliwogs" are replaced with "teddy bears" in Enid Blyton than there is if "nigger" is replaced by "slave" in *Huckleberry Finn*: Hemingway never said all modern American literature came from one book by Enid Blyton.

The treatment of the poor as objects of rich people's charity carried on unabated in *A Little Princess*. Halina Skrobiszewska defended the book, saying that it was no longer a historical novel about a "late nineteenth century England swollen by colonial wealth" but a quasi-realistic fairy tale (Skrobiszewska 1971: 540). Because of the changes in Poland, contemporary readers, she argues, will not see the philanthropy in the book as a social method but simply as an instinctive desire to do good (Skrobiszewska 1971: 541). The story in translation is intact, containing all the episodes in which the heroine, Sara Crewe, displays her charity, and in which the poor display their poverty, for example: "The little ravening London savage was still snatching and devouring when she turned away. She was too ravenous to give any thanks, even if she had ever been taught any politeness – which she had not. She was only a poor little wild animal" (Burnett 1994: 125). The post-war translation keeps the reference to "savage" and her lack of politeness but softens the blow a little by translating the last sentence (using diminutives) as a simile: "she was like a poor little wild animal" (Burnett 1963: 131) (Pacyniak 2009: 56-58).

A more noticeable effect of the changes in Poland on the translation is – arguably – the decision by the translator here and in many other children's books not to reproduce the dialects of the lower classes. In *A Little Princess* this means, for example, Becky, a servant in the school Sara Crewe attends, speaks like Sara. There are many examples scattered throughout the book but Katarzyna Pacyniak has analysed one passage in some detail, where Becky says: "'Once I see a princess. I was standin' in the street with the crowd outside Covin' Garden, watchin' the swells go inter the operer...'" (Burnett 1994: 45). Pacyniak shows that the pre-war translation (by Józef Birkenmajer) attempts to capture this speech by using an old-fashioned style of Polish with some non-standard grammatical forms like "patrzaj" for "look" (imperative) instead of the correct "patrz". The post-war translation by Wacława Komarnicka (Burnett 1963: 46) uses far less incorrect grammar to render Becky's speech, while there is no attempt at all to show class markers in the cook's speech: "'No savin's of mine never goes into no mines – particular diamond ones'" (Burnett 1994: 113; Burnett 1963: 118) (Pacyniak 2009: 64-67, 70-71).

A similar reluctance to differentiate the speech of working class characters and the less well educated can be seen in many children's books. For example, in chapter six of L.M. Montgomery's *Anne's House of Dreams* we meet "Captain Jim", a nautical type, who speaks very differently from Anne or the narrator: "'…your husband doesn't introduce me jest exactly right. […] you might as well begin as you're sartain to end up. […] Looking at you sorter makes me feel that I've jest been married myself'" (Montgomery 1986: 471). If anything the Polish Captain Jim is more ceremonious than the average educated speaker. For "'I mostly has to eat my meals alone, with the reflection of my ugly old phiz in a looking-glass opposite for company'" (Montgomery 1986: 471) the translation has "'Musi pani wiedzieć, że najczęściej spożywam obiad w towarzystwie mej własnej podobizny odbitej w wiszącym naprzeciw zwierciadle'" ("You must know that I usually consume dinner in the company of my own visage reflected in the mirror hanging opposite") (Montgomery 1985: 33). This is not the slightly rough diamond of the original. In his analysis of the translation of *Anne of Green Gables* Piotr Oczko points out that the exalted language of characters is – in the source text but often not in the Polish translation – punctured by a sober narrative voice (Oczko 2013: 51-52).

Tommy Stubbins, the cobbler's son in *Voyages of Doctor Dolittle*, moves in working class circles (he himself is too poor to go to school) and it is there that he learns English:

> 'Yon crittur's got a broken leg,' he [Joe, the mussel-man] said – 'and another badly cut an' all. I can mend you your boats, Tom, but I haven't the tools nor the learning to make a broken squirrel seaworthy. This is a job for a surgeon – and for a right smart one an' all. There be only one man I know who could save yon crittur's life. And that's John Dolittle.'
> 'Who is John Dolittle?' I asked. 'Is he a vet?'
> 'No,' said the mussel-man. 'He's no vet. Doctor Dolittle is a nacheralist.'
> 'What's a nacheralist?' (Lofting 1923: 21).

In translation the mussel-man speaks standard Polish and describes Dolittle as a "przyrodnik", i.e. a naturalist, not a "nacheralist" (Lofting 1985: 10-11).

Edith Nesbit's children in *The Story of the Amulet* also brush up against the lower orders from time to time, often so that they can try to do them some good:

> 'Oh, dear!' said Anthea, jumping up. 'Whatever is the matter?'
> She put her hand on the little girl's arm. It was rudely shaken off.
> 'You leave me be,' said the little girl. 'I ain't doing nothing to you.'

'But what is it?' Anthea asked. 'Has someone been hurting you?'

'What's that to you?' said the little girl fiercely. '*You're* all right.'

'Come away,' said Robert, pulling at Anthea's sleeve. 'She's a nasty, rude little kid.'

'Oh, no,' said Anthea. 'She's only dreadfully unhappy. What is it?' she asked again.

'Oh, *you're* all right,' the child repeated; '*You* ain't agoin' to the Union.'

'Can't we take you home?' said Anthea; and Jane added, 'Where does your mother live?'

'She don't live nowheres – she's dead – so now!' (Nesbit 1959: 178-179).

The gulf between the children and the little girl here is indicated by the unfolding events of the story so the lack of linguistic differentiation in the Polish (for lacking it is) does not drastically alter the sense or mood of the book. However, social differences are not always spelled out as clearly as they are in this chapter. Sometimes speech is the major or only indicator of class differences. When the children try to buy the Sand-fairy from a pet shop, the shopkeeper speaks so: "'Lookee here. I ain't agoin' to have you a comin' in here a turnin' the whole place outer winder, an' prizing every animile in the stock just for your larks, so don't think it!'" (Nesbit 1959: 24). In translation he speaks standard Polish and the reader has to guess that this ill-tempered, devious, grasping man is a representative of London's "lower orders". Like the "animal" in *A Little Princess* he is "one of the populace".

Even *A Bear Called Paddington*, written in a less class-divided Britain than Nesbit's, displays this linguistic differentiation between working class and middle class people. The London Underground employee, for example, drops his aitches, saying, "'There's a young bear 'ere...'" (Bond 1985: 48). He speaks standard Polish (Bond 1988: 44). Nor is it just English books in translation that are affected. Jack London's *White Fang* also distinguishes sharply between the language of the narrator and that of the frontiersmen in chapter two, for instance: "'I might have knowed it, [...] I've hearn sailors talk of sharks followin' a ship, [...] they ain't a-holdin' our trail this way for their health'" (London s.d.: 26-27). This is all standardised in Polish (London 1975: 30-31).

It is no easy task to translate Cockney or authentic frontier talk into Polish equivalents and it would be a stern judge who said failure to do so was a form of ideological censorship, especially since the reading public (or rather, its parents) complained about dialect words in children's books written in Polish, let alone translations (Skrobiszewska 1978: 9). But it is unlikely that in any but a small minority of cases the reason for this neglect was that the translator simply did not notice the stylisation. Even a beginning translator must notice all the apostrophes indicating omitted letters and when the working class/middle class divide is not at issue, translators show themselves capable of stylising the Polish in response to stylised English. For instance there is Peter's challenge to single combat in *Prince Caspian* that runs, in part, "*Wherefore we most heartily provoke, challenge and defy your Lordship to the said combat and monomachy...*'" (Lewis s.d.: 156). This is translated into a similarly courtly Polish, though the translator does miss, or deliberately omit, Lewis's joke when Peter reminds the scribe to spell "abominable" with an "h". Instead the translator has him remind the scribe of the *correct* way to write the word, perhaps for fear of teaching children bad habits (Lewis 1985: 125).

There is the possibility – faint after 1956 – that translators were mindful of Stalin's views on dialect (see chapter one). Two other explanations for the lack of stylisation of working class speech suggest themselves. One is that translators and publishers avoided "bad" Polish for educational reasons: books for children are to be written in good Polish so that their readers can learn their language properly. German translations of Michael Bond's *Paddington* books also corrected deliberate spelling mistakes (O'Sullivan 2005: 88), while Emer Delaney suggests the Italian translations of the William books by Richmal Crompton correct bad English from a combination of fear of setting a bad example and paucity of Italian equivalents (Delaney 2013: 114).

C.S. Lewis has been criticised for writing poor English by, among others, Moorcock (1987) and Peter Hunt, who notes that in one passage of no more than a hundred words from *The Lion, the Witch, and the Wardrobe*, Susan "finds herself" somewhere a total of three times, while Lewis's adjectives are no more adventurous than "little" and "strange" (Hunt 1991: 108). An examination of *Prince Caspian* and its translation suggests that the Polish translator tried to improve on such deficiencies. The final paragraph of chapter one starts "Pressing their way between the laden branches they reached the wall. It was very old, and broken down in places..." (Lewis s.d.: 16). In Polish it is "Clearing a path for themselves through the mounds of fallen branches they reached the wall. It was very old, in places crumbling and cracked..." ("Torując sobie drogę wśród zwałów opadłych gałęzi dotarli do muru. Był bardzo stary, miejscami wykruszony i popękany...") (Lewis 1985: 12). "Laden branches" is replaced with three words (changing the meaning) and "broken down" becomes "crumbling and cracked". A few lines later (after – yes – finding themselves there), we read that the children "stepped out into the middle of" a "wide open place" (Lewis s.d.: 16). One can step into a small open place; into the middle of a wide open place one must take a few steps, i.e. walk. In the translation the verb used is "dojść" ("reach, arrive, walk up to etc."), though they do "find themselves" in the Polish version (Lewis 1985: 12). Or there is this sentence, with its repeated "and": "They came in a glade to an old hollow oak tree covered with moss, and Trufflehunter tapped with his paw three times on the trunk and there was no answer" (Lewis s.d.: 67). In Polish this is "They came to an old and rotten oak covered in moss and evidently hollow because Trufflehunter knocked on the trunk three times. There was, however, no answer" ("Doszli do starego, zmurszałego dębu, pokrytego mchem i najwidoczniej pustego w środku, ponieważ Truflogon zapukał w pień trzy razy. Nie było jednak żadnej odpowiedzi") (Lewis 1985: 54).

The pressure on translators and writers of children's literature to write good, correct Polish appears quite strong – perhaps stronger than in English speaking countries. As seen above, the Polish spoken by Captain Jim in *Anne's House of Dreams* is considerably more ornate than the English. The language of the translation of *The Wonderful Wizard of Oz* is also frequently more sophisticated than the original English. Where Frank Baum wrote "supper" (Baum 1997: 114) the translator has the bookish, vocabulary-expanding "wieczerza" (Baum 1972: 72). Where Baum has simply "When he saw Dorothy ..." (Baum 1997: 117) the Polish has the formal, literary perfective participle form of one of the rarer of Polish's many words for "to see": "Ujrzawszy Dorotę..." (Baum 1972: 74). The same can be said for the translation of *The Jungle Book*. The *thees* and *thous* of the original find a counterpart in Polish, as when Toomai says, "'When thou art old, Kala Nag, there will come some rich Rajah, and he will buy thee...'" (Kipling 1939: 209). In the Polish translation the contracted forms of the possessive pronoun ("twą" and "twe") give the text a similarly dignified feel (Kipling 1963: 142). However, leaving aside the *thees* and *thous*, *The Jungle Book* is usually quite straightforward but the Polish translation often embellishes it, as when the original has "'Quick, Chuchundra, or I'll bite you!'" (Kipling 1939: 180) and the Polish has, in back translation, "'Don't grumble, Chuchundra, because my teeth are sharp and I can bite with them!'" (Kipling 1963: 126). Before the war, Birkenmajer had in fact been criticised for enriching the text needlessly in his translation (Kurowska 1987: 167).

Another possible explanation for the elimination of linguistic variety is that by making the speech of the working classes as "good" as that of everyone else, the translators avoid or seek to avoid patronising the workers. In his essay on Rudyard Kipling, Orwell argues that "one can often improve Kipling's poems, make them less facetious and less blatant, by simply going through them and translating them from Cockney into standard speech" (Orwell 1998, vol. 13: 154). A solution to the problem of translating dialect variation often suggested by students is to translate, say, frontier American English, with the dialect of Polish spoken in the Tatra Mountains. Perhaps professional translators felt, like Orwell, that this would be facetious, or even absurd. Clifford Landers's advice on the translation of dialects, for example, is a flat "don't" (Landers 2001: 117). Whatever the precise cause or causes, the smoothing out of such linguistic differences can leave children unaware that the heroes on their hols and the beneficiaries of their good will belong to different social classes.

"Other books traditionally included in the canon of children's literature, such as Lewis's Narnia series, Tolkien's *The Hobbit*, and Kipling's *Jungle Book* have been criticised on the grounds that the values they contain are too exclusively male and white", writes Tony Watkins (Watkins 1999: 35). All of these books were translated into Polish under a system that claimed to uphold equality of the sexes and races. The cruder, more obvious forms of racism were combated by the censor but in the struggle against paternalism the nature of the Polish language itself was a perhaps unexpected ally. It is certainly true that English language writers of an older stamp often used "men" to mean – well, "men", as if women did not count. The Polish for "man" is "mężczyzna" and for "men" is "mężczyźni" but when speaking of people in general, the words "człowiek" ("person") and "ludzie" ("people") are nearly always used. "Ludzie" is not gender-specific and it is the word of choice in translations.

So, for example, *Prince Caspian* has "'No men – or very few – lived in Narnia before the Telmarines took it'" (Lewis s.d.: 44), while the Polish, by using "ludzie", avoids the suggestion that perhaps women (and children, for that matter) might have once lived in Narnia but are not worth talking about. The effect of the source text is unintentionally comical from a modern-day point of view. The speaker says a little later, "'I said there were very few *men* in Narnia'" (Lewis s.d.: 45), wishing to stress that other *creatures* lived there. Because the Polish uses less sexist language the implication that he means creatures of some kind (and not women or children) is clearer (Lewis 1985: 36). "'You have seen what no man now alive has seen'" (Lewis s.d.: 47-48) is translated with non-sexist language (Lewis 1985: 38-39) and so forth. Similarly in *The Jungle Book*: when Mowgli says, "'I will go to men'" and the narrator says Mowgli "went down the hillside alone, to meet those mysterious things that are called men" (Kipling 1939: 40, 41) the Polish uses the word "ludzie", i.e. people of both sexes (Kipling 1963: 32).[9] The word "mężczyźni" does occur in the Polish translation (Kipling 1963: 94), in the passage where Matkah, the female seal, tut-tuts about her husband's behaviour: "'Oh, you men, you men!'" (Kipling 1939: 130). Here it is specifically the males that are being referred to and "mężczyźni" is an appropriate translation.

The Polish use of "ludzie" appears to be the natural choice in the contexts given above. That is, to write in Polish that Mowgli went to meet "those mysterious things called 'mężczyźni'" would mean he was deliberately going to avoid women, perhaps because they are not at all mysterious. This would be absurd since it is obviously *humans* that are mysterious to Mowgli, who has been brought up by animals. But what does it mean that "ludzie" is the "natural choice"? How far can the use of "ludzie" be attributed to something inherent in the Polish language and how far to the consciousness of writers, translators and people in general that women are people too – a consciousness partially attributable to socialism, or socialist propaganda if one prefers? It may be less a case of translators consciously toning down the sexism of the source texts and more a question of English usage only recently catching up with what had for a long time been accepted in Polish.

For all that, though, it remains a fact that in the Polish version of *The Hobbit*, Bilbo Baggins and all his companions are male. In *Prince Caspian* it is Peter, not Susan or Lucy, who takes on Miraz in single combat and his gift is a shield and sword, while Lucy's is a healing potion, and Susan's a bow and arrow and a horn that can summon help (Lewis s.d.: 27). The surface level sexism is attenuated but the underlying structures and presumptions are there: females get to heal and to summon help, and if they must fight it is from a distance.[10] This is as true of the Polish translations as it is of the English originals but there are limits to the male chauvinism in *Prince Caspian* that translators will tolerate. "Peter leaned forward, put his arms round the beast and kissed the furry head: it wasn't a girlish thing for him to do, because he was the High King" (Lewis s.d.: 152) is a line that has attracted the ire of some readers for its denigration of females. The Polish translates the word "girlish" as "childish" ("dziecinny") (Lewis 1985: 123), an unmistakeable intervention, whether from translator, editor or censor. However, references in the original to talking "'like an old woman'" and "'womanish counsels'" (Lewis s.d.: 160, 161) are translated complete with stereotypes (Lewis 1985: 129, 130). Similarly, the gist of Lewis's dismissal of ugly schoolgirls is also translated faithfully: "Then she [Miss Prizzle] saw the Lion, screamed and fled, and with her fled her class, who were mostly dumpy, prim little girls with fat legs" (Lewis s.d.: 175). For "dumpy" the Polish uses "przysadzisty" ("stocky, squat"), which is perhaps a little less nasty, and there is a diminutive for "legs" ("nóżki") but this does little to change the text's message (Lewis 1985: 142). However, someone obviously felt obliged to intervene more directly a few lines later when Gwendolen (not one of the ugly girls) joins the Maenads, who "whirled her round in a merry dance and helped her take off some of the unnecessary and uncomfortable clothes that she was wearing" (Lewis s.d.: 176). In Polish they help the child take off parts of her school uniform (Lewis 1985: 143). The suggestion that the child has gone off to dance naked is a little weaker: she could have taken off her blazer or hat.

Such interventions are quite superficial and translators do not try any sophisticated ways to prevent the reader from identifying with any implicit reactionary message the books might have. John Stephens has argued that focalisation and narrative viewpoint construct "implied readers who must be expected to share" ideological assumptions (Sarland 1999: 48). In omniscient narrative, for example, the presentation of characters and settings "may contribute towards the construction of an ethos (and hence ideology), and so may encode a societal ideology" (Stephens 1992: 57). Stephens assumes that readers will identify with the main character, through whom any focalisation is usually channelled, and therefore accept that character's values. Whether this actually happens is another matter (though it seems to me more likely to occur with children). Noël Carroll, for one, argues that readers often do not share the emotions of the characters, which he suggests would be necessary for such identification (Carroll 1990: 91). Nonetheless, Stephens puts forward some questions that are of relevance in examining translations of the ideology inherent in fiction. For example: who sees? Who interprets? Are non-middle class, white cultures and experiences shown as inferior? Does the book assume that standard English is superior? (Stephens 1992: 27, 83). The very presence in children's books of servants and the assumption that children will be familiar with them projects an implied reader belonging to a certain, upper, class. But Polish translators (censors, editors etc.) neither remove them altogether (and imply that the child-heroes are more working class) or beef up their roles. They were unconcerned with the fact that children in socialist Poland read books that assumed familiarity with upper middle class capitalist life. Nor have I found any evidence of translators trying to prevent children from identifying with certain characters and the ideology hidden in their actions by, for example, avoiding expressions like "our hero". Put simply, Polish translators were too scrupulously faithful to the source texts to change the identity of the person who interprets. If the answer to "who sees?" in the source text is "a Tory" then it is generally a Tory who sees in the Polish target text.

Randomly chosen passages show almost no change in the assumptions hidden behind the point of view of the narrator. *The Wonderful Wizard of Oz* contains the line "There were few birds in this part of the forest, for birds love the open country" (Baum 1997: 67), which casually assumes that humans know what birds like and attributes to them an emotion known to humans but not necessarily to birds. The Polish does likewise, though it drops the word "love", reading in back translation "...for birds prefer open space" (Baum 1972: 42). When the Tin Woodman says, a few lines later, that they "must" protect Toto (Baum 1997: 68), the same modal verb is used in the Polish (Baum 1972: 43), preserving the idea that the strong have a duty to the weak. In "The White Seal" story in *The Jungle Book* it remains the case in the Polish that Matkah, the female character, hangs back while the male seals do the hard and dangerous work of finding a place on the beach. When she joins her bloody and battered mate she alternately flatters him and complains of their location. She coos, "'How thoughtful of you! You've taken the old place again'", to follow up a few seconds later with "'I've often thought we should be much happier if we hauled out at Otter Island instead of this crowded place'" (Kipling 1939: 130). She is duplicitous and manipulative, preparing child readers for the stereotypes of women they will meet in later life. This is all there in the Polish, as is – in fairness to Kipling – the irony and the male character's insufferable pomposity and petit-bourgeois snobbery. There is one small change, though. In the same passage Kipling writes, "Now that all the seals and their wives were on the land..." (Kipling 1939: 131). The Polish avoids the appendage "and wives", translating it as "males and females" (Kipling 1963: 94).

In *The Voyages of Doctor Dolittle,* the narrator longs to seek his fortune in foreign lands. The sight of the ships setting sail prompts the following: "What strange things would they have seen, I wondered, when next they came back to anchor at Kingsbridge! And, dreaming of the lands I had never seen, I'd sit on there, watching till they were out of sight" (Lofting 1923: 17-18). The grosser verbal abuse of the people he might meet there, as seen, is removed from the Polish translation, but in both the translation and the original he does not dream of the people he might meet there: only of the "things" and "lands".[11]

To finish this chapter I consider the fortunes in Poland of two authors, briefly mentioned above, whose books "became" children's books, though they did not write for children: Owen Wister and James Fenimore Cooper. Wister's *The Virginian* re-appeared in post-war Poland in 1964. The third edition, in 1977, was published by Iskry, in a series called "Classics for the Young" that included books like *White Fang, Anne of Green Gables* and Robert Louis Stevenson's *Kidnapped.* Several passages are omitted from *The Virginian.* The translator skips some remarks about the "Rime of the Ancient Mariner" ("These lines are the pure gold", the narrator says (Wister 1988: 211)). It is quite common in children's books for Polish translators to substitute passing culture-specific references with more general terms so that, for example, "last December's *Bradshaw,* and an odd volume of Plumridge's *Commentary on Thessalonians*" in *The Story of the Amulet* (Nesbit 1959: 15-16) becomes "an old ancient history handbook and a yearbook of an illustrated magazine" (Nesbit 1963: 10). However, omitting a passage like this, in which the author dilates on his topic, is quite unusual.

The most noticeable change to *The Virginian* is the cutting of overt racism. "'White men, that is. Can't do nothing with niggers or Chinese. But you're white, all right'" (Wister 1988: 29), says a travelling salesman at one point. It is translated as follows: "'Mówię o białych twarzach, bo Murzyni i Chińczycy wydają mi się wszyscy na jedno kopyto'" ("I'm talking about white faces because Negroes and Chinese all seem the same to me") (Wister

1977: 25-26). The reference to being white is cut here and later on, when Scipio le Moyne assures his interlocutors that he and his people are "white" despite his foreign (French) name. It is a little surprising that the Virginian's song about Jim Crow only dilutes the derogatory reference to black people in translation. In the original there is mention of a "nigger" (Wister 1988: 163) and in the translation we have "Czarny jak wszystkie Murzyny" ("Black like all Negroes") (Wister 1977: 186). The noun, "Murzyn", has been declined as if it were feminine, which is a mark of disrespect in Polish, although the translator may have been trying to render the Virginian's irregular grammar and pronunciation (which is a parody of African American English). Although, as seen above, censors were tolerant of words like "savage" and "Indian" there were limits to their patience and so a "scarlet and black Navajo blanket, striped with its splendid zigzags of barbarity" (Wister 1988: 257) is in Polish just splendid and Navajo – not barbaric (Wister 1977: 302).

Also missing from the Polish version is the narrator's paean to the American (or at least his own) idea of democracy, summed up by the motto, "Let the best man win, whoever he is" (Wister 1988: 116). It is conceivable that such a passage might have been left untouched in a book directed at adults. What harm in letting an American reactionary rave about "the quality and the equality"? It should only serve to strengthen in Polish readers the worst stereotypes about the cutthroat, capitalist, United States of America – a desirable outcome for a socialist ideologue fighting a propaganda battle against the West. However, censors had a tendency to treat all readers paternally: the passage may have been cut because children might read it and, identifying with the Virginian of the title, believe it represents a good social order (*pace* Stephens) or it may have been cut because *adults* might read it and believe it represents a good social order. The cutting was done quite clumsily. In Polish the whole opening meditation of chapter 13 reads in back translation: "There can be no doubt that America is divided into two classes: the go-getters and the equal. The above remarks..." (Wister 1977: 130). The use of the plural "remarks" alerts the reader to the fact that something has been cut out and may be interpreted as an act of resistance by the translator or editor. The right to indicate parts of texts that had been cut was only gained in 1981.

Paternalism may also explain the cutting of most, but not all, of the defence of lynching in chapter 33. Polish propaganda liked to dwell on such sins of the USA but perhaps the censors feared Wister's defence might be too persuasive for a young mind to resist. Nonetheless, something remains of Judge Henry's defence of the Virginian for lynching cattle rustlers. Critics have pointed out that children are capable of all kinds of "aberrant" readings (Sarland 1999: 49-51). An aberrant reading that suggests itself here would lend itself admirably to anti-American propaganda. The judge argues that although the Virginian did not follow the correct procedures (i.e. give the accused a trial etc.) the procedures themselves only flow from the will of the people and since it was the will of the people that cattle rustlers be hanged, no harm was done. In effect, he argues that US justice (the propagandist would put the word in inverted commas), for all its pomp, is simply mob justice. Rather than dignify the Virginian's actions by comparing them to the American justice system, he has denigrated the American justice system by comparing it to the Virginian's cold blooded murder of two alleged thieves. This part is present in the Polish translation. Whether youngsters read it aberrantly or not is another matter.

James Fenimore Cooper was popular in Poland. The 1988 Iskry edition of *Last of the Mohicans* was the tenth edition (the fifth of the abridged version) and had a print run of 100,000. Regardless of Mark Twain's acerbic comments (see below), Cooper fell under the heading of classic literature and therefore was, at least in theory, free from the attentions of the Main Office for the Control of Press, Publications and Public Performances. There were many pre-war versions of Cooper's books, some of them adaptations rather than translations, and in the late 1940s some were reissued. However, in the 1950s fresh translations were commissioned and these became the standard Polish versions – or the standard basis for abridged versions. A comparison of *Last of the Mohicans* and the 1950s translation shows little or nothing that can be attributed to institutional censorship with the exception of paratexts in earlier, post-war editions.

Had Cooper been a contemporary writer and had *Last of the Mohicans* not presented the native Americans in a favourable light one might expect to see fewer or no mentions of Hawkeye's pure-bloodedness but they are usually intact, though some of them fall by the wayside in the abridged version. Cooper's acknowledgment of the equality of native Americans might seem a little watery by modern standards ("'There is reason in an Indian, though nature has made him with a red skin!' said the white man [Hawkeye]" (Cooper 2002: 20)) but given the times in which it was written the censor was content to let it pass.

The 1956 version includes an afterword to set readers straight. It starts by describing the oppression of the native Americans (referred to here as "redskins" ("czerwonoskórzy"), which does not seem to have been perceived as derogatory) as well as the attempts by the colonisers to wipe out the "'savage' tribes". The inverted commas dissociate the author, Kazimierz Piotrowski, and by implication Cooper, from the racism of America's colonisers (Piotrowski 1956a: 447). Piotrowski invokes Engels to combat the accusation that Cooper idealised the native Americans (Piotrowski 1956a: 453-454) and ends by praising Hawkeye's values as ones to which young readers should aspire in a passage which is a nod in the direction of socialism's insistence on becoming engaged in the work for a better future: Hawkeye's "manliness, courage and nobility may certainly appeal to those who do not look on passively at our times but take a manly and self-sacrificing part in the shaping of a new life and they may appeal to – above all – our young" (Piotrowski 1956a: 458). Cooper had been somewhat grudgingly published under Stalinism, with no editions of any of his books from 1950 to 1953 inclusive. The foreword also mentions Balzac, Mark Twain and the conventions of the romantic novel so the socialist irruptions may be seen as an attempt to rehabilitate Cooper in the eyes of the authorities.

In the foreword to the translation of *Deerslayer* (also by Kazimierz Piotrowski), which finds room to discuss briefly the Korean War, Cooper is praised for his progressiveness. True, it was limited, bourgeois progressiveness, and he was a backslider, but for his times, Cooper was definitely on the side of right, and this time he receives the imprimatur of Gorky, as well as Balzac, Goethe, Lermontov and Bielinsky (Piotrowski 1956b: 5-22).

Despite the precaution of the afterword, a few very small changes were made to the translation of *Last of the Mohicans*, and they concern the question of race relations. For example, Cora Munro is at one point described as "chaste" in the English (Cooper 2002: 93) but as "honest" ("uczciwa") in the Polish (Cooper 1956a: 139). This is in a scene in which the native American Magua is threatening to take Cora as his wife, and by changing "chaste" to "honest" some of the sexual tension is reduced. Elsewhere, Munro reproaches Heyward for – as Munro mistakenly believes – not wanting to marry his daughter Cora because she is not 100% white: "'You scorn to mingle the blood of the Heywards with one so degraded, lovely and virtuous though she be?'" (Cooper 2002: 147). In translation "degraded" is gone, replaced with "of such descent" (Cooper 1956a: 212). There is also a small change (though it may have been an oversight) in the lines "the tell-tale blood stole over her [Cora's] features" (Cooper 2002: 58). In Polish this reads "blood treacherously coloured her cheeks and forehead" (Cooper 1956a: 90). That is, in the Polish she simply blushed but in the English her descent from black slaves is hinted at. As David Blair shows in his introduction to the 2002 English edition, Cooper draws "repeated attention" to the nature of Cora's blood (Blair 2002: xx). Nonetheless, it must be said that the censor's hand – whether institutionally imposed or self-imposed – is hardly to be detected.

Eliza Łuszczewska shows how the Polish translation of Cooper's *The Pioneers* changes some of the original's objectionable parts, for example neutralising references to "niggers". Cooper also calls the native American a "savage" and refers to their "animal existence". This is changed to the less charged "Indians and their life" (Łuszczewska 2012: 81). The change is perhaps over-zealous as the words occur in a passage that very clearly condemns the white settlers for bringing ruin upon the natives. In the context "animal existence" might be taken to mean their physical or biological existence: "the power and inroads of the whites had reduced some of the tribes to a state of dependence, that rendered not only their political, but, considering the wants and habits of a savage, their animal existence also, extremely precarious" (Cooper 1985, vol. 1: 82). Łuszczewska also gives an interesting example of a translation bringing out the exploitation of the American continent more clearly than the original. Leatherstocking says, "'This comes of settling a country!'" but in the translation he uses the word "kolonizacja" ("colonisation") a much less innocent word than "settling" ("osiedlanie się") (Łuszczewska 2012: 80).

Mark Twain's famous essay "Fenimore Cooper's Literary Offences" was not unknown in Poland. One of his objections is to the inconsistency of Deerslayer's speech in the novel of the same name: "In the *Deerslayer* story he [Cooper] lets Deerslayer talk the showiest kind of book talk sometimes, and at other times the basest of base dialects" (Twain 1996: 111-112). It is shown elsewhere that Polish translations had a tendency to iron out the wrinkles of different language varieties in the English source texts and this can be seen working to Cooper's advantage (at least in Twain's eyes) in the translation of *Deerslayer*. Twain complains that Deerslayer at times speaks thus –

> 'She's in the forest – hanging from the boughs of the trees, in a soft rain – in the dew on the open grass – the clouds that float about in the blue heavens – the birds that sing in the woods – the sweet springs where I slake my thirst – and in all the other glorious gifts that come from God's Providence!'

– and at times thus: "'It consarns me as all things that touches a fri'nd consarns a fri'nd'" (Twain 1996: 112). In the 1950s Polish translation the first of the two quoted passages is similarly high-flown (Cooper 1956b: 167-168) but the second is also literary, not marked as the speech of an uneducated person (for example, it uses "mego", a high-register version of "mojego", for "my") (Cooper 1956b: 167). Another example Twain gives is "'If I was Injin born, now, I might tell of this, or carry in the scalp and boast of the expl'ite afore the whole tribe; or if my inimy had only been a bear'" (Twain 1996: 112). This is marked in translation as literary rather than uneducated speech: a giveaway again being the use of a contracted form of the possessive pronoun ("mych") (Cooper 1956b: 152). Chingachgook speaks ungrammatical English and this is rendered with ungrammatical Polish but when Hurry says, "'It's but a little deerskin, a'ter all, and cut this-a-way or that-a-way, it's not a skear-crow to frighten true hunters from their game. What say you, Sarpent, shall you or I canoe it?'" (Cooper 1985, vol. 2: 809) this comes out as standard Polish (Cooper 1956b: 382).

Twain also complains of Munro, in *Last of the Mohicans*, "comporting himself in the field like a windy melodramatic actor" (Twain 1996: 112) when his daughters reach the fort he is defending. His speech in Polish may fairly be called windy and melodramatic, if perhaps slightly less so. Where in the original Munro says, "'pull not a trigger, lest ye kill my lambs!'" (Cooper 2002: 133), in Polish he says "'Nie ruszać cyngli, bo zabijecie moje drogie owieczki'" ("Don't touch your triggers or you'll kill my dear little lambs") (Cooper 1956a: 193). The use of a diminutive does seem out of place coming from "a veteran Scotch Commander-in-Chief" (Twain 1996: 112) but the Polish is more modern than the English and in other places, too, a preference can be seen for standard – though often quite flowery – Polish. For example, Cooper was fond of reversing the normal word order for direct questions ("'Seek you any here?'", "'Think you so?'" (Cooper 2002: 13, 29)). These are unmarked in translation (Cooper 1956a: 27, 50), though the translator does try to capture Gamut's highly individual style of talking.

Twain gives a long list of words which he believes Cooper used incorrectly in *Deerslayer*. It is not possible to locate them all in the text but it does seem that the translations, rather than preserve the mistakes, are written in correct Polish. When Twain complains that Cooper wrote "decreasing" when he meant "deepening" (Twain 1996: 114) it seems he meant the line where Cooper contrasts morning light with evening light: "The witchery of an increasing, a thing as different as possible from the *decreasing* twilight" (Cooper 1985, vol. 2: 805), where it is – if not exactly clear from the context, certainly probable – that he meant "deepening". The Polish refers to evening twilight (Cooper 1956b: 378) – poor style, perhaps, since "zmierzch" ("twilight") can only occur in the evening anyway – but not plain wrong, as in the original. Twain also complains of "embedded" being used where "enclosed" should have been (Twain 1996: 114). The word occurs twice in the novel, each time referring to a body of water and while Twain may be accused of splitting hairs, the Polish translation in both cases chooses uncontroversial words (Cooper 1956b: 137, 377). It is not possible to be sure if Twain (1996: 114) had in mind the following line when he complained that "precision" was used for "facility" and "phenomena" for "marvels" but it seems a likely candidate: "The precision with which those, accustomed to watchfulness, or lives of disturbed rest, sleep, is not the least of the phenomena of our mysterious being" (Cooper 1985, vol. 2: 789). In Polish this is much more lucid. In back translation it runs: "The punctuality with which people used to staying on watch or rising in the night wake is one of the most interesting phenomena of unfathomable human life" (Cooper 1956b: 360).

The above discussion has taken us far from institutional censorship but it could be argued that with so much riding on Cooper there was pressure on the translator to (a) improve on the language and (b) make the book more accessible. Under socialist realism there was a strong emphasis on accessibility (Jarosiński 1999: 55). In the Party's Central Committee files there is a report entitled "From Comrade Molotov's Speech at the All-Union Publishing Council, February 17th 1955" praising socialist realist literature from socialist and communist countries and calling for it to be translated. As to *how* it should be translated, the document contains the memorable phrase "Better to harm the writer than the reader", though this may be taken to apply to the selection criteria: it is a little difficult to make out from the context (K-237viii-270: 226). Books were to reach out to the factory hand and the farm labourer, not just the children of the pre-war intelligentsia. *Nowe Książki* rated *Last of the Mohicans* grade I, which meant it was considered accessible to any reader with a primary school education (Rev. of *Pogromca...* 1954: 379). A desire to protect the reputation of a by now officially approved author would explain why the linguistic faults that Twain found are not in the Polish version. But it is not only translators working under the strictures of socialist realism that opt to improve their texts and the avoidance of Cooper's errors may be ascribed to nothing more sinister than professionalism, to taking pride in one's work as a translator. Let the foregoing serve, then, if as nothing else, as an illustration of the difficulty in drawing the line between editing and censoring.

---

[1] Piotr Nowak has found and quoted similar judgements in the Poznań censors' archives. In a review of a Polish children's book the censor wrote "the fairy tale is not desirable reading matter for children because of the supernatural phenomena and the educationally unsuitable way in which the shoemaker is rewarded for his 'work'". Nowak explains that in the offending tale the shoemaker is rewarded with gold for making shoes with the help of angels (Nowak 2012: 58).

[2] In Wells's *Kipps*, the brand name of a bicycle, "Red Flag" (Wells 1941: 185), is elided in translation (Wells 1950: 224).

[3] Objections to fairy tales go back at least as far as the eighteenth century in Europe (see Lathey 2010: 61-65).

[4] Nor did this apply only to children's literature. George Orwell commented in his 1940 essay "Charles Dickens" that "the ordinary town proletariat, the people who make the wheels go round, have always been ignored by novelists. When they do find their way between the covers of a book, it is nearly always as objects of pity or as comic relief" (Orwell 1998, vol. 12: 21).

[5] "Major wstał chwiejnie na nogi, a krew płynąca mu z gardła czerwieniła się na śniegu szeroką strugą" (London 1975: 196).

[6] "...ludzie poczęli tłuc foki pałkami po głowach – waląc ile wlazło. W dziesięć minut później mały Kotik już nie mógł rozpoznać żadnego ze swych kamratów: pozostały z nich jeno skóry, zdarte od nozdrzy aż po płetwy tylnych odnóży..." (Kipling 1963: 102)

[7] See also Jan Kott's introduction to the 1953 Polish edition.

[8] The censors wrote of *Treasure Island*: "'...it is difficult to find in it even one positive character'" (Rogoż 2013: 109) – but they did permit its publication, in 1950.

---

[9] Where Kipling refers to animals as people, the Polish uses "tribe".

[10] But see Monika B. Hilder's *The Feminine Ethos in C.S. Lewis's Chronicles of Narnia*, Peter Lang: New York (2012) for an alternative view.

[11] I am grateful to my students in Lublin for their discussion of these passages in class.

Chapter 7
Translators

Teresa Kieniewicz says of inter-war translations of American literature that they were often bad, displaying ignorance of American life, the English language, and even of Polish. She attributes these low standards to commercial pressures. Translations via French or German were frequent and there was much competition among translators, driving down wages and quality (Kieniewicz 1977: 86-87). Unscrupulous publishers would sometimes issue "new" translations identical to the old ones and issued books in two volumes in order to bump up prices (Wnęk 2006: 62n, 28). Elżbieta Kurowska attributes some of the blame for the poor quality of translations from English in this period to the historical dominance of French: the first chair of English in a Polish university was founded only in 1911 and there were few students of English, although the language gained ground in the 1930s. Critics complained about bad English translations, with Andrzej Mikułowski claiming there *were* no English translators. Publishers, Kurowska maintains, remained deaf to such complaints (Kurowska 1987: 37-38).

Against this background, People's Poland appears like a shining beacon. Along with improved literacy there was an increase in the number of copies of books printed. The average print run of a book in the inter-war period has been estimated by Andrzej Zawada at 4,000 (he does not specify whether he means all books or fiction) (Zawada 1995: 184). Kurowska estimates an average run of 2,000 to 2,500 copies for translations from English (Kurowska 1987: 43). The typical literary fiction novel studied here had an initial print run of just over 10,000, with some novels going through many editions (the sixth edition of *Grapes of Wrath* was printed in 40,290 copies). As noted before, translations flew off the shelves, with classics (not just from English) sold at below cost in the 1950s (Szkup 1972: 33).

The standard of translations from English after World War Two rose. Jerzy Borejsza of Czytelnik publishers came out against the practice of relay translation on the pages of *Nowa Kultura* in 1951 (Borejsza 1951: 9). In 1958, by which time he had broken with communism, Czesław Miłosz wrote approvingly of the course translation had taken in Poland since the war. The greatest writers had been put off by the low pay before the war and if they did undertake translation they did it "slapdash" but now translation was better paid (Miłosz 2007: 203-204). Other commentators have noted an improvement in the quality of translations in People's Poland, though it could be argued that, given the existence of censorship, they were not or could not be entirely frank. Jerzy Szkup contrasts the quality of translations issued by private publishers immediately after the war with those of state publishers (Szkup 1972: 11-12), which eventually pushed aside the private houses. Before 1950, private publishers had often used pre-war editions, sometimes anonymous and abridged, or bearing the legend "on the basis of…". After 1950, new or improved translations appeared (Szkup 1972: 36). Zdzisław Najder, in a 1975 article about the Polish translations of Conrad, claimed the quality of translations from English had shot up over the previous 25 years (Najder 1975: 202). In 1959, Bronisław Zieliński mentioned among problems facing translators the lack of good dictionaries and personal knowledge of the USA (Zieliński 1959: 49) but his own translations show that these problems were surmountable. Much later, Wacław Sadkowski claimed that People's Poland "disciplined" publishing, causing a marked improvement in the translation of belles lettres. For example, publishers carefully compared translations with the originals, which meant much fewer omissions caused by oversight (Sadkowski 2002: 113-4). Bogumiła Staniów, writing in 2013, claims that "paradoxically, [sic] state control contributed to the decent quality of translations" (Staniów 2013: 164).

Censors sometimes played the role of proof readers or editors, commenting not only on the politics of the books they had to review but also on their literary value. Jack Lindsay's *1649: A Novel of a Year*, one wrote, had longueurs and no harm would be done if the last few lines were cut (G-145, 31/26: 555-556); the translation of Cronin's *Three Loves* was "beneath criticism" and should be thoroughly proofed again (G-173c, 32/44: 122); Lloyd Brown's *Iron City* was well written but the translation often let it down (G-375, 31/32: 925); Sean O'Casey's *I Knock at the Door* was boring and should not be published (G-771, 132/106). As seen, the authorities tried to stamp out trashy books, though many were let back in. There is an interesting parallel between the state authorities and individual translators: Stalinists simply eliminated second rate literature (replacing it with their own). The translators and editors – and sometimes censors – can sometimes be seen trying to improve second rate literature.

At the risk of broadening the definition of censorship too much one might propose the existence in People's Poland of a "censorship of quality". Translators were sometimes more scrupulous than the authors they were translating. In 1952, the translator Irena Tuwim wrote that language in children's literature must be clear and flawless: if the language was not good in the original this was no excuse for the translator to write bad Polish

(Tuwim 2007: 185). Maria Dąbrowska, who translated Pepys's diaries, wrote in 1954: "with the Polish reader's interests in mind, there is no way one should, for example, preserve all the mistakes and arbitrariness in Pepys's syntax, which sometimes obscure the sense to the point where the sentence becomes a conundrum" (Dąbrowska 2007: 189).

Dąbrowska was not the only one who cleared up conundrums in translation. For example, in *Georgia Boy* the narrator's father says, "'I need you to give me a lift right away'" (Caldwell 1950: 4) but in Polish he says, "'Potrzebny mi jesteś'" ("I need you") (Caldwell 1973: 5). This gives a more accurate picture of what is going on: the narrator's father wants help in lifting a baling machine. He does not need to be driven or lifted anywhere. This "adjustment upwards" could have happy effects, as, for example, in Krystyna Tomorowicz's translation of Carter Dickson's "locked room" mystery, *The Reader is Warned*. The translation is written in better Polish than the original is in English, as a few examples will show. Take the translation of "it started out in a smooth upward run of smooth dark-red brick" (Dickson 1951: 13). In conformity with norms of good written Polish, the translation avoids repeating "smooth" (Dickson 1972: 16). Repetition is a problem elsewhere too. Carter Dickson displays a fondness for the phrase "with the air": "'Ah sir!' said Masters, coming into the parlour with the air of a galleon under full sail" (Dickson 1951: 63); "'What would you say to poison, now?' suggested Masters, with the air of one making a fair business proposition" (Dickson 1951: 66); "His [Masters's, again] air was one of elaborate off-handedness" (Dickson 1951: 72); "'You [Masters] have been putting on an air of false and forced geniality'" (Dickson 1951: 78); "there was a somewhat breathless air about her [...]. Despite her deprecating air" (Dickson 1951: 215). In each one of these examples the Polish uses a different phrase, avoiding the monotony of Dickson's limited vocabulary (Dickson 1972: 77, 81, 89, 96, 270).

Dickson perpetrates on his readers the following sentence: "Lawrence Chase looked surprised and doubtful (of her) and somewhat fretful" (Dickson 1951: 18). The translation is written so well that it does not need to explain itself in parentheses; nor does it repeat "and": "Twarz Lawrence'a Chase'a wyrażała zdziwienie, powątpiewanie i trochę poirytowania" ("Lawrence Chase's face expressed surprise, doubt and a little annoyance") (Dickson 1972: 22). Despite the conjunction, it is difficult to see the connection (because there is none) between the lighting and the laughter in the following: "There was only one light on in the room, the lamp by the bedside, and this was behind her head. But she choked with something like laughter" (Dickson 1951: 109). The Polish makes sense of the passage, the second sentence reading, in back translation, "But even in the semi-darkness it could be seen she was trying to stifle laughter" (Dickson 1972: 137). The Polish tendency to embellish reporting verbs is seen to some advantage in the translation of this exchange between Masters and Sanders: "'But either they were wiped off afterwards or else they were never there.' Sanders refused to be drawn. 'So now I'm accused of seeing things?'" (Dickson 1951: 179). Of course it sounds like he *has* been drawn: Sanders is inviting Masters to insult him. The Polish translator has Sanders "mumble" or "growl" his piece "wearily" ("mruknął ze znużeniem") (Dickson 1972: 226).

The translator of *The Reader is Warned* also corrects the word "nigger" in one character's speech: "'If I can dress for dinner among a lot of damned niggers, surely I can dress for dinner in my own house?'" (Dickson 1951: 38). The translator uses the word "Murzyn" (Dickson 1972: 48). The words are repeated later in the book and again "Murzyn" is used in the translation (Dickson 1951: 223; 1972: 280). On both these occasions "damned" is translated "przeklęty" (i.e. "damned") but in other places the translation tends to conform to the practice, detailed elsewhere, of leaving God out of the picture, or substituting the devil, as when the original has "'some of the god-damnedest cases'" (Dickson 1951: 84) while in Polish the cases are simply "damned" – by whom being left unsaid (Dickson 1972: 105).

Two final observations about the censorship of this book are in order, lest it be thought that People's Poland brought only sweetness and light. A Mr. Pennick claims to have the ability to kill people by the power of thought alone but only if they are less intelligent than himself. Masters remarks that this caveat would seem to "'rule out bumping off Hitler or Mussolini or Stalin or any of the big pots'" (Dickson 1951: 100). Stalin is missing from the Polish translation, which also translates the old fashioned "big pots" with "fat fish", the standard Polish equivalent of "big shots" (Dickson 1972: 125). Later, Henry Merrivale, the master detective, admits that if his plan goes wrong he will be "'departin' for Siberia'" (Dickson 1951: 146). In the Polish version, it is to the Sahara that he may be bound (Dickson 1972: 184).

Translators may have improved on Carter Dickson, Myra Page and C.S. Lewis but the emphasis on good Polish is sometimes deleterious. It makes itself felt in translations that are sometimes a little too polished, most noticeable in the translations of direct speech. Demotic, dialectal, sometimes ungrammatical English is often standardised in Polish translations. Krzysztof Filip Rudolf comes out against this quite strongly in a 2014 article: if the author has taken the trouble to write non-standard English the translator should not then standardise it in the target language. He calls this a truism but one that often goes unobserved (Rudolf 2014: 29). In Polish, the tradition is of almost universal standardisation. Monika Adamczyk-Garbowska notes the use of a small amount of stylisation but even this, Rudolf claims, is an overstatement. Neutralisation is usually complete, as in the translation of the speech of Joseph in *Wuthering Heights* (Rudolf 2014: 34-35). Rudolf goes on to present ways devised by students in the University of Gdańsk in which Joseph's speech could be better translated, stressing that it is not a question of absolute philological fidelity to a particular variety of Polish but simply a matter of consistently marking the character's speech as different. The examples given are far more radical than anything I have read in professional translations and include not just rural lexical items, which one does occasionally find in the work of professional translators, but also phonetic transcriptions of simplified, fast speech, e.g. "myślo" instead of "myślą" ("they think") and "nieestem" instead of "nie jestem" ("I am not") (Rudolf 2014: 39, 45). Also suggested are purely visual pointers, such as writing "tfój" instead of the correct "twój" ("your") (Rudolf 2014: 45). Not all scholars are as bullish as Rudolf, however.

The effect of neutralisation on the target text (TT) is not always trivial. Eliza Łuszczewska writes of the translation of *Elmer Gantry*:

> the American linguistic variety is lost in the TT as the majority of expressions spelled in the vernacular mode have not been rendered. [...] The vernacular expressions typically used by lower working classes, that may show Ad Locust's social background, are not preserved in the TT. Thus, the TT reader is not able to conclude that he could have been a member of [a] lower social class who has managed to become a successful Peugeot Farm Implement Company agent and [...] therefore a living example of [the] American Dream (Łuszczewska 2012: 51).

Lisiecka (1964: 81) credits the socialist realist "production novel" with introducing the language of miners and peasants to Polish literature but the tendency of translations to reduce dialogue with its regional and social class markers to standard literary Polish would have strengthened beliefs that the USA was a classless society.

Lord Jim was re-translated in 2001 by Michał Kłobukowski, who was unhappy with Aniela Zagórska's 1933 version, which eliminated differences between dialects in the original (Sadkowski 2002: 159). Zagórska's version was the one in circulation throughout the duration of People's Poland. Other examples of standardisation have been remarked in passing in various parts of the book and it is determined attempts by translators to reproduce bad or non-standard English that stand out. One such brave exception is Wacław Niepokólczycki's translation of *Call it Sleep*, which contains the following piece of dialogue: "'Wot's your fodder?' 'Mine fodder is a printer'" (Roth 1991: 21). The translation keeps the sense and is similarly ungrammatical: "'Czym jest twój tata?' 'Mój tata jest drukarz'" (Roth 1975: 22).[1] Zofia Kierszys also attempts to render dialect variation in her translation of *Sanctuary*, where, for example, "'One day mo! Aint no place fer you in heavum!'" (Faulkner 1997: 150) is rendered "'Jeszcze jeden dzień! Nima [nie ma] miejsca dla ciebie w niebiesiech [niebie]'" ("One day more. There is no place for you in heaven") (Faulkner 1957: 124). However, in *Manhattan Transfer* Congo says, "'Hell I'm going out to Senegal and get to be a nigger'" and "'When I very leetle I first go to sea dey call me Congo because I have curly hair an dark like a nigger'" (Dos Passos 1986: 44: 207). As seen, in translation Congo does not use racist words but not only that: he also speaks grammatically, like an educated Pole (Dos Passos 1958: 51, 280). In Flannery O'Connor's "Greenleaf" Scofield says, "'Mamma don't like to hear me say it'" (O'Connor 1971: 315) but in Polish he uses the correct grammatical forms, just as the narrator does, increasing the "levelling" effect described in chapter five. Neglect of social class speech markers in the translations of Nesbit, Montgomery, Lofting and Bond were detailed in the chapter on children's literature.

The results of this domestication can sometimes even be ridiculous, as in the translation of the Charlie Chan novel, *The Chinese Parrot*. Low-brow though the book may be, it is technically better written than Dickson's *The Reader is Warned*. However, Charlie Chan speaks perfect Polish. The characteristic "'All time big Pacific Ocean suffer sharp pain down below, and toss about to prove it. Maybe from sympathy, I am in same fix'" (Biggers 1987: 21) comes out as "'Wielki Pacyfik cały czas odczuwał boleści gdzieś tam w dole i rzucał się na wszystkie strony. Ja, prawdopodobnie przez sympatię, czułem się podobnie" ("All the time the great Pacific felt pains somewhere below and hurled itself about in all directions. I, probably in sympathy, felt the same") (Bigger 1979: 25). The effect created by bringing into collision a literary metaphor and irregular English is lost in translation. Later on, Chan, playing the part of a Chinese servant, says, "'Maybe you wantee catch 'um moah fish, hey, boss?'" (Biggers 1987: 52). Any irony or humour or sophisticated comment on stereotyping to be derived from Chan's change of role and speech is lost on the Polish reader. The translation cuts the line (which goes unanswered anyway) (Biggers 1979: 63). Another unfortunate example comes in chapter six. To begin with, Chan is still playing the part of the Chinese servant:

> 'You come 'long, boss,' said his confederate [i.e. Chan] loudly. 'You ac' lazy bimeby you no catch 'um bleckfast.'
> Having said which, Charlie gently closed the door and came in, grimacing as one who felt a keen distaste.
> 'Silly talk like that hard business for me,' he complained (Biggers 1987: 58).

The Polish translation is correct – too correct, meaning the reader is left wondering what is so very silly about saying, "'Pan idzie prędko na śniadanie... bo kto lenieje, ten nie je'" ("Come quickly to breakfast...the lazy man does not eat") (Biggers 1979: 69).

The Charlie Chan example shows high-handedness on the part of the translator, who seems to have placed respect for language (the Polish language) higher than respect for the source text, since it is "only" pulp fiction. Ross Macdonald's Lew Archer mystery, *Sleeping Beauty*, translated in 1978, comes from the higher reaches of detective fiction but a similar lack of respect for the source text may have led to the following hiccup in the translation, when a character corrects himself: "'Laurel and me – Laurel and I had one or two discussions about it'" (Macdonald 1973: 202). In Polish there is no correction. It reads, in back translation, "Laurel and I... Laurel and I had one or two conversations about it" (Macdonald 1978: 223), making the speaker sound merely hesitant. This is a small but significant point. The speaker is Laurel's husband, Tom Russo, who married into a wealthy family and is aware of his humble origins. His self-correction is a small sign of his feelings of inferiority. Afraid to speak his own, "inferior" brand of English, he "levels up" to that of his interlocutor – in this case a private investigator. This is missing in the Polish, whether through an oversight or because of the tendency to write correct Polish.

The problem is by no means restricted to popular fiction (the Polish edition of *The Chinese Parrot* had a print run of 100,300. 120,320 copies of *Sleeping Beauty* were printed). Jerzy Jarniewicz has shown how Zygmunt Allan's desire to write good Polish (avoiding repetition, for example) meant that his translation of Joyce's *Portrait of the Artist as a Young Man* fails to capture the child's voice in which some of the book is told. "Queer", "strange" and "nice" recur at the start of the book, testifying, Jarniewicz says, to the "immaturity of the narrator's style. They have broad, imprecise semantic fields. This is a problem for the translator, whose first reaction would be to replace the recurring words with synonyms or pronouns". In addition, there is the risk that the faithful translator (not Stephen Dedalus) will be blamed for poor writing style (Jarniewicz 2012: 240).

A certain conservatism can also be seen in Zofia Kierszys's translation of *Pylon*, by William Faulkner. Faulkner commits some sins against good Polish, such as repetition: "Then he looked at his hands; he looked at them as if he had just discovered he had them..." (Faulkner 1951: 71). The Polish is "Potem spojrzał na swoje ręce takim wzrokiem, jakby dopiero teraz odkrył, że je ma..." ("Then he looked at his hands as if he had just discovered he had them") (Faulkner 1967: 108). Faulkner's prose in *Pylon* is dense and hard to penetrate, with twists in the direction taken by sentences, as in the following disconcerting example: "He [Jiggs] rolled over to face the room and the daylight and saw Shumann standing over him, dressed save for his shirt, and the parachute jumper awake too, lying on his side..." (Faulkner 1951: 68-69). Jiggs faces the room, the daylight and – and here Faulkner puts in a verb instead of the noun that might be expected and might be counted as good, clear prose style. The Polish is written in a conventionally good, clear prose style and is much easier to follow: "Odwrócił się od ściany i w pełnym świetle dnia zobaczył, że stoi nad nim Shumann, ubrany do pasa, tylko bez koszuli, i że spadochroniarz [...] również już nie śpi" ("He turned away from the wall and in the full light of day saw that Shumann, dressed but without a shirt, was standing over him and that the parachutist [...] was also awake") (Faulkner 1967: 104). Part of the ease of reading comes from the fact that Polish is an inflected language forcing clarity on the relations between different parts of the sentence. For example, in English there is "Shumann now herded them all before him. Then he paused and looked back at Jiggs, dressed, neat, profoundly serious beneath the new hat which Jiggs might still have been looking at through plate glass" (Faulkner 1951: 72). Who is dressed and neat? Jiggs or Shumann? The Polish translation – as it must – puts Jiggs in the accusative case and "dressed and neat" in the nominative case so it is immediately clear that it is Shumann who is dressed and neat (Faulkner 1967: 109).

Some of this clarity comes from Kierszys's "correction" of Faulkner's style. For example, "but he said nothing: he just said, 'What happened last night?'" (Faulkner 1951: 69), is in Polish "ale nic nie powiedział. Tylko zapytał po chwili: 'Co się tu działo w nocy?'" ("but he said nothing. Only after a moment he asked, 'What happened here last night?'") (Faulkner 1967: 105). The translator added "after a moment" to avoid the flat self-contradiction present in the original. Even the translation of the title of the chapter from which these examples come ("Tomorrow") shows a strong tendency to normalise the text. In Polish it is the more logical "Nazajutrz" ("The Following Day"). From the reader's point of view the events related in the chapter take place the day after the previous events and cannot, in fact, take place "tomorrow". Paradoxes and non-sequiturs occasionally throw translators, as when Evelyn Waugh has a character say, "'Heavens, how nasty this stuff [yoghurt] is. I wish you'd take to it, John'" (Waugh 1951: 7). The incongruity did not elude the translator but he decided to make sense of the words. In back translation it reads, "How nasty! Even still, I wish you would get used to yoghurt" (Waugh 1957: 13).[2] It could be argued that these are not good quality translations – but they are good quality *Polish*.

László Scholz, after Haraszti, notes a similar tendency to "'write well'" in post-war Hungary. This carried over into translations, where clarity was highly prized (Scholz 2011: 209, 212). The desire to write well is "in reality the inevitable consequence of the concept of art and directed art that values content over form" (Scholz 2011: 209, after Haraszti). Some of the practical results of this in Hungarian translations of Spanish fiction should sound familiar. Scholz writes:

The most common linguistic-stylistic taboo in Hungarian literature of the postwar period was the use of obscenities, vulgarities, and indecent slang. Such language was ignored or, in the majority of cases, substituted with more decent or euphemistic phrases according to the clichés of 'good writing,' evidence of the general tendency toward literarization and of the monolithic imposition of an official taste (Scholz 2011: 214).

There are numerous examples of this kind of euphemistic language in Polish translations from English. Scholz also writes, "neither does one see any attempt to stray from the canonical norms on a syntactic level; the 'irregularities' are almost always corrected", giving examples similar to those above from Dos Passos, of non-standard language being translated into correct Hungarian (Scholz 2011: 215). Scholz traces the causes of this back to the social function which art was supposed to have in Hungary:

The unquestionable social function of art carried evident consequences. No effort could exist to produce works of *l'art pour l'art*, playful, experimental or self-reflective texts removed from the pre-established goal; there was no room left for attempts at artistic innovations and changes of genre. The other fundamental requirement was clarity. An artistic work that contained elements that were difficult to define or understand were considered unpublishable, first by the aforementioned organs of control, and then by the artists themselves, who, with time, came to practice self censorship without hesitation (Scholz 2011: 208).

In People's Poland, too, art was to have a social function. However, the regime was more liberal, especially after 1956, when leave was given by the authorities for "sensible experiments", and the effects of conservatism were much less pronounced in People's Poland. In the popular saying Poland was "najweselszy barak w socjalistycznym obozie", which can be loosely translated as "the happiest tent/ barrack in the socialist camp". Andrzej Walicki puts it somewhat differently in his *Od komunistycznej utopii do neoliberalnej utopii*, where the People's Republic of Poland is described as "the least orthodox and the least repressive version of 'people's democracy'" (Walicki 2013: xi). For people from East Germany – or the German Democratic Republic if one prefers – Poland was "'the West, a land of freedom'" (Helena Flam, qtd. in Walicki 2013: 80). For this reason it is difficult to draw hard and fast conclusions from the data, especially concerning the years after 1956. Racist language, swearing, and blaspheming against God and against communism were all frowned on but translators had much room to manoeuvre and there are many exceptions.

Scholz writes of a "striking uniformity of literary translations from Spanish into Hungarian" in this period (Scholz 2011: 205) but in Polish translations of English language fiction there is more variety. Dehnel gave us standard literary Polish in the speech of emigrants in *Manhattan Transfer* and Sujkowska transformed the dialect spoken in *Wuthering Heights* into standard Polish but Juliusz Kydryński, the translator of Albert Maltz's "Season of Celebration", tried to show that the characters in the story are not speaking high-flown English. One of them, Zets, is Russian (Polish in the translation) and speaks thus in the original: "'Boy bad sick maybe. You give him bicarb? Bicarb good for belly'" (Maltz 1938: 54). The translator keeps the sense and, like the source text, leaves out two verbs, giving an unusual effect.[3] And while Faulkner's experimentation may have suffered at the hands of Zofia Kierszys, Wacław Sadkowski rates Kalina Wojciechowska's translations of *Wild Palms* and *Sartoris* highly (Sadkowski 2002: 128).

Uniform Poland may not have been but a tendency to write conventionally good (grammatical, well-structured, logical, unadventurous) Polish did exist and when it coincided with a genteel avoidance of swear words, racist abuse and blasphemy it could result in slightly anaemic translations. However, not all critics will consider domestication censorship.

Translations from English got off lightly because there was a risk of comparison with the source text but they also escaped the worst of the censors' lash because so many of them were properly critical of capitalism and the western way of life. Charles Dickens is an obvious example and propagandists often tried to claim him for their own, socialist cause but one does not have to reach for the greatest of the great to find such criticism of capitalism. Here is a throwaway remark in Ross Macdonald's *Sleeping Beauty*: "'Other people burn their bridges behind them. We do things on a grander scale in our family. We burn ships and spill oil. It's the all-American way'" (Macdonald 1973: 76). *Sleeping Beauty* is detective fiction or family drama if you prefer: to suggest it was selected by the Polish authorities because of its devastating critique of the American Dream is absurd. The fact is that questioning and criticism of the American way can be found in much of the American and British fiction that is worth being translated in the first place. Here is Mario Puzo, hardly a communist propaganda tool: "Like many businessmen of genius he [Don Corleone] learned that free competition was wasteful, monopoly efficient" and "It [the Mafia in Sicily] had become a degenerate capitalist structure, anti-communist, anti-liberal, placing its own taxes on every form of business endeavour no matter how small" (Puzo 1969: 213, 327). Both these sentiments and the lines from *Sleeping Beauty* are translated into Polish without any obfuscation (Puzo 1979: 281, 433; Macdonald 1978: 87). So, too, for that matter, is the unflattering "It [gangsterism] was ten times worse than communism" (Puzo 1969: 69; Puzo 1979: 89). It might be argued that such books implicitly support the American Way but as has been seen over and again censors were less concerned with the underlying themes of books than what was there on the surface.

A book might be an all-out attack on totalitarianism but even then it is often possible to claim it has a universal application and is not directed only at the USSR or communism. For instance, the following lines, all of which were translated accurately into Polish, might read like a satire of the show trials of the Soviet Union but they do not come from *Darkness at Noon* or *1984*: "The case [...] was open and shut. The only thing missing was something to charge him with"; "'Didn't you whisper that we couldn't punish you to that other dirty son of a bitch we don't like?'"; "'What will I be charged with?' 'What the hell difference does that make?'"; "'That's a very serious crime you've committed, Father,' said the major. 'What crime?' 'We don't know yet,' said the colonel. 'But we're going to find out. And we sure know it's very serious'"; "'I'm not guilty!' 'Then why would we be questioning you if you weren't guilty?'" They come from *Catch-22* (Heller 1964: 81-82, 88, 90, 402, 406) and it is easy enough to argue that the book is an indictment of McCarthyism. In Albert Maltz's testimony before the House Un-American Activities Committee the questioning goes in short order from "Are you a member of the Screen Writers Guild?" to "Are you now or have you ever been a member of the Communist Party?" When Maltz declined to satisfy his interrogator on constitutional grounds, the interrogator said, "Excuse the witness. No more questions. Typical Communist line" ('Hearings' 1947: 366-367).

And it could have been the same Albert Maltz – in bottom dog mode – who wrote:

> He wondered how many people were destitute that same night even in his own prosperous country, how many homes were shanties, how many husbands were drunk and wives socked, and how many children were bullied, abused or abandoned. How many families hungered for food they could not afford to buy? How many hearts were broken? How many suicides would take place that same night, how many people would go insane? How many cockroaches and landlords would triumph?

Again, though, it was Joseph Heller in *Catch-22* (1964: 435-436). This, too, was translated faithfully into Polish (Heller 1978: 445). Albert Maltz is tainted by association with the Soviet Union and its jargon of "genuine people's writers" and "critical realism" (Ruggles 1961: 431) but *Catch-22*, in contrast, is "a disturbing insight into the larger struggle of today: the survival of mankind" (Heller 1964: n. pag.). After all, Heller remembered to add the words "What a lousy earth!" to his criticism of Yossarian's own country (Heller 1964: 435).

Any thoughtful writer will be critical of the status quo and although writers such as Jeffrey Archer, Irwin Shaw, Dean Koontz, James Clavell and Ken Follett were translated in People's Poland, the authorities leaned towards more thoughtful literature. A search of the Polish National Library's online catalogue turns up no pre-1989 mentions of popular fiction writers Robert Ludlum, Jilly Cooper, Stephen King, Georgette Heyer, Tom Clancy, Catherine Cookson, Barbara Cartland, Rosamunde Pilcher, Maeve Binchy, Jackie Collins, Harold Robbins, Clive Cussler, Michael Crichton, Danielle Steel, Shirley Conran, Judith Krantz, Colleen McCullough, Sidney Sheldon, Irving Wallace, Mary Higgins Clark, Thomas Harris, or Marion Zimmer Bradley. A perusal of the author index of the *Bibliography of Literature Translated into Polish Published Between 1945 and 1976* makes it immediately apparent that more serious writers were favoured.

The bias towards high brow fiction means that writers with something serious and – perhaps inevitably – critical to say about their home countries are over-represented in Polish translation. Such writers are attractive to those who would discredit the other side on the crude principle of "my enemy's enemy is my friend". The Russian regime welcomed *The Catcher in the Rye* because it was "a damning critique of contemporary American society and its institutions", while the Russian intelligentsia applied it to Russia (Baer 2012: 97). This explains why Tadeusz Jakubowicz was allowed to translate and Czytelnik to publish "'Your commune in France was the beginning ... socialism failed. It's for the anarchists to strike the next blow'" in *Manhattan Transfer* (Dos Passos 1986: 45). Jay McInerney describes Dos Passos's novel as "a passionate but not a systematic critique of American capitalism in the early twenties" (McInerney 1986: 9). The novel's criticism of the US outweighs this dismissal of socialism by one of its characters. The tendency of writers to be critical of their own countries also helps explain why books translated from Russian far outnumber books translated from English in *samizdat* publications. Czachowska and Dorosz list just 20 editions of US translations (1977-1989), including books by Nabokov and Ayn Rand as well as Roth's *The Prague Orgy* and Vonnegut's *Mother Night*. There are 51 from British literature but Orwell's works account for 34 of them. There are roughly 150 entries for Russian books (Czachowska and Dorosz 1991). Russians were writing bad things about Russia, which drove them underground; Americans wrote bad things about America, which meant they were acceptable to the Polish authorities.

Then there is the question of the applicability of any criticism in a novel. Simplifying, a socialist reviewer of, say, *Catch-22* will describe the interrogations of Clevinger and the chaplain as criticism of McCarthyism while a capitalist reviewer will cite the trials of Bukharin and Zinoviev. The reader – Polish and American – is in the happy position of having full access to the book precisely because it can be argued over in this way.[4] If the book were crude, one-sided propaganda then the chances are greater that one side at least would be deprived of access. The James Bond film *Thunderball* was banned in Poland; so were *The Battle of the Bulge* and *The Longest Day* (for praising US heroism at a time when the Vietnam War was being fought) (G-846, 86/1: 4, 72); and so were *Rambo II* and *Rocky IV*, the latter for its "caricature-like depiction of the USSR" (G-2115, 438/8: 239). As ever, there were exceptions to the rule: the film version of Graham Greene's *The Comedians*, which is hardly one-sided propaganda, was banned for allegedly absolving the US of the moral responsibility for the dictatorship in Haiti (G-848, 86/3: 16). *The Spy Who Came in From the Cold* was only available as a *samizdat* publication, from 1986 (Czachowska and Dorosz 1991), though it cannot be accused of glorifying the British intelligence services.

The censor will have much more work to do with a thoughtful Polish writer. It was alright when a western writer questioned the spiritual emptiness of modern life: this can be seen as an attack on the western milieu or – if the writer is really good – as a statement on the human condition. But a Polish author depicting such spiritual emptiness is obviously having a go at her own, eastern milieu and protestations that her book is about the human condition risk being written off as attempts to cloak criticism of communism.

Polish writers often sought refuge in Aesopian language but translators of English fiction had little need for such tricks and I have found few instances of resistance to censorship on their part. Another tactic used by Polish writers was to overload their work with very obviously debatable material in the hope that it would be stopped while more subtle criticisms would pass. There is a passage from *The Maltese Falcon* that *may* be an example of this in translated literature too. The passage mentions "'the natural contrariness of a Russian general'" (Hammett 2010: 123). In Polish the general is still Russian but his contrariness is his own, not that of Russians. However, the speaker is permitted to refer to him as a "'stupid soldier'" ("głupi żołdak") on the same page (Hammett 1963: 129). This is quite a daring move on the part of the translator, since "żołdak" is pejorative, carrying the additional meaning of "looting", which many Poles would have associated with the Red Army. I have not been able to find any reviews of this book in the archives but it is at least possible that the translator wrote both of Russian contrariness and the tendency to loot in the hope that at least one swipe at Russian soldiers would pass the censor – as it did.

Samantha Sherry argues, after Judith Butler, that texts may be translated in such a way as to tip the reader off to the existence of censorship (Sherry 2012: 155-156). However, this can lead to fairly generous definitions of "resistance". For example, the replacement, in the Russian translation of *Catcher in the Rye*, of "fuck you" with "an obscenity" is

> a metalinguistic device that draws the reader's attention to the absence. It could be posited that the censorial act is also a perlocutionary act: the censor seeks to draw the reader's attention to the act of censorship and hint at what has been removed. The reader can then attempt to reconstruct the original (Sherry 2012: 154).

If translation by means of euphemism is a form of resistance then Polish translators did indeed resist, and quite strongly. But what, precisely, were they resisting? Western literary norms? Or were they conforming to norms of Polish literature and socialist decorum? To argue that in bowdlerising a text the translator is actually striking a blow for freedom of speech seems a little too much like having your cake and eating it. The definition of resistance – like that of censorship – has become perilously broad. Walton demonstrates how bowdlerisation can alert the reader to the influence of censorship – but he wonders if it is censorship (Walton 2007: 156). Similarly, Zygmunt Hubner lists the use of allusions in theatre as a way of circumventing censorship but he adds: "Who is outsmarting whom? The theatre usually emerges victorious, but let us not forget that the allusion is a form of self-censorship" (Hubner 1992: 63). If we remove Stalin's name from a list of "every enemy that freedom ever had" we make him conspicuous by his absence but it is still censorship, just not very effective censorship. Some examples have been given here of drawing attention to censorship – such as the passage from *To Be A Pilgrim* that mysteriously lacks an antecedent – but they are few and far between.

There is virtually no sabotage of texts, few attempts to narrow the author's criticism of life, the universe and everything down to a criticism of communist life in translations from English. A censor's review of a serialised German novel by Manfred Gregor called *The Bridge* and set during the Second World War contains an intriguing hint at resistance on the part of the translator. The censor writes that "the translation is very weak and naïve. For example, the translator uses our Party terminology for the fascist party". Publication was not recommended (G-588, 55/1: 118). One wonders if the translator really was so naïve or if he or she deliberately tried to draw a parallel between Nazism and communism by using the latter's terminology to describe the former.

Catch-22 might be considered an exception to the no-sabotage rule. The title was translated as *Paragraf 22*, which means "Paragraph 22", as in a paragraph or section of the legal code. What in the original is left very vague is in the Polish translation concretised as a statute. There is a saying, often attributed by Poles to the Stalinist prosecutor Andrei Vyshinsky: "Give me the man; there'll be a paragraph for him" ("Dajcie mi człowieka, a paragraf się znajdzie"). Zbigniew Lewicki recognised the translation as a concretisation but he criticised it: the subtitle of his review article reads bluntly, "a catch is not a paragraph" (Lewicki 1976: 338). If Heller's translator, Lech Jęczmyk, was deliberately trying to steer the book's satire towards eastern totalitarianism by using the word "paragraf" his attempt was not appreciated – or at any rate not acknowledged.

---

[1] "Czym" is used for referring to objects, not people and "drukarz" ("printer") should be in the instrumental case ("drukarzem").

[2] For other examples of this tendency to make sense of illogical source texts see Looby (2013).

[3] "'Chłopak pewnie bardzo chory. Dajesz mu sodę? Soda dobra na brzuch'" (Maltz 1951: 46).

[4] Wacław Sadkowski tells how he was roundly criticised in 1989 for emphasising the universality of *Animal Farm* in his afterword for the Polish edition (Sadkowski 2002: 150).

Bibliography

Archival Sources

All archival sources come from the Central Archives of Modern Records (Archiwum Akt Nowych) in Warsaw.

G: Zespół (collection) number 1,102. *Główny Urząd Kontroli Prasy, Publikacji i Widowisk* (GUKPPiW), (Main Office for Control of the Press, Publications and Public Performances).

K: Zespół (collection) 1,354. *Komitet Centralny, Polska Zjednoczona Partia Robotnicza* (KC PZPR), (Central Committee of the Polish United Workers' Party).

M: Zespół (collection) 366. *Ministerstwo Kultury i Sztuki* (Ministry for Culture and Art).

C: Zespół (collection) 367. *Centralny Urząd Wydawnictw, Przemysłu Graficznego i Księgarstwa* (Central Office of Publishers, the Typographic Industry and Bookselling).

Primary

Amis, Kingsley. 1954. *Lucky Jim: A Novel*. London: Victor Gollancz [1954].

Amis, Kingsley. 1958. *Jim szczęściarz* (tr. Bronisława Jackiewicz and Cecylia Wojewoda). Warsaw: Państwowy Instytut Wydawniczy.

Anderson, Sherwood. 1946. *Winesburg, Ohio: A Group of Tales of Ohio Small-Town Life*. New York: Penguin [1919].

Anderson, Sherwood. 1977. *Miasteczko Winesburg. Obrazki z życia w stanie Ohio* (tr. Jerzy Krzyszton). Warsaw: Czytelnik.

Baldwin, James. 1966. *Głoś to na górze* (tr. Krystyna Tarnowska). Warsaw: PAX.

Baldwin, James. 1991. *Go Tell it on the Mountain*. London: Penguin [1954].

Baum, Frank. 1972. *Czarnoksiężnik ze szmaragdowego grodu*, 2nd edn. (tr. Stefania Wortman). Warsaw: Nasza Księgarnia [1962].

Baum, Frank. 1997. *The Wonderful Wizard of Oz* (ed. Susan Wolstenholme). Oxford and New York: Oxford University Press [1900].

Behan, Brendan. 1982. *Więzień Borstalu* (tr. Krystyna Korwin-Mikke). Kraków: Wydawnictwo Literackie.

Behan, Brendan. 1990. *Borstal Boy*. London: Arrow Books [1958].

Biggers, Earl Derr. 1979. *Chińska papuga* (tr. Izabella Dąmbska). Warsaw: Iskry.

Biggers, Earl Derr. 1987. *The Chinese Parrot*. New York: Mysterious Press [1926].

Bond, Michael. 1985. *A Bear Called Paddington* (omnibus edition). London: Chancellor Press [1958].

Bond, Michael. 1988. *Miś zwany Paddington*, 2nd edn. (tr. Kazimierz Piotrowski). Warsaw: Krajowa Agencja Wydawnicza [1971].

Bradbury, Ray. 1960. *451° Fahrenheit* (tr. Adam Kaska). Warsaw: Czytelnik.

Bradbury, Ray. 1980. *Fahrenheit 451*. New York: Ballantine [1953].
Braine, John. 1957. *Room at the Top*. London: Eyre & Spottiswoode.
Braine, John. 1960. *Wielka kariera* (tr. Henryk Krzeczkowski). Warsaw: Państwowy Instytut Wydawniczy.
Burnett, Frances Hodgson. 1963. *Mała księżniczka*, 2nd edn. (tr. Wacława Komarnicka). Warsaw: Nasza Księgarnia [1959].
Burnett, Frances Hodgson. 1994. *A Little Princess*. Ware, Hertfordshire: Wordsworth Classics.
Caldwell, Erskine. 1947. *Tobacco Road*. New York: Signet.
Caldwell, Erskine. 1949. *Druga Ameryka* (tr. J. Łaszczowa and M. Żurowski (*Tobacco Road*) and J. Łaszczowa and T. Borowski (*Trouble in July*)). s.l.: Czytelnik.
Caldwell, Erskine. 1950. *Georgia Boy*. New York: Duell, Sloan and Pearce [1943].
Caldwell, Erskine. 1961. *Ziemia tragiczna* (tr. Krzysztof Zarzecki). Warsaw: Państwowy Instytut Wydawniczy.
Caldwell, Erskine. 1973. *Chłopiec z Georgii*, 3rd edn. (tr. Mira Michałowska). Warsaw: Państwowy Instytut Wydawniczy [1962].
Caldwell, Erskine. 1979. *Tragic Ground & Trouble in July*. New York: New American Library [1940 & 1944, respectively].
Caldwell, Erskine. 1984. *Najlepsze nowele* (various translators). Warsaw: Iskry.
Carroll, Lewis. 1972. *Przygody Alicji w Krainie Czarów* (tr. Maciej Słomczyński). Warsaw: Czytelnik.
Carroll, Lewis. 1986. *Alicja w Krainie Czarów i Po drugie stronie Lustra* (tr. Robert Stiller). Warsaw: Wydawnictwo Alfa.
Cary, Joyce. 1958. *First Trilogy: Herself Surprised, To Be A Pilgrim* and *The Horse's Mouth*. New York: Harper and Brothers [1942].
Cary, Joyce. 1959. *Kostur pielgrzyma* (tr. Wacław Niepokólczycki). Warsaw: Państwowy Instytut Wydawniczy.
Chesterton, G.K. 1937. *The Man Who was Thursday: A Nightmare*. Harmondsworth: Penguin [1908].
Cooper, James Fenimore. 1956a. *Ostatni Mohikan* (tr. Tadeusz Evert). Warsaw: Iskry.
Cooper, James Fenimore. 1956b. *Pogromca zwierząt, czyli pierwsza ścieżka wojenna* (tr. Kazimierz Piotrowski). Warsaw: Iskry.
Cooper, James Fenimore. 1985. *The Leatherstocking Tales* (ed. Blake Nevius), 2 vols. New York: The Library of America.
Cooper, James Fenimore. 2002. *The Last of the Mohicans*. Ware, Hertfordshire: Wordsworth Editions.
Cronin, A.J. 1956. *The Keys of the Kingdom*. New York: Bantam [1941].
Cronin, A.J. 1974. *Klucze Królestwa*, 3rd edn. (tr. Stanisław Morgenthal). Warsaw: PAX [1954].
Curwood, James Oliver. 1982. *Włóczęgi Północy*, 10th edn. (tr. Jerzy Marlicz). Warsaw: Iskry [1955].
De Boissiere, Ralph. 1953. *Klejnot korony* (tr. Janusz Grabowski). Warsaw: Czytelnik.
De Boissiere, Ralph. 1956. *Crown Jewel*. Leipzig: Paul List Verlag.
Dick, Philip K. 1981. *Człowiek z Wysokiego Zamku* (tr. Lech Jęczmyk). Warsaw: Czytelnik.
Dick, Philip K. 2001. *The Man in the High Castle*. London: Penguin [1962].
Dickens, Charles. 1951. *Wielkie nadzieje* (tr. Karolina Beylin). Warsaw: Książka i Wiedza.
Dickens, Charles. 1992. *Great Expectations*, London: Everyman's Library, Random Century.
Dickson, Carter. 1951. *The Reader is Warned*. Harmondsworth: Penguin [1939].
Dickson, Carter. 1972. *Ostrzegam czytelnika...* (tr. Krystyna Tomoworicz). Warsaw: Czytelnik.
Dos Passos, John. 1931. *Manhattan Transfer* (tr. Tadeusz Jakubowicz). Warsaw: Rój.
Dos Passos, John. 1958. *Manhattan Transfer* (tr. Tadeusz Jakubowicz). Warsaw: Czytelnik.
Dos Passos, John. 1986. *Manhattan Transfer*. Harmondsworth: Penguin [1925].
Drabble, Margaret. 1976. *Klatka latem w ogrodzie* (tr. Irena Doleżal-Nowicka). Warsaw: Czytelnik.

Drabble, Margaret. 1984. *A Summer Bird Cage*. Harmondsworth: Penguin [1963].

Dreiser, Theodore. 1959a. *Sister Carrie* (ed. Claude Simpson). Boston: Houghton Mifflin [1900].

Dreiser, Theodore. 1959b. *Siostra Carrie*, 2nd edn. (tr. Zofia Popławska). Poznań: Wydawnictwo Poznańskie [1949].

Eliot, George. 1960. *Młyn nad Flossą* (tr. Anna Przedpełska-Trzeciakowska). Warsaw: Czytelnik.

Eliot, George. s.d. *The Mill on the Floss*. Garden City, New York: Doubleday.

Farrell, Michael. 1963. *Thy Tears Might Cease*. London: Hutchinson.

Farrell, Michael. 1967. *Łzy twoje przestałyby płynąć* (tr. Maria Boduszyńska-Borowikowa, verses translated by Ludmiła Marjańska). Warsaw: Państwowy Instytut Wydawniczy.

Fast, Howard. 1949. *Departure and Other Stories*. Boston: Little, Brown & Co.

Fast, Howard. 1950. *Odjazd* (tr. M. Michałowska). Katowice: Czytelnik.

Fast, Howard. 1952. *Droga do wolności*, 2nd edn. (tr. Zofia Meissner). Warsaw: Książka i Wiedza [1949].

Fast, Howard. 1979. *Freedom Road*. London: Futura [1944].

Faulkner, William. 1951. *Pylon*. New York: Signet [1935].

Faulkner, William. 1954. *The Wild Palms* and *The Old Man*. New York: Signet [1939].

Faulkner, William. 1957. *Azyl* (tr. Zofia Kierszys). Warsaw: Państwowy Instytut Wydawniczy.

Faulkner, William. 1967. *Punkt zwrotny* (tr. Zofia Kierszys). Warsaw: Państwowy Instytut Wydawniczy.

Faulkner, William. 1987. *Dzikie palmy* i *Stary* (tr. Kalina Wojciechowska). Warsaw: Iskry [*Dzikie palmy* first published 1958].

Faulkner, William. 1997. *Sanctuary*. New York: Random House [1931].

Fielding, Helen. 1997. *Bridget Jones's Diary: A Novel*. London: Picador.

Fielding, Helen. 2001. *Dziennik Bridget Jones* (tr. Zuzanna Naczyńska). Poznań: Zysk i S-ka.

Fielding, Henry. 1953. *Przygody Józefa Andrewsa* (tr. Maria Korniłowicz). Warsaw: Państwowy Instytut Wydawniczy.

Fielding, Henry. 1980. *Joseph Andrews* and *Shamela* (ed. Douglas Brooks-Davies). Oxford: Oxford University Press [1742].

Fitzgerald, F. Scott. 1973. 'Diament wielki jak góra' in *Diament wielki jak góra*, 2nd edn. (tr. Adam Kaska). Warsaw: Książka i Wiedza [1967].

Fitzgerald, F. Scott. 1986. 'The Diamond as Big as the Ritz' in *The Collected Short Stories of F. Scott Fitzgerald*. Harmondsworth: Penguin. 74-109.

Gaskell, Elizabeth. 1970. *Panie z Cranford* (tr. Aldona Szpakowska). Warsaw: Czytelnik.

Gaskell, Elizabeth. s.d. *Cranford*. London: Thomas Nelson and Sons [1853].

Greene, Graham. 1948. *The Heart of the Matter*. Heinemann: Melbourne.

Greene, Graham. 1950. *Sedno sprawy* (tr. Jacek Woźniakowski). Warsaw: PAX.

Greene, Graham. 1956. *Moc i chwała* (tr. Bolesław Taborski). Paris: Instytut Literacki.

Greene, Graham. 1966. *Spokojny Amerykanin*, 2nd edn. (tr. Jacek Woźniakowski). Warsaw: PAX [1956].

Greene, Graham. 1970a. *Podróże z moją ciotką* (tr. Zofia Kierszys). Warsaw: PAX.

Greene, Graham. 1970b. *Our Man in Havana*. London: Heinemann and Bodley Head [1958].

Greene, Graham. 1971. *Travels with my Aunt*. Harmondsworth: Penguin [1969].

Greene, Graham. 1975. *Nasz człowiek w Hawanie*, 2nd edn. (tr. Maria Skibniewska). Warsaw: PAX [1960].

Greene, Graham. 1977. *The Quiet American*. London: Penguin [1955].

Greene, Graham. 1985. *Moc i chwała*, 4th edn. (tr. Bolesław Taborski). Warsaw: PAX [1967].

Greene, Graham. 1991. *The Power and the Glory*. London: Penguin [1940].

Hammett, Dashiell. 1963. *Sokół Maltański* (tr. Wacław Niepokólczycki). Warsaw: Iskry.

Hammett, Dashiell. 1984. 'The Farewell Murder' in *The Continental Op* (ed. Steven Marcus). London: Picador. 219-255.

Hammett, Dashiell. 1987. *Dwie martwe Chinki* (tr. Ariadna Demkowska-Bohdziewicz). Warsaw: Iskry.

Hammett, Dashiell. 1988. *Osmalona fotografia* (tr. Wacław Niepokólczycki) and *Idiotyczna sprawa* (tr. Krzysztof Zarzecki). Warsaw: Iskry.

Hammett, Dashiell. 1990. 'Morderstwo w Farewell' in *Od Stevensona do Hammetta. Opowiadania kryminalne* (tr. and ed. Jan S. Zaus). Poznań: Nakom. 157-203.

Hammett, Dashiell. 2005. *The Big Knockover*. London: Orion.

Hammett, Dashiell. 2010. *The Maltese Falcon*. London: Orion.

Hawthorne, Nathaniel. 1947. *Szkarłatna litera* (translation revised by Adam Laterner). Warsaw: Syrena.

Hawthorne, Nathaniel. 1994a. *The Scarlet Letter*. London: Penguin.

Hawthorne, Nathaniel. 1994b. *Szkarłatna litera* (tr. Bronisława Bałutowa). Wrocław: Wydawnictwo Dolnośląskie.

Heller, Joseph. 1964. *Catch-22*. London: Corgi.

Heller, Joseph. 1978. *Paragraf 22*, 2rd edn. (tr. Lech Jęczmyk). Warsaw: Państwowy Instytut Wydawniczy.

Hemingway, Ernest. 1971. *Śmierc po południu* (tr. Bronisław Zieliński). Warsaw: Państwowy Instytut Wydawniczy.

Hemingway, Ernest. 2000. *Death in the Afternoon*. London: Vintage [1932].

Joyce, James. 1981. *Ulisses*, 3rd edn. (tr. Maciej Słomczyński). Warsaw: Państwowy Instytut Wydawniczy.

Joyce, James. 1994. *Ulysses*. London: Secker and Warburg [1922].

Kipling, Rudyard. 1926. *Kim* (tr. Józef Birkenmajer). Lwów and Poznań: Wydawnictwo Polskie.

Kipling, Rudyard. 1939. *The Jungle Book*. London: Macmillan.

Kipling, Rudyard. 1963. *Księga dżungli*, 6th edn. (tr. Józef Birkenmajer). Warsaw: Nasza Księgarnia [1946].

Kipling, Rudyard. s.d. *Kim*. Leipzig: Bernhard Tauchnitz [1901].

Lessing, Doris. 1956. *Mrowisko* (tr. Agnieszka Glinczanka). Warsaw: Państwowy Instytut Wydawniczy.

Lessing, Doris. 1960. *Five Short Novels*. Harmondsworth: Penguin [1953].

Lewis, C.S. 1985. *Książę Kaspian* (tr. Andrzej Polkowski). Warsaw: PAX.

Lewis, C.S. s.d. *Prince Caspian: the Return to Narnia*. London: Geoffrey Bles [1951].

Lewis, Sinclair. 1935. *Elmer Gantry*. Hamburg and Paris: The Albatross [1927].

Lewis, Sinclair. 1961a. *Babbitt*. New York: New American Library [1922].

Lewis, Sinclair. 1961b. *Babbitt* (tr. Zofia Popławska). Warsaw: Państwowy Instytut Wydawniczy.

Lewis, Sinclair. 1987. *Elmer Gantry*, 2nd edn. (tr. Adam Kaska). Warsaw: Wydawnictwo MON (Ministry of Defence) [1959].

Linklater, Eric. 1936. *Ripeness is All*. Hamburg, Paris and Bologna: Albatross.

Linklater, Eric. 1962. *Rogi obfitości* (tr. Tadeusz Evert). Warsaw: Czytelnik.

Lofting, Hugh. 1923. *The Voyages of Doctor Dolittle*. London: Jonathan Cape.

Lofting, Hugh. 1985. *Podróże doktora Dolittle*, 6th edn. (tr. Janina Mortkowiczowa). Warsaw: Nasza Księgarnia [1946].

London, Jack. 1962. *A Daughter of the Snows* (ed. I.O. Evans). London: Arco.

London, Jack. 1975. *Biały kieł*, 8th edn. (tr. Anna Przedpełska-Trzeciakowska). Warsaw: Iskry [1955].

London, Jack. 1986. *Córka śniegów*, 2nd edn. (tr. Stanisława Kuszelewska). Warsaw: Ludowa Spółdzielnia Wydawnicza [1948].

London, Jack. s.d. *White Fang*. London: Thomas Nelson and Sons.

Macdonald, Ross. 1973. *Sleeping Beauty*. New York: Alfred A. Knopf.

Macdonald, Ross. 1978. *Śpiąca królewna* (tr. Wacław Niepokólczycki). Warsaw: Czytelnik.

Maltz, Albert. 1938. *The Way Things Are and Other Stories*. New York: International Publishers.

Maltz, Albert. 1940. *The Underground Stream*. Boston: Little, Brown & Co.
Maltz, Albert. 1949. *Te trzy dni. Opowieść amerykańska*, 2nd edn. (tr. Józef Brodzki). Katowice: Czytelnik.
Maltz, Albert. 1951. *Człowiek na drodze i inne opowiadania* (tr. Juliusz Kydryński). Warsaw: Czytelnik.
Maugham, William Somerset. 1935. *The Moon and Sixpence*. Melbourne and London: Heinemann [1919].
Maugham, William Somerset. 1959. *Księżyc i miedziak* (tr. Jadwiga Olędzka). Warsaw: Państwowy Instytut Wydawniczy.
McCarthy, Mary. 1964. *The Group*. New York: Signet.
McCarthy, Mary. 1985. *Grupa*, 2nd edn. (tr. Cecylia Wojewoda). Kraków and Wrocław: Wydawnictwo Literackie.
Melville, Herman. 1971. *Moby-Dick, czyli biały wieloryb*, 4th edn. (tr. Bronisław Zieliński). Warsaw: Czytelnik.
Melville, Herman. 1994. *Moby-Dick*. London: Penguin [1851].
Montgomery, Lucy Maud. 1985. *Wymarzony dom Ani*, 7th edn. (tr. Stefan Fedyński). Warsaw: Nasza Księgarnia [1959].
Montgomery, Lucy Maud. 1986. *Anne of Green Gables. Three Volumes in One: Anne of Green Gables, Anne of Avonlea, Anne's House of Dreams*. New York: Avenel Books.
Mrożek, Sławomir. 2000. *Słoń*, 2nd edn. Warsaw: Noir sur Blanc.
Mrożek, Sławomir. 2010. *The Elephant* (tr. Konrad Syrop). London: Penguin [1962].
Nesbit, Edith. 1959. *The Story of the Amulet*. Harmondsworth: Penguin.
Nesbit, Edith. 1963. *Historia amuletu* (tr. Irena Tuwim). Warsaw: Nasza Księgarnia.
O'Brien, Edna. 1963. *The Country Girls*. London: Penguin [1960].
O'Brien, Edna. 1964. *Girl With Green Eyes*. Harmondsworth: Penguin [1962].
O'Brien, Edna. 1978a. *Czekając na miłość*, 2nd edn. (tr. Maria Zborowska). Warsaw: Książka i Wiedza [1974].
O'Brien, Edna. 1978b. *Dziewczyna o zielonych oczach*, 3rd edn. (tr. Maria Zborowska). Warsaw: Książka i Wiedza [1973].
O'Casey, Sean. 1956. *Red Roses for Me* in *Six Great Modern Plays*. New York: Dell. 259-353 [1943].
O'Casey, Sean. 1961. *Czerwone róże dla mnie* (tr. Cecylia Wojewoda and Włodzimierz Lewik). *Dialog* 6(10): 50-85.
O'Casey, Sean. 1963. *Pukam do drzwi* (tr. Maria Traczewska). Kraków: Wydawnictwo Literackie.
O'Casey, Sean. 1971. *Autobiography Volume 1: I Knock at the Door*. London: Pan Books [1939].
O'Connor, Flannery. 1971. *The Complete Short Stories*. New York: Farrar, Straus and Giroux.
O'Connor, Flannery. 1975. *W pierścieniu ognia* (tr. Maria Skibniewska). Warsaw: Państwowy Instytut Wydawniczy.
O'Connor, Frank. 1963. *My Oedipus Complex and Other Stories*. Harmondsworth: Penguin.
O'Connor, Frank. 1971. *Święte Wrota* (tr. Maria Boduszyńska-Borowikowa). Warsaw: Państwowy Instytut Wydawniczy.
Page, Myra. 1950a. *With Sun in our Blood*. New York: Citadel Press.
Page, Myra. 1950b. *Słońce nad kopalnią* (tr. Ewa Fiszer and Eleonora Romanowicz). Katowice: Czytelnik.
Portis, Charles. 1973. *Troje na prerii* (tr. Zofia Uhrynowska). Warsaw: Iskry.
Portis, Charles. 2011. *True Grit*. London: Bloomsbury [1968].
Prichard, Katharine. 1951. *Skrzydlate ziarna* (tr. Tadeusz Dehnel). Warsaw: Czytelnik.
Prichard, Katharine. 1984. *Winged Seeds*. London: Virago [1950].
Puzo, Mario. 1969. *The Godfather*. Greenwich, Conn.: Fawcett Crest.

Puzo, Mario. 1979. *Ojciec chrzestny*, 2nd edn. (tr. Bronisław Zieliński). Warsaw: Czytelnik [1976].

Roth, Henry. 1975. *Nazwij to snem* (tr. Wacław Niepokólczycki). Warsaw: Państwowy Instytut Wydawniczy.

Roth, Henry. 1991. *Call it Sleep*. New York: Farrar Straus and Giroux.

Roth, Philip. 1969. *Portnoy's Complaint*. New York: Random House.

Roth, Philip. 1986. *Kompleks Portnoya* (tr. Anna Kołyszko). Kraków: Wydawnictwo Literackie.

Salinger, J.D. 1953. *The Catcher in the Rye*. New York: New American Library [1951].

Salinger, J.D. 1967. *Buszujący w zbożu*, 3rd edn. (tr. Maria Skibniewska). Warsaw: Iskry [1961].

Saxton, Alexander. 1951. *Stacja Great Midland* (tr. Ewa Fiszer). Warsaw: Państwowy Instytut Wydawniczy.

Saxton, Alexander. 1997. *The Great Midland*. Urbana and Chicago: University of Illinois Press.

Shelley, Mary. 1989. *Frankenstein*, 2nd edn. (tr. Henryk Goldmann). Poznań: Wydawnictwo Poznańskie.

Shelley, Mary. 1994. *Frankenstein or, the Modern Prometheus*. London: Penguin.

Sillitoe, Alan. 1973. *Men, Women and Children*. London and New York: W.H. Allen.

Sillitoe, Alan. 1979. *Mężczyźni, kobiety, dzieci* (tr. Jadwiga Milnikiel). Warsaw: Książka i Wiedza.

Sinclair, Upton. 1928. *Nazywają mnie cieślą* (no translator credited). Lwów: Ludowe Spółdzielcze Towarzystwo Wydawniczego.

Sinclair, Upton. 1971. *They Call Me Carpenter: A Tale of the Second Coming*. Bath: Cedric Chivers [1922].

Smith, Zadie. 2001. *White Teeth*. London: Penguin [2000].

Smith, Zadie. 2003. *Białe zęby* (tr. Zbigniew Batko). Warsaw: Świat Książki.

Spark, Muriel. 1965. *The Prime of Miss Jean Brodie*. Harmondsworth: Penguin [1961].

Steinbeck, John. 1939. *Grapes of Wrath*. London and Melbourne: Heinemann.

Steinbeck, John. 1959. *Grona gniewu*, (tr. Alfred Liebfeld). Warsaw: Państwowy Instytut Wydawniczy.

Steinbeck, John. 1963. *Na wschód od Edenu* (tr. Bronisław Zieliński). Warsaw: Państwowy Instytut Wydawniczy.

Steinbeck, John. 1992. *East of Eden*. London: Penguin [1952].

Stevenson, Robert Louis. 1939. *Treasure Island*. New York: Pocket Books.

Stevenson, Robert Louis. 1974. *Wyspa skarbów*, 8th edn. (tr. Józef Birkenmajer). Warsaw: Iskry.

Stowe, Harriet Beecher. 1909. *Uncle Tom's Cabin*. London and Toronto: Dent.

Stowe, Harriet Beecher. 1958. *Chata wuja Toma* (tr. Irena Tuwim and Julian Stawiński). Warsaw: Iskry.

Swift, Jonathan. 1971. *Podróże Gulliwera* (tr. Anon). Warsaw: Państwowy Instytut Wydawniczy.

Swift, Jonathan. 1979. *Podróże do wielu odległych narodów świata* (tr. Maciej Słomczyński). Kraków: Wydawnictwo Literackie.

Swift, Jonathan. 1986. *Gulliver's Travels*. Oxford: Oxford University Press.

Thackeray, William Makepeace. 1960. *Targowisko próżności* (tr. Tadeusz Dehnel). Warsaw: Państwowy Instytut Wydawniczy.

Thackeray, William Makepeace. 1983. *Vanity Fair: A Novel without a Hero* (ed. John Sutherland). Oxford: Oxford University Press.

Tolkien, J.R.R. 1985. *Hobbit czyli tam i z powrotem*, 2nd edn. (tr. Maria Skibniewska, verses translated by Włodzimierz Lewik). Warsaw: Iskry [1960].

Tolkien, J.R.R. 1997. *The Hobbit, or There and Back Again*. London: Harper Collins [1937].

Tuwim, Julian. 1985. 'Ball at the Opera (Bal w operze)' (tr. Madeline G. Levine and Steven I. Levine), *The Polish Review* 30(1): 5-23.

Tuwim, Julian. 1986. *Wiersze wybrane*. Biblioteka Narodowa, series 1: 184, 4th edn. Wrocław: Zakład im. Ossolińskich.

Twain, Mark. 1898. *Przygody Huck'a* (tr. T. Prażmowska). Warsaw: Granowski & Sikorski.

Twain, Mark. 1966. *Przygody Hucka*, 3rd edn. (tr. Krystyna Tarnowska). Warsaw: Iskry [1955].

Twain, Mark. 2001. *The Adventures of Tom Sawyer* and *The Adventures of Huckleberry Finn*. Ware, Hertforshire: Wordsworth Editions [1884].

Updike, John. 1973. *Museums and Women and Other Stories*. London: André Deutsch.

Updike, John. 1978. *Muzea i kobiety oraz inne opowiadania* (tr. Maria Skibniewska). Warsaw: Państwowy Instytut Wydawniczy.

Vonnegut, Kurt. 1963. *Cat's Cradle*. New York and Chicago: Holt, Rinehart and Wilson.

Vonnegut, Kurt. 1971. *Kocia kołyska* (tr. Lech Jęczmyk). Warsaw: Państwowy Instytut Wydawniczy.

Waugh, Evelyn. 1951. *A Handful of Dust*. Harmondsworth: Penguin [1934].

Waugh, Evelyn. 1957. *Garść prochu* (tr. Jerzy Olgar). Warsaw: PAX.

Waugh, Evelyn. 1962. *Brideshead Revisited: The Sacred and Profane Memories of Captain Charles Ryder*. London: Penguin [1945; this, revised edition 1960].

Waugh, Evelyn. 1970. *Znowu w Brideshead. Bogobojne i bluźniercze wspomnienia kapitana Karola Rydera* (tr. Irena Doleżal-Nowicka). Warsaw: PAX.

Weatherwax, Clara. 1952. *Będzie nas więcej* (tr. Irena Doleżal-Nowicka). Warsaw: Czytelnik.

Wells, H.G. 1941. *Kipps*. Harmondsworth: Penguin [1905].

Wells, H.G. 1950. *Kipps* (tr. Celina Wieniewska). Warsaw: Czytelnik.

West, Nathanael. 1963. *Dzień szarańczy* i *Miss Lonelyhearts* (tr. Maria Skibniewska). Warsaw: Czytelnik.

West, Nathanael. 1975. *The Day of the Locust*. New York: Bantam [1939].

Wister, Owen. 1977. *Wirgińczyk. Jeździec z równin*, 3rd edn. (tr. Janina Sujkowska). Warsaw: Iskry [1964].

Wister, Owen. 1988. *The Virginian: a Horseman of the Plains*, (unabridged). Pleasantville, NY: Reader's Digest Association [1902].

Wolfe, Thomas. 1940. *You Can't Go Home Again*. New York: Grosset & Dunlap [1934].

Wolfe, Thomas. 1959. *Nie ma powrotu* (tr. Maria Skibniewska). Warsaw: Czytelnik.

Woolf, Virginia. 1948. *The Years*. London: Pan Books [1937].

Woolf, Virginia. 1958. *Lata* (tr. Małgorzata Szercha). Warsaw: Czytelnik.

Paratexts

Bałutowa, Bronisława. 1959. Posłowie tłumaczki. *Dom o Siedmiu Szczytach*. By Nathaniel Hawthorne (tr. Bronisława Bałutowa). Warsaw: Czytelnik. 310-315.

Baum, Frank. 1997. Introduction. *The Wonderful Wizard of Oz*. By Baum (ed. Susan Wolstenholme). Oxford and New York: Oxford University Press. 3-4.

Bauman, Zygmunt. 1956. Posłowie. *Mary Barton*. By Elizabeth Gaskell (tr. Krystyna Tarnowska). Warsaw: Państwowy Instytut Wydawniczy. 459-470.

Bidwell, George. 1955. Posłowie. *Niezwykłe przygody Roderyka Randoma*. By Tobiasz Smollett (tr. Bronisław Zieliński). Warsaw: Państwowy Instytut Wydawniczy. Vol. 2: 269-279.

Blair, David. 2002. Introduction. *The Last of the Mohicans*. By James Fenimore Cooper. Ware, Hertfordshire: Wordsworth Editions. v-xxxiii.

Chwalewik, Witold. 1958. 'O *Tristramie Shandy* L. Sterne'a.' Preface to *Życie i myśli JW Pana Tristrama Shandy* by Lawrence Sterne (tr. Krystyna Tarnowska). Warsaw: Czytelnik. Vol. 1: 5-43.

Dobrzycka, Irena. 1955. Posłowie. *Rodzina Newcome'ów*. By William Thackeray (tr. Tadeusz Dehnel). Warsaw: Państwowy Instytut Wydawniczy. Vol. 2: 533-541.

Dobrzycka, Irena. 1963. Posłowie. *Juda nieznany*. By Thomas Hardy (tr. Ewa Kołaczkowska). Warsaw: Państwowy Instytut Wydawniczy. 478-482.

Draczko, Stefania. 1948. Przedmowa. *Powrót Krzyżowca (Ivanhoe).* By Walter Scott (tr. Stefania Draczko). Warsaw: Chłopski Świat. 5-8.

Ferens, Czesław. 1960. Posłowie. *Droga człowiecza.* By Samuel Butler (tr. Jerzy Schwakopf). Warsaw: Państwowy Instytut Wydawniczy. 641-650.

Helsztyński, Stanisław. 1949. Przedmowa. *Tajemnica opactwa.* By Walter Scott (tr. Erazm Rykaczewski). Warsaw: Stanisław Cukrowski. 5-16.

Karst, Roman. 1954. Przedmowa. *Sprawy firmy Dombey i Syn. Hurt. Detal. Export.* By Charles Dickens (tr. Zofia Sroczyńska and Roman Adamski). Warsaw: Czytelnik. Vol. 1: 5-13.

Kieruzalska, Ewa. 1977. Foreword. *Wirgińczyk. Jeździec z równin,* 3rd edn. By Owen Wister (tr. Janina Sujkowska). Warsaw: Iskry. 5-9.

Kołyszko, Anna. 1986. Przedmowa. *Kompleks Portnoya.* By Philip Roth (tr. Anna Kołyszko). Kraków: Wydawnictwo Literackie. 5-10.

Kott, Jan. 1949. Przedmowa. *Podróże Gulliwera w rózne kraje dalekie.* By Jonathan Swift (tr. Anon). Warsaw: Książka i Wiedza. v-xix.

Kott, Jan. 1953. Przedmowa. *Przypadki Robinsona Kruzoe.* By Daniel Defoe (tr. Józef Birkenmajer (vol. 1) and Anon (vol. 2)). Warsaw: Państwowy Instytut Wydawniczy. 5-40.

Krzeczkowski, Henryk. 1960. Posłowie. *Ambasadarowie.* By Henry James (tr. Maria Skibniewska). Warsaw: Czytelnik. Vol. 2: 359-367.

Kydryński, Juliusz. 1979. Posłowie. *Podróże do wielu odległych narodów świata.* By Jonathan Swift (tr. Maciej Słomczyński). Kraków: Wydawnictwo Literackie. 318-325.

Lewik, Włodzimierz. 1953. Posłowie. *Przygody Józefa Andrewsa.* By Henry Fielding (tr. Maria Korniłowicz). Warsaw: Państwowy Instytut Wydawniczy. 437-445.

Lichniak, Zygmunt. 1954. 'Sens dziejów angielskiego Judyma.' Foreword to *Cytadela* by A.J. Cronin (tr. Józef Szpecht). Warsaw: PAX. 5-9.

Lindsay, Jack. 1950. Wstęp. *Ciężkie czasy.* By Charles Dickens (tr. Wanda Gojawiczyńska-Nadzinowa). Warsaw: Książka i Wiedza. 5-18.

McInerney, Jay. 1986. Introduction. *Manhattan Transfer.* By John Dos Passos. Harmondsworth: Penguin. 7-11.

Michalski, Marian. 1954. Słowo wstępne. *Klucze Królestwa.* By A.J. Cronin (tr. Stanisław Morgenthal). Warsaw: PAX. v-vii.

Modjeska, Drusilla. 1984. Introduction. *Winged Seeds.* By Katharine Prichard. London: Virago. v-xvi.

Piotrowski, Kazimierz. 1956a. Posłowie. *Ostatni Mohikan.* By James Fenimore Cooper (tr. Tadeusz Evert). Warsaw: Iskry. 445-458.

Piotrowski, Kazimierz. 1956b. Przedmowa. *Pogromca zwierząt, czyli pierwsza ścieżka wojenna* (tr. Kazimierz Piotrowski). Warsaw: Iskry. 5-22.

Słomczyński, Maciej. 1972. 'Od tłumacza.' Preface to *Przygody Alicji w Krainie Czarów* by Lewis Carroll (tr. Maciej Słomczyński). Warsaw: Czytelnik. 5-6.

Wilhelmi, Janusz. 1960. Posłowie. *Opowieść o dwóch miastach.* By Charles Dickens (tr. Tadeusz Dehnel). Warsaw: Czytelnik. 439-444.

Willingham, Calder. 1979. 'Genius of the Ribald.' Introduction to *Tragic Ground & Trouble in July* by Erskine Caldwell. New York: New American Library. v-xiv.

'Wstęp.' 1950. *Wichrowe wzgórza.* By Emily Brontë (tr. Janina Sujkowska). Warsaw: Czytelnik. v-vii.

Żurawiec, Mateusz. 1954. 'Zamiast przedmowy. List do przyjaciela.' Preface to *Gwiazdy patrzą na nas* by A.J. Cronin (tr. Józef Szpecht). Warsaw: PAX. Vol. 1: v-viii.

Secondary

Aaron, Daniel. 1977. *Writers on the Left.* Oxford: Oxford University Press [1961].

Bibliography

Adamczyk-Garbowska, Monika. 1988. *Polskie tłumaczenia angielskiej literatury dziecięcej. Problemy krytyki przekładu.* Wrocław: Ossolineum.

Adamowski, Janusz and Andrzej Kozieł. 1999. 'Cenzura w PRL' in Miernik, Grzegorz (ed.) *Granice wolności słowa. Materiały konferencji naukowej Kielce 4-5 Maja 1995r.* Kielce and Warsaw: Kieleckie Towarzystwo Naukowe. 57-71.

'Adnotacje.' 1952. *Nowe Książki* 4(4): 198.

Agnosiewicz, Mariusz. 2010. 'Kościół, Partia, współżycie' in Majmurek, Jakub and Piotr Szumlewicz (eds) *PRL bez uprzedzeń.* Warsaw: Książka i Prasa. 137-165.

'Amerykański przyjaciel.' 1953. Review by WISZ of Saxton (1951) in *Życie Literackie* 3(6): 6.

Baer, Brian. 2012. 'Response' in *Translation Studies* 5(1): 95-99.

Barańczak, Stanisław. 1984. 'Taking Revenge on Language: Julian Tuwim's *Ball at the Opera*' in *Slavic and East European Journal* 28(2): 234-250.

Bates, John. 2002. 'Cenzura wobec problemu niemieckiego w literaturze polskiej (1948-1955)' in Dąbrowska, Danuta and Piotr Michałowski (eds) *Presja i ekspresja. Zjazd szczeciński i socrealizmu.* Szczecin: Wydawnictwo Naukowe Uniwersytetu Szczecińskiego. 79-92.

Bates, John. 2004a. 'The Censorship of Polish Literature in the Stalinist Period 1948-1954' in Berry, R., J. Bates and C. McManus (eds) *Proceedings of The Scottish Society for Russian and East European Studies: Papers from the Annual Conferences 1998 and 1999.* Scottish Society for Russian and East European Studies. 11-33.

Bates, John 2004b. 'From State Monopoly to a Free Market of Ideas? Censorship in Poland 1976-1989' in Müller, Beate (ed.) *Censorship and Cultural Regulation in the Modern Age.* Amsterdam and New York: Rodopi. 141-167.

Bates, John. 2011. 'Censoring English Literature in People's Poland, 1948-1967' in O'Leary, Catherine and Alberto Lázaro (eds) *Censorship across Borders: The Reception of English Literature in Twentieth-Century Europe.* Newcastle: Cambridge Scholars Publishing. 59-72.

Bayó Belenguer, Susana, Eiléan Ní Chuilleanáin and Cormac Ó Cuilleanáin. 2013. Introduction. *Translation Right or Wrong.* By Bayó Belenguer, Ní Chuilleanáin and Ó Cuilleanáin (eds). Dublin: Four Courts Press. 9-35.

Bereta, Katarzyna. 2013. 'O prozie realizmu socjalistycznego dla młodego odbiorcy' in Heska-Kwaśniewicz, Krystyna and Katarzyna Tałuć (eds) *Literatura dla dzieci i młodzieży (1945-1989),* vol. 3. Katowice: Wydawnictwo Uniwersytetu Śląskiego. 70-93.

Rev. of *Będzie nas więcej* by Clara Weatherwax. 1953. *Nowe Książki* 5(5): 154.

Białek, Józef. 1978. 'Elementy nowatorskie we współczesnej prozie dla dzieci i młodzieży' in Białek, Józef and Maria Guśpiel (eds) *Literatura dla dzieci i młodzieży. Teoria i krytyka. Wybór tekstów.* Kraków: Wydawnictwo Naukowe WSP. 120-135.

Białkowska, Barbara. 1991. 'Książki niechciane – książki "groźne" dla dzieci w Polsce Ludowej, czyli o czystkach w księgozbiorach bibliotecznych' in *Nowe Książki* 7: 60-61.

Bibliografia literatury tłumaczonej na język polski wydanej w latach 1945-1976, vol. 1. 1977. Warsaw: Czytelnik.

Bibliografia literatury tłumaczonej na język polski wydanej w latach 1945-1977, vol. 2. 1978. Warsaw: Czytelnik.

Bibliografia literatury tłumaczonej na język polski wydanej w latach 1977-1980, vol. 3. 1983. Warsaw: Czytelnik.

Bidwell, George. 1952. 'Obsesje Grahama Green'a [sic],' review of Greene (1950) in *Nowa Kultura* 3(15): 10.

Bielecka, Daniela. 1989. 'Dickens in Poland' in Zagórska, Anna and Grażyna Bystydzieńska (eds) *Literatura angielska i amerykańska. Problemy recepcji.* Lublin: UMCS. 119-135.

Rev. of *Bitwa pod Valley Forge* by Howard Fast. 1950. *Nowe Książki* 2(1): 13.

Błoński, Jan. 1995. 'Aneks: Censor jako Czytelnik' in *Wszystkie sztuki Sławomira Mrożka.* Kraków: Wydawnictwo Literackie. 269-281.

211

Bober, Sabina. 2011. *Walka o dusze dzieci i młodzieży w pierwszym dwudziestoleciu Polski Ludowej*, Lublin: Wydawnictwo KUL.

Bocheński, Jacek. 1995. 'Cenzura-nie-cenzura' in *Przegląd Polityczny* 27/28: 62-63.

Boguta, Grzegorz. 1999. [Contribution to] 'Dyskusja panelowa' in Miernik, Grzegorz (ed.) *Granice wolności słowa. Materiały konferencji naukowej Kielce 4-5 Maja 1995r.* Kielce and Warsaw: Kieleckie Towarzystwo Naukowe. 129-144.

Borejsza, Jerzy. 1951. 'Cervantes, Neruda i przekłady' in *Nowa Kultura* 2(27): 9.

Bromberg, Adam. 1966. *Książki i wydawcy. Ruch wydawniczy w Polsce Ludowej w latach 1944-1964*, 2nd edn. Warsaw: Państwowy Instytut Wydawniczy.

Brzoza, Czesław and Andrzej Leon Sowa. 2003. *Wielka historia Polski*, vol. 5. Kraków: Fogra.

Budrowska, Kamila. 2009. *Literatura i pisarze wobec cenzury PRL 1948-1958*. Białystok: Wydawnictwo Uniwersytetu w Białymstoku.

Budrowska, Kamila. 2012. 'Cenzura, tabu i wstyd. Cenzura obyczajowa w PRL-u (1948-1958)' in *Tabu i wstyd* (Napis 18). Warsaw: Wydawnictwo DiG. 229-244.

Budrowska, Kamila. 2013. *Zatrzymane przez cenzurę. Inedita z połowy wieku XX*. Warsaw: Instytut Badań Literackich.

Bystydzieńska, Grażyna. 2005. 'Recepcja Jane Austen w Polsce' in *Acta Philologica. Konstrukcje, rekonstrukcje, dekonstrukcje* 31: 109-115.

Carroll, Noël. 1990. *The Philosophy of Horror, or Paradoxes of the Heart*. New York and London: Routledge.

Cenzura PRL. Wykaz książek podlegających niezwłocznemu wycofaniu 1.X.1951r. 2002. Wrocław: Wydawnictwo Nortom.

Chilewska, Anna. 2009. *The Translated Child: Children's Literature in Translation in Communist and Post-Communist Poland*. PhD thesis. University of Alberta.

Chotomska, Wanda. 2013. 'Matka na przychodne, autorka na stałe' in *Wysokie Obcasy*, supplement to *Gazeta Wyborcza* (1 June 2013).

Ciećwierz, Mieczysław. 1989. *Polityka prasowa 1944-1948*. Warsaw: Państwowe Wydawnictwo Naukowe.

Cieśla, Joanna. 2011. 'Kolega. Kim właściwie jest nowy poseł Killion Munyama' in *Polityka*, (2 November 2011).

Couvares, Francis G. 2006. Introduction. *Movie Censorship and American Culture*, 2nd edn. By Couvares. Amherst and Boston: University of Massachusetts Press. 1-15.

Czabanowska-Wróbel, Anna. 2013. '[Ta dziwna] instytucja zwana literaturą dla dzieci. Historia literatury dla dzieci w perspektywie kulturowej' in *Teksty Drugie* 5: 13-24.

Czachowska, Jadwiga and Beata Dorosz (eds). 1991. *Literatura i krytyka poza cenzurą, 1977-1989 (Bibliografia druków zwartych)*. Wrocław: Wydawnictwo Wiedza o Kulturze.

Czachowska, Jadwiga. 1992. 'Zmagania z cenzurą słowników i bibliografii literackich w PRL' in Kostecki, Janusz and Alina Brodzka (eds) *Piśmiennictwo – systemy kontroli – obiegi alternatywne*, vol. 2. Warsaw: Biblioteka Narodowa. 214-36.

Czarnik, Oskar Stanisław. 1993. *Między dwoma Sierpniami. Polska kultura literacka w latach 1944-1980*. Warsaw: Wiedza Powszechna.

Czarnik, Oskar Stanisław. 2001. 'Control of Literary Communication in the 1945-1956 Period in Poland' in *Libraries & Culture* 36(1): 104-115.

Czeszko, Bohdan. 1957. Review of Steinbeck (1959) in *Przegląd kulturalny* 6(6): 3.

Dąbrowska, Maria. 2007. 'Parę myśli o pracy przekładowej' in Balcerzan, Edward and Ewa Rajewska (eds) *Pisarze polscy o sztuce przekładu 1440-2005. Antologia*. Poznań: Wydawnictwo Poznańskie. 186-191 [1954].

Delaney, Emer. 2013. 'Bowdlerization as translation: dual readership and the translation of children's literature' in Bayó Belenguer, Susana, Eiléan Ní Chuilleanáin and Cormac Ó Cuilleanáin (eds) *Translation Right or Wrong*. Dublin: Four Courts Press. 107-121.

'Dickens, jakiego nie znamy.' 1950. Review by A.W. of *Our Mutual Friend* and *Hard Times* in *Dziś i Jutro* 6(43): 12.

Rev. of *Dom pod Starym Łucznikiem* by Albert Halper. 1950. *Nowe Książki* 2(10): 24.

Drewnowski, Tadeusz. 1998. 'Cenzura PRL a współczesne edytorstwo' in Pelc, Janusz and Marek Prejs (eds) *Autor – tekst – cenzura*. *Prace na Kongres Slawistów w Krakowie w roku 1998*. Warsaw: Wydawnictwo Uniwersytetu Warszawskiego. 13-23.

Dudziński, Bolesław. 1950. 'Studium o gangsteryzmie,' review of *Tucker's People* in *Nowa Kultura* 1(21): 11.

Dudziński, Bolesław. 1951. 'Ostatnia powieść T. Dreisera,' review of *The Bulwark* in *Nowa Kultura* 2(38): 10.

Dudziński, Bolesław. 1952. 'Sprawcy i ofiary wyzysku,' review of *Ragged Trousered Philanthropists* in *Wieś* 9(38): 2.

'Dwaj amerykańscy klasycy.' 1949. Review by K.W. of *The Spy* by James Fenimore Cooper and *Moby-Dick* in *Tygodnik Powszechny* 5(29): 9.

'Dwie Ameryki.' 1951. Review by T.W. of Maltz (1951) and Fast (1950) in *Świetlica* 2(6): 17-19.

Elektorowicz, Leszek. 1971. 'The Latecomers: American Literature in Poland' in *Polish Perspectives* 14(1): 17-26.

Ermolaev, Herman. 1997. *Censorship in Soviet Literature, 1917-1991*. Lanham, Maryland: Rowman and Littlefield.

Ferman, James. 1980. 'Film Censorship in Britain Today' in *Film Directions* 9(3): 4-8.

Fik, Ignacy. 1979. 'Literatura choromaniaków.' *Wybór pism krytycznych*, 2nd edn. Ed. Andrzej Chruszczyński. Warsaw: Książka i Wiedza. 125-134 [1935].

Fik, Marta. 1989. *Kultura polska po Jałcie. Kronika lat 1944-1981*. London: Polonia.

Fik, Marta. 1993. 'Z archiwum GUKPPiW (V-XII-1971)' in *Kwartalnik Filmowy* 16(3): 181-187.

Fik, Marta. 1996. 'Cenzor jako współautor' in Wojnowska, Bożena (ed.) *Literatura i władza*. Warsaw: Instytut Badań Literackich. 131-47.

Freshwater, Helen. 2004. 'Towards a redefinition of Censorship' in Müller, Beate (ed.) *Censorship and Cultural Regulation in the Modern Age*. Amsterdam and New York: Rodopi. 225-245.

Friszke, Andrzej. 2003. 'Kultura czy ideologia? Polityka kulturalna kierownictwa PZPR w latach 1957-1963' in Friszke, Andrzej (ed.) *Władza a społeczeństwo w PRL. Studia historyczne*. Warsaw: Instytut Studiów Politycznych PAN. 115-145.

Friszke, Andrzej. 2013. 'To był człowiek katolickiej lewicy' in *Gazeta Wyborcza* (29 October 2013).

Frycie, Stanisław. 1978. *Literatura dla dzieci i młodzieży w latach 1945-1970. Tom I*. Warsaw: Wydawnictwo Szkolne i Pedagogiczne.

Frycie, Stanisław. 1982. *Literatura dla dzieci i młodzieży w latach 1945-1970. Tom II*. Warsaw: Wydawnictwo Szkolne i Pedagogiczne.

Gaszyńska-Magiera, Małgorzata. 2011. *Recepcja przekładów literatury iberoamerykańskiej w Polsce w latach 1945-2005 z perspektywy komunikacji międzykulturowej*. Kraków: Wydawnictwo Uniwersytetu Jagiellońskiego.

Gazda, Grzegorz. 2008. *Dwudziestolecie międzywojenne. Słownik literatury polskiej*. Gdańsk: Gdańskie Wydawnictwo Oświatowe and słowo/obraz/terytoria.

Gibbels, Elisabeth. 2009. 'Translators, the Tacit Censors' in Ní Chuilleanáin, Eiléan, Cormac Ó Cuilleanáin and David Parris (eds) *Translation and Censorship: Patterns of Communication and Interference*. Dublin: Four Courts Press. 57-75.

Gilbert, Nora. 2012. 'Thackeray, Sturges, and the Scandal of Censorship' in *PMLA* 127(3): 542-557.

Głowiński, Michał. 1990. *Nowomowa po polsku*. Warsaw: PEN.

Głowiński, Michał. 1993. *Peereliada. Komentarze do słów 1976-1981*. Warsaw: Państwowy Instytut Wydawniczy.

Głowiński, Michał. 1996. 'Władza ludowa przemawia do pisarzy' in Wojnowska, Bożena (ed.) *Literatura i władza*. Warsaw: Instytut Badań Literackich. 115-129.

Gomułka, Władysław. 1959. 'Referat sprawozdawczy Komitetu Centralnego wygłoszony w dniu 10 marca 1959r. na III Zjeździe PZPR' in *Nowe Drogi* 13(4): 6-92.

Gomułka, Władysław. 1967. 'Przemówienie na XIV Zjeździe Związku Literatów Polskich w Lublinie wygłoszone 18.IX.1964r.' in *Przemówienia. Lipiec 1964-grudzień 1966*. Warsaw: Książka i Wiedza. 53-73.

Grenby, M.O. 2008. *Children's Literature*. Edinburgh: Edinburgh University Press.

Grodzieńska, Wanda and Seweryn Pollack. 1951. 'O nową literaturę dla dzieci' in *Twórczość* 7(8): 132-150.

Groten-Sonecka, Erwina. 1950. 'W obronie człowieka,' review of Maltz (1951) in *Nowa Kultura* 1(38): 8.

Grzeniewski, Ludwik. 1950. 'Ku czyjej chwale?' review of *All Glorious Within* in *Nowa Kultura* 1(3): 6.

Grzeniewski, Ludwik. 1955. 'Dzieisęć lat *Drogi do wolności* Howarda Fasta' in *Po Prostu* 6: 5, 7.

Rev. of *A Guide to Soviet Russian Translations of American Literature* by Glenora W. Brown and Deming B. Brown. 1955. *Russian Review*, 3 (14): 271.

Günther, Hans. 1990. 'Education and Conversion: The Road to the New Man in the Totalitarian *Bildungsroman*' in Günther, Hans (ed.) *The Culture of the Stalin Period*. Basingstoke: Macmillan. 193-209.

Hubner, Zygmunt. 1992. *Theatre and Politics* (tr. and ed. Jadwiga Kosicka). Evanston Illinois: Northwestern University Press.

Hunt, Peter. 1991. *Criticism, Theory, and Children's Literature*. Oxford: Basil Blackwell.

Hunt, Peter (ed.). 1999. *Understanding Children's Literature: Key Essays from the* International Companion Encyclopedia of Children's Literature. London and New York: Routledge.

Hunt, Peter. 2001. *Children's Literature*. Oxford: Blackwell.

Inggs, Judith A. 2011. 'Censorship and translated children's literature in the Soviet Union: The example of the Wizards *Oz* and *Goodwin*' in *Target* 23(1): 77-91.

Iwaszkiewiczowa, Anna. 1951. 'Jeszcze o *Sednie sprawy*' in *Tygodnik Powszechny* 7(49): 6.

Jabłońska, Joanna. 2007. 'Tabuizmy w przekładzie literackim. Wybrane przekłady dzieł literatury anglojęzycznej na język polski' in Fast, Piotr and Natalia Strzelecka (eds) *Tabu w przekładzie*. Katowice and Częstochowa: Śląsk and Wydawnictwo Wyższej Szkoły Lingwistycznej. 187-200.

Jakowlew, L. 1950. 'Literatura marazmu' in *Literatura Radziecka* 6: 161-167.

Jakubiak, Katarzyna. 2011. 'The Black Body in Translation: Polish Productions of Lorraine Hansberry's *A Raisin in the Sun* in the 1960s' in *Theatre Journal* 63(4): 541-569.

Jarniewicz, Jerzy. 2012. 'Parada języków. Autokomentarz tłumacza *Portrety artysty w wieku młodzieńczym* Jamesa Joyce'a' in *Gościnność słowa. Szkice o przekładzie literackim*. Kraków: Wydawnictwo Znak. 232-247 [2005].

Jarosiński, Zbigniew. 1999. *Nadwiślański socrealizm*. Warsaw: Instytut Badań Literackich.

Jasienica, Paweł. 1950a. 'Jeszcze o Marshall'u' in *Dziś i Jutro* 6(20): 2, 12.

Jasienica, Paweł. 1950b. 'Wokół książki Greene'a' in *Dziś i Jutro* 6(32): 7.

Rev. of *Jasny dzień* by A.J. Cronin. 1949. *Nowe Książki* 1(3): 10.

Kalendarium dziejów Polski. 2007. Warsaw: Państwowe Wydawnictwo Naukowe.

Kalinowska, Izabela. 2009. 'Seks, polityka i koniec PRL-u: o cielesności w polskim kinie lat osiemdziesiątych' in Jagielski, Sebastian and Agnieszka Morstin-Popławska (eds) *Ciało i seksualność w kinie polskim*. Kraków: Wydawnictwo Uniwersytetu Jagiellońskiego. 63-78.

Karpiński, Jakub. 1978. 'Dwa szkice o cenzurze, 1. Kierunki badań cenzuroznawczych. 2. Cenzury i Historia. Zapisy i praktyka' in *Zapis* 5: 94-97.

Karst, Roman. 1950. 'Spotkanie z Dickensem' in *Nowa Kultura* 1(11): 5.

Kieniewicz, Teresa. 1977. *Recepcja literatury amerykańskiej w Polsce w dwudziestoleciu międzywojennym*. Warsaw: Wydawnictwo Uniwersytetu Warszawskiego.

Kisielewski, Stefan. 1983. 'Przeciw cenzurze – legalnie (Garść wspomnień)' in *Bez cenzury*, 2nd edn. Paris: Editions Spotkania. 79-88.

Kitrasiewicz, Piotr and Łukasz Gołębiewski. 2005. *Rynek książki w Polsce 1944-1989*. Warsaw: Biblioteka Analiz.

Klemperer, Victor. 2006. *The Language of the Third Reich: LTI – Lingua Tertii Imperii: A Philologist's Notebook* (tr. Martin Brady). London and New York: Continuum [1957].

'Kolejarze z Chicago.' 1951. Review by G.K. of Saxton (1951) in *Dziś i Jutro* 7(33): 9.

Kondek, Stanisław Adam. 1999. *Papierowa rewolucja. Oficjalny obieg książek w Polsce w latach 1948-1955*. Warsaw: Biblioteka Narodowa.

Kondek, Stanisław. 2006. 'Literatura popularna w ofercie czytelniczej polskiego socrealizmu' in Stępnik, Krzysztof and Magdalena Piechota (eds) *Socrealizm. Fabuły – komunikaty – ikony*. Lublin: Wydawnictwo UMCS. 23-32.

Kos, Wincenty. 1954. 'Stacja wiernej przyjaźni,' review of Saxton (1951) in *Tygodnik Powszechny* 10(16): 14.

Kossewska, Elżbieta (ed.). 2005. *Cenzura na Warmii i Mazurach w latach 1945-1946. Sprawozdania Wojewódzkiego Urzędu Informacji i Propagandy w Olsztynie (1945-1947)*, vol. 1. Warsaw: Oficyna Wydawnicza ASPRA-JR.

Kott, Jan. 1961. 'Caldwell bez smaku,' review of Caldwell (1961) in *Przegląd Kulturalny* 10(36): 5.

Kozłowski, Krzysztof. 2013. 'Udało nam się, bo byliśmy rozumni' in *Gazeta Wyborcza* (30 March - 1 April 2013).

Krajewski, Andrzej. 2004. *Między współpracą a oporem. Twórcy kultury wobec systemu politycznego PRL (1975-1980)*. Warsaw: Trio.

'Kronika.' 1977. *Zapis* 4: 207-215.

Kruszewska-Kudelska, Anna. 1978. 'Problemy narracji i funkcja narratora w polskiej powieści dla dziewcząt' in Białek, Józef and Maria Guśpiel (eds) *Literatura dla dzieci i młodzieży. Teoria i krytyka. Wybór tekstów*. Kraków: Wydawnictwo Naukowe WSP. 111-119.

Kuhiwczak, Piotr. 2011. 'Translation and Censorship' in *Translation Studies* 4(3): 358-366.

Kuhn, Annette. 1988. *Cinema, Censorship and Sexuality, 1909-1925*. London and New York: Routledge.

Kujawska-Lis, Ewa. 2008. 'Turning *Heart of Darkness* into a Racist Text: A Comparison of Two Polish Translations' in *Conradiana* 40(2): 165-178.

Kuliczkowska, Krystyna. 1978. 'Wokół "przygody". Model bohatera a konwencje gatunkowe i narracyjne' in Białek, Józef and Maria Guśpiel (eds) *Literatura dla dzieci i młodzieży. Teoria i krytyka. Wybór tekstów*. Kraków: Wydawnictwo Naukowe WSP. 99-110.

Kuroń, Jacek and Jacek Żakowski. 1996. *PRL dla początkujących*. Wrocław: Wydawnictwo Dolnośląskie.

Kurowska, Elżbieta. 1987. *Recepcja literatury angielskiej w Polsce (1932-1939)*. Wrocław: Ossolineum.

Landers, Clifford E. 2001. *Literary Translation: A Practical Guide*. Clevedon: Multilingual Matters.

Lasota, Grzegorz. 1951. 'O sytuacji w literaturze dla młodzieży' *Twórczość* 7(8): 113-132.

Lathey, Gillian. 2010. *The Role of Translators in Children's Literature: Invisible Storytellers*. New York and London: Routledge.

Leighton, Lauren G. 1991. *Two Worlds, One Art: Literary Translation in Russia and America*. Dekalb: North Illinois University Press.

Rev. of *Lewanty* by Andrzej Braun. 1953. *Nowe Książki* 5(5): 152.

Lewicki, Zbigniew. 1976. 'Podwójne widzenie Hellera, czyli hak to nie paragraf' in *Literatura na Świecie* 6: 328-347.

Lichański, Stefan. 1954. 'Katolicyzm uśmiechnięty,' review of Cronin (1974) in *Dziś i Jutro* 10(20): 4.
Lisiecka, Alicja. 1964. *Pokolenia 'Pryszczatych.'* Warsaw: Państwowy Instytut Wydawniczy.
Looby, Robert. 2008. 'Looking for the Censor in the Works of Sean O'Casey (and Others) in Polish Translation' in *Translation and Literature* 17(1): 47-64.
Looby, Robert. 2013. 'The Stifling of Edna O'Brien in the People's Republic of Poland' in Piątkowska, Katarzyna and Ewa Kościałkowska-Okońska (eds) *Correspondences and Contrasts in Foreign Language Pedagogy and Translation Studies*. Cham: Springer. 159-168.
Lyra, Franciszek. 1989. 'Toward a History of American Literature in Poland' in Anna Zagórska and Grażyna Bystydzieńska (eds) *Literatura angielska i amerykańska. Problemy recepcji*. Lublin: UMCS. 194-208.
Łapiński, Zdzisław and Wojciech Tomasik (eds). 2004. *Słownik realizmu socjalistycznego*. Kraków: Universitas.
Łopieńska, Barbara. 1981. 'Ja, cenzor' (interview with a former censor, "K-62") in *Tygodnik Solidarności* (8 May 1981).
Łuszczewska, Eliza. 2012. *Censorship and Translation in the People's Republic of Poland in 1956-1970, American Novel*. MA thesis. Catholic University of Lublin.
Maciejewski, Janusz. 2009. 'Cenzura w Polsce w latach 1957-1980 i sposoby jej omijania przez pisarzy' in *Umysły zniewolone. Literatura pod presją* (Napis 15). Warsaw: Wydawnictwo DiG. 327-336.
MacLeod, Anne Scott. 2006. 'Censorship and Children's Literature' in Hunt, Peter (ed.) *Children's Literature: Critical Concepts in Literary and Cultural Studies*, vol. 3 Cultural Concepts. London and New York: Routledge. 120-131 [1983].
Madej, Alina. 1994. *Mitologie i konwencje. O Polskim kinie fabularnym dwudziestolecia międzywojennego*. Kraków: Universitas.
Matras-Mastelarz, Wanda. 2012. '*Przekrój* Mariana Eilego w opinii i ocenie krakowskich cenzorów (1948-1953)' in Degen, Dorota and Marcin Żynda (eds) *Nie po myśli władzy. Studia nad cenzurą i zakresem wolności słowa na ziemiach polskich od wieku XIX do czasów współczesnych*. Toruń: Wydawnictwo Naukowe UMK. 197-214.
Mazurkiewicz, Adam. 2009. 'Kapitalizm w odwrocie. O socrealistycznym epizodzie polskiej fantastyki naukowej' in *Pamiętnik Literacki* 100(2): 109-124.
Mędelski, Stanisław. 1950. 'Banda Tuckera,' review of *Tucker's People* in *Wieś* 7(8): 5.
Michalik-Nedelković, Krystyna. 1949. 'Krzywe zwierciadło anglosaskiej krytyki literackiej' in *Wieś* 6(47): 7.
Michnik, Adam. 1998. *Kościół, lewica, dialog*. Warsaw: Świat Książki [1976].
Mielczarek, Tomasz. 2010. 'Pisarze w PRL: "pieszczochy władzy" czy ofiary systemu' in Degen, Dorota and Jacek Gzella (eds) *Niewygodne dla władzy. Ograniczanie wolności słowa na ziemiach polskich w XIX I XX wieku*. Toruń: Wydawnictwo Naukowe UMK. 213-231.
Miłosz, Czesław. 1983. *The History of Polish Literature*, 2nd edn. Berkeley: University of California Press.
Miłosz, Czesław. 2007. 'Przekłady i Gałczyński' in Balcerzan, Edward and Ewa Rajewska (eds) *Pisarze polscy o sztuce przekładu 1440-2005. Antologia*. Poznań: Wydawnictwo Poznańskie. 203-208 [1958].
Monticelli, Daniele and Anne Lange. 2014. 'Translation and totalitarianism: the case of Soviet Estonia' in *The Translator* 20(1): 95-111.
Moorcock, Michael. 1987. *Wizardry and Wild Romance: A Study of Epic Fantasy*. London: Victor Gollancz.
Morstin-Górska, Maria. 1948. 'Nowe powieści Cronina,' review of Cronin (1974) and *The Green Years* in *Tygodnik Powszechny* 4(7): 9.
Morstin-Górska, Maria. 1949. 'Cztery prezkłady' in *Tygodnik Powszechny* 5(2): 9.

Müller Beate. 2004. 'Censorship and Cultural Regulation: Mapping the Territory' in Müller, Beate (ed.) *Censorship and Cultural Regulation in the Modern Age*. Amsterdam and New York: Rodopi. 1-31.

Myślik, Tadeusz. 1954. 'O książce, która jest buntem,' review of *The Stars Look Down* in *Dziś i Jutro* 10(22): 3.

Nadolna-Tłuczykont, Marta. 2013. *Powrót książek 'zakazanych' do współczesnych odbiorców (wybrane zagadnienia)*. Katowice: Wydawnictwo Uniwersytetu Śląskiego.

Najder, Zdzisław. 1975. 'Conrad w przekładach Anieli Zagórskiej' in Pollak, Seweryn (ed.) *Przekład artystyczny. O sztuce tłumaczenia. Księga druga*. Wrocław: Ossolińskich. 197-210.

Nałęcz, Daria (ed.). 1994. *Główny Urząd Kontroli Prasy 1945-1959*. Warsaw: Instytut Studiów Politycznych, Polska Akademia Nauk.

Napiontkowa, Maria. 1990. '"Odwilż" w Warszawie' in Kuchtówna, Lidia (ed.) *Warszawa teatralna*. Warsaw: Polska Akademia Nauk. 220-234.

Rev. of *Niezwyciężony* by Howard Fast. 1950. *Nowe Książki* 2(12): 24.

Nikolowski-Bogomoloff, Angelika. 2009. 'More than a Childhood Revisited? Ideological Dimensions in the American and British Translations of Astrid Lindgren's *Madicken*' in Ní Chuilleanáin, Eiléan, Cormac Ó Cuilleanáin and David Parris (eds) *Translation and Censorship: Patterns of Communication and Interference*. Dublin: Four Courts Press. 173-183.

Nowak, Piotr. 2012. *Cenzura wobec rynku książki. Wojewódzki Urząd Kontroli Prasy, Publikacji i Widowisk w Poznaniu w latach 1946-1955*. Poznań: Wydawnictwo Naukowe UAM.

Nowak, Piotr. 2013. 'Cenzura w PRL jako nieefektywna kopia radzieckiej hybrydy leninowsko-stalinowskiej. Nowe spojrzenie na Główny Urząd Kontroli Prasy, Publikacji i Widowisk' in Gzella, Grażyna and Jacek Gzella (eds) *'Nie należy dopuszczać do publikacji.' Cenzura w PRL*. Toruń: Wydawnictwo Naukowe UMK. 39-52.

'Nowości Państwowego Instytutu Wydawniczego.' 1949. *Nowe Książki* 1(1): n. pag.

Ó Cuilleanáin, Cormac. 2009. '... *comme des nègres*: whitewashed in translation' in Ní Chuilleanáin, Eiléan, Cormac Ó Cuilleanáin and David Parris (eds) *Translation and Censorship: Patterns of Communication and Interference*. Dublin: Four Courts Press. 184-204.

O'Drisceoil, Donal. 2011. 'Frank O'Connor and Irish Literary Censorship' in O'Leary, Catherine and Alberto Lázaro (eds) *Censorship across Borders: The Reception of English Literature in Twentieth-Century Europe*. Newcastle: Cambridge Scholars Publishing. 27-41.

O'Higgins, Paul. 1972. *Censorship in Britain*. London: Nelson.

O'Sullivan, Emer. 2005. *Comparative Children's Literature*. London and New York: Routledge.

Oczko, Piotr. 2013. 'Anna z domu o zielonym dachu. O cyklu powieściowym Lucy Maud Montgomery' in *Teksty Drugie* 5: 42-61.

Oesterloef, W.K. 1951. 'Obok torów,' review of Saxton (1951) in *Nowa Kultura* 1(23): 11.

Orwell, George. 1998. *The Complete Works, Vols 1-20*, ed. Peter Davison. London: Secker and Warburg.

Ostasz, Maria. 1999. *Oblicze powojennej krytyki literatury dla dzieci i młodzieży 1945 - 1956*. Kraków: Wydawnictwo Naukowe WSP.

Ostrowski, Witold. 1953. 'Klucz do Cronina' in *Tygodnik Powszechny* 9(26): 1-2.

Pacławski, Jan and Marek Kątny. 1996. *Literatura dla dzieci i młodzieży*, 2nd edn. Kielce: Wszechnica Świętokrzyska.

Pacyniak, Katarzyna. 2009. *Domestication and Foreignisation in* A Little Princess *by Frances Hodgson Burnett: an Analysis of Three Polish Translations*. MA thesis. Catholic University of Lublin.

Paul, Lissa. 1999. 'From Sex-Role Stereotyping to Subjectivity: Feminist Criticism' in Hunt (1999): 112-123.

Pawlicka, Katarzyna. 2004. *Polityka władz wobec Kościoła katolickiego (grudzień 1970 - październik 1978)*. Warsaw: Wydawnictwo TRIO.

Phelps, Guy. 1975. *Film Censorship*. London: Victor Gollancz.

Rev. of *Pieniądz i zdrada* by Theodore Dreiser. 1949. *Nowe Książki* 1(2): 9.

Rev. of *Pogromca zwierząt* by James Fenimore Cooper. 1954. *Nowe Książki* 6(24): 763.

'Powszednie dni Brooklynu.' 1952. Review by a.r. of *Spit and the Stars* in *Nowa Kultura* 3(15): 10.

Pytlos, Barbara. 2013. 'Powieść dla dziewcząt w latach 1945-1968. Co powinny czytać dziewczęta?' in Heska-Kwaśniewicz, Krystyna and Katarzyna Tałuć (eds) *Literatura dla dzieci i młodzieży (1945-1989)*, vol. 3. Katowice: Wydawnictwo Uniwersytetu Śląskiego. 106-132.

Remmer, Alexander. 1989. 'A Note on Post-Publication Censorship in Poland 1980-1987' in *Soviet Studies* 41(3): 415-425.

Reynolds, Matthew. 2007. 'Semi-censorship in Dryden and Browning' in Billiani, Francesca (ed.) *Modes of Censorship and Translation: National Contexts and Diverse Media*. Manchester: St. Jerome. 187-204.

Rideout, Walter. 1956. *The Radical Novel in the United States 1900-1954: Some Interrelations of Literature and Society*. Cambridge: Harvard University Press.

Rockett, Kevin. 2004. *Irish Film Censorship: A Cultural Journey from Silent Cinema to Internet Pornography*. Dublin: Four Courts Press.

Rogoziński, Julian. 1961. 'Szkice do autoportretu,' review of *Włóczędzy o zachodzie słońca* by Thomas Wolfe in *Przegląd Kulturalny* 10(18): 6.

Rogoż, Michał. 2013. 'Przekłady zagranicznej literatury dla dzieci i młodzieży w okowach polskiej cenzury. Ocena książek skierowanych do wydania w latach 1948-1956' in Gzella, Grażyna and Jacek Gzella (eds) *'Nie należy dopuszczać do publikacji.' Cenzura w PRL*. Toruń: Wydawnictwo Naukowe UMK. 99-122.

Romanow, M. 1949. 'Zagadnienia postępowej literatury w USA' in *Literatura Radziecka* 5: 164-170.

Roszkowski, Wojciech. 1991. *Historia Polski 1914-1990*. Warsaw: Wydawnictwo Naukowe PWN.

Różdżyński, Jan. 1994. 'Raporty cenzorów. Do Polski wysłano "doświadczonych towarzyszy"' in *Życie Warszawy* (18-19 June 1994).

Ruch Wydawniczy w Liczbach XXXV: 1989 (Polish Publishing in Figures). 1990. Warsaw: Biblioteka Narodowa.

Rudolf, Krzysztof Filip. 2014. '"Szejset czydzieści pienć upatkuf tumacza" – czyli nieistniejąca stylizacja w polskich przekładach literatury angielskiej' in *Tekstualia* 36(1): 29-45.

Ruggles, Melville J. 1961. 'American Books in Soviet Publishing' in *Slavic Review* 20(3): 419-435.

Rzendowski, Leon. 1994. 'Pierwszy censor Polski Ludowej' in *Rzeczpospolita* (16 July 1994). On line at: http://archiwum.rp.pl/artykul/21034-Pierwszy-cenzor-Polski-Ludowej. html?_=Rzeczpospolita-21034?_=3 (consulted 02.10.2014).

Sadkowski, Wacław. 2002. *Odpowiednie dać słowu słowo. Zarys dziejów przekładu literackiego w Polsce*. Warsaw: Prószyński i S-ka.

Sarland, Charles. 1999. 'The Impossibility of Innocence: Ideology, Politics, and Children's Literature' in Hunt (1999): 39-55.

Scholz, László. 2011. 'Squandered Opportunities: On the Uniformity of Literary Translations in Postwar Hungary' in Baer, Brian James (ed.) *Contexts, Subtexts and Pretexts: Literary Translation in Eastern Europe and Russia*. Amsterdam and Philadelphia: John Benjamins. 205-217.

Sherry, Samantha. 2010. 'Censorship in Translation in the Soviet Union: The Manipulative Rewriting of Howard Fast's *The Passion of Sacco and Vanzetti*' in *Slavonica* 16(1): 1-14.

Sherry, Samantha. 2012. *Censorship in Translation in the Soviet Union in the Stalin and Khrushchev Eras*. PhD Thesis. University of Edinburgh.

Sherry, Samantha. 2013. 'Better Something Than Nothing: The Editors and Translators of *Inostrannaia literatura* as Censorial Agents' in *Slavonic and East European Review* 91(4): 731-758.

Siekierski, Stanisław. 1998. 'Drugi obieg jako efekt działania cenzury PRL?' in Pelc, Janusz and Marek Prejs (eds) *Autor – tekst – cenzura. Prace na Kongres Slawistów w Krakowie w roku 1998*. Warsaw: Wydawnictwo Uniwersytetu Warszawskiego. 25-38.

Siemion, Piotr. 2010. 'The Obsolescence of Vice.' Paper presented at *Of Pynchon and Vice: America's Inherent Others: International Pynchon Week Conference* (Uniwersytet Marii Curie-Skłodowskiej, Lublin, 11 June 2010).

Rev. of *Siostra Carrie* by Theodore Dreiser. 1950. *Nowe Książki* 2(1): 13.

Skórzyński, Jan. 1991. 'Odwilż w cenzurze' in *Krytyka* 34-35: 102-116.

Skotnicka, Gertruda. 2008. *Barwy przeszłości. O powieściach historycznych dla dzieci i młodzieży 1939-1989*. Gdańsk: Słowo/obraz terytoria.

Skrobiszewska, Halina. 1971. *Książki naszych dzieci, czyli o literaturze dla dzieci i młodzieży*. Warsaw: Wiedza Powszechna.

Skrobiszewska, Halina. 1973. *Literatura i wychowanie. O literaturze dla starszych dzieci i młodzieży*. Warsaw: Ludowa Spółdzielnia Wydawnicza.

Skrobiszewska, Halina. 1978. 'Współczesna polska krytyka literatury dla dzieci. Jej typy, funkcje i powinności' in Białek, Józef and Maria Guśpiel (eds) *Literatura dla dzieci i młodzieży. Teoria i krytyka. Wybór tekstów*. Kraków: Wydawnictwo Naukowe WSP. 5-21.

Staniów, Bogumiła. 2013. 'Przekłady z literatur obcych w latach 1945-1989' in Heska-Kwaśniewicz, Krystyna and Katarzyna Tałuć (eds) *Literatura dla dzieci i młodzieży (1945-1989)*, vol. 3. Katowice: Wydawnictwo Uniwersytetu Śląskiego. 149-165.

Starowieyska-Morstinowa, Zofia. 1950. 'Grzech zdemaskowany,' review of Greene (1950) in *Tygodnik Powszechny* 6(31): 3.

Stephens, John. 1992. *Language and Ideology in Children's Fiction*. London and New York: Longman.

Stowarzyszenie PAX 1945-1985, Informator. 1985. Warsaw: PAX.

'Styron i Vonnegut: Rozmowa.' 1986. Trans. and ed. Andrzej Ceynowa in *Literatura na Świecie* 1: 296-310.

'Szarlatan i inne...' 1957. Review by B. Cz. of *Szarlatan* by Erskine Caldwell in *Przegląd Kulturalny* 6(48): 3.

Szkup, Jerzy. 1972. *Recepcja prozy amerykańskiej w Polsce Ludowej w latach 1945-1965*. Warsaw: Uniwersytet Warszawski.

Szonert, Ewa. 1952. 'Powieść o poszukiwaczach złota,' review of Prichard Trilogy in *Dziś i Jutro* 8(38): 11.

Szymanowski, Antoni. 1952. 'Zamach na Robesona,' review of *Peekskill USA* in *Nowa Kultura* 3(23): 9.

Szymańska, Adriana. 1972. 'Z prozy irlandzkiej,' review of O'Connor (1971) in *Twórczość* 28(5): 159-160.

Szymańska, Irena. 2001. *Miałam dar zachwytu. Wspomnienia wydawcy*. Warsaw: Czytelnik.

Świstak, Mateusz. 2010. 'Niepolityczny tabu PRL, czyli o cenzurze obyczajowej lat 80.' in Skorupa, Ewa (ed.) *Przeskoczyć tę studnię strachu. Autor i dzieło a cenzura PRL*. Kraków: Wydawnictwo Uniwersytetu Jagiellońskiego. 115-131.

Tajne dokumenty Państwo – Kościół 1960-1980. 1996. London: Aneks.

Tax-Choldin, Marianna. 1986. 'The New Censorship: Censorship by Translation in the Soviet Union' in *The Journal of Library History (1974-1987)* 21(2), Libraries, Books, & Culture II: 334-349.

Tokarzówna, Krystyna. 1992. 'Cenzura w *Polskiej Bibliografii Literackiej*' in Kostecki, Janusz and Alina Brodzka (eds) *Piśmiennictwo – systemy kontroli – obiegi alternatywne*, vol. 2. Warsaw: Biblioteka Narodowa. 237-250.

Tomasik, Wojciech. 1988. *Polska powieść tendencyjna 1949-1955. Problemy perswazji literackiej*. Wrocław: Ossolineum.

Toury, Gideon. 1995. *Descriptive Translation Studies and Beyond*. Amsterdam and Philadelphia: John Benjamins.

Trawińska, Marta. 2010. 'Współczesne polskie feministki o możliwościach upodmiotowienia kobiet w okresie PRL-u' in Majmurek, Jakub and Piotr Szumlewicz (eds) *PRL bez uprzedzeń*. Warsaw: Książka i Prasa. 185-196.

Tribe, David. 1973. *Questions of Censorship*. London: George Allen and Unwin.

Tuwim, Irena. 2007. '[Między tłumaczeniem a adaptacją]' in Balcerzan, Edward and Ewa Rajewska (eds) *Pisarze polscy o sztuce przekładu 1440-2005. Antologia*. Poznań: Wydawnictwo Poznańskie. 185-186 [1952].

Twain, Mark. 1996. 'Fenimore Cooper's Literary Offences' in *How To Tell a Story and Other Essays*, New York and Oxford: Oxford University Press. 93-116.

Rev. of *Umarli pozostają młodzi* by Anna Seghers. 1949. *Nowe Książki* 1(2): 10.

Urbańczyk, Andrzej. 1953. 'Chiny – Japonia – Trinidad,' review of De Boissiere (1953) in *Życie Literackie* 3(52): 14.

Urbański, Andrzej. 1992. 'Cenzura – kontrola kontroli (system lat siedemdziesiątych)' in Kostecki, Janusz and Alina Brodzka (eds) *Piśmiennictwo – systemy kontroli – obiegi alternatywne*, vol. 2. Warsaw: Biblioteka Narodowa. 251-265.

Walicki, Andrzej. 2013. *Od projektu komunistycznego do neoliberalnej utopii*. Kraków: Universitas.

Wallicht, Leonard. 1950. 'Z życia robotników amerykańskich,' review of *The Foundry* in *Wieś* 7(37): 7.

Walton, J. Michael. 2007. 'Good Manners, Decorum and the Public Peace: Greek Drama and the Censor' in Billiani, Francesca (ed.) *Modes of Censorship and Translation: National Contexts and Diverse Media*. Manchester: St. Jerome. 143-166.

Watkins, Tony. 1999. 'The Setting of Children's Literature: History and Culture' in Hunt (1999): 30-38.

Weber, Adam. 1950. 'Płk. Willoughby wygrał wojnę dla siebie,' review of *The Crusaders* in *Dziś i Jutro* 6(17): 9.

Wegner, Jacek. 1973. 'Western z lat czterdziestych,' review of *House in the Uplands* in *Kultura* 11(44): 9.

Werblan, Andrzej. 2009. *Stalinizm w Polsce*. Warsaw: Towarzystwo Wydawnicze i Literackie [1991].

Westdickenberg, Michael. 2004. *Die 'Diktatur des anständigen Buches.' Das Zensursystem der DDR für belletristische Prosaliteratur in den sechziger Jahren*. Wiesbaden: Harrassowitz Verlag.

Rev. of *Wiedeńska wiosna* by Aleksander Jackiewicz. 1953. *Nowe Książki* 5(5): 152.

Wilczyński, Marek. 1993. 'Formy obecności literatury amerykańskiej w Polsce w latach 1945-1992' in *Przegląd Zachodni* 49(2): 133-149.

Witt, Susanna. 2011. 'Between the Lines: Totalitarianism and Translation in the USSR' in Baer, Brian James (ed.) *Contexts, Subtexts and Pretexts: Literary Translation in Eastern Europe and Russia*. Amsterdam and Philadelphia: John Benjamins. 149-170.

Wnęk, Jan. 2006. *Polskie przekłady literatury zagranicznej 1918-1939*. Kraków: MCDN.

Wojsław, Jacek. 2013. 'Miejsce cenzury w ocenach aparatu partyjnego w okresie politycznej konfrontacji lat 1980-1981' in Gzella, Grażyna and Jacek Gzella (eds) *'Nie należy dopuszczać do publikacji.' Cenzura w PRL*. Toruń: Wydawnictwo Naukowe UMK. 195-215.

Woods, Michelle. 2010. 'Václav Havel and the Expedient Politics of Translation' in *New Theatre Quarterly* 26(1): 3-15.

Woźniak-Łabieniec, Marzena. 2013. 'Cenzura w okresie odwilży jako temat tabu' in *Acta Universitatis Lodziensis* 1: 89-97.

'Wśród książek.' 1950. Review by b.d. of *Ostatni liść* by O. Henry in *Nowa Kultura* 1(37): 11.

'Wśród książek.' 1951. Review by b.d. of *The Foundry* in *Nowa Kultura* 2(33): 11.

'Zabijanie słowa. O cenzurze w PRL z Aleksandrem Pawlickim, Tomaszem Strzemboszem i Wiesławem Władyką rozmawia Władysław Bułhak i Barbara Polak.' 2004. *Biuletyn Instytutu Pamięci Narodowej* 37(2): 4-26.

Zaborowski, Tadeusz. 2003. 'Dyskutowaliśmy o moralności' in *Czas Kultury* 19(2-3): 65-67.

Zaitsev, Mark. 1975. 'Soviet Theater Censorship' in *The Drama Review: TDR* 19(2), Political Theatre Issue: 119-128.

Zawada, Andrzej. 1995. *Dwudziestolecie literackie*. Wrocław: Wydawnictwo Dolnośląskie.

Zengel, Ryszard. 1958. 'O Caldwellu – krytycznie,' review of *God's Little Acre* and *Szarlatan* by Erskine Caldwell in *Życie Literackie* 8(21): 10.

Zieliński, Bronisław. 1959. 'American and British Literature in Poland' in *The Polish Review* 4(1-2): 47-49.

Żak, Stanisław. 1999. 'Cenzura wobec humanistyki w PRL' in Miernik, Grzegorz (ed.) *Granice wolności słowa. Materiały konferencji naukowej Kielce 4-5 Maja 1995r*. Kielce and Warsaw: Kieleckie Towarzystwo Naukowe. 73-90.

Żylińska, Jadwiga. 1953. 'Dickens nieznany' in *Życie Literackie* 3(14-15): 6-7.

Internet Sources

Curwood, James Oliver. 2003. *Nomads of the North*, n. pag. Project Gutenberg. Web. http://www.gutenberg.org/files/4704/4704-h/4704-h.htm

'Hearings regarding the communist infiltration of the motion picture industry. Hearings before the Committee on Un-American Activities, House of Representatives, Eightieth Congress, first session. Public law 601 (section 121, subsection Q (2)) (1947).' 1947. Government Printing Office: Washington. Web. https://archive.org/details/hearingsregardin1947aunit

Index

More titles: www.rodopi.nl